American Indian Studies Program Guide

Post Doctoral Research Project

Dr. Byron Lee Blackwell, JD, Ed.D

I want to dedicate this American Indian Studies Program Guide to Doris Oxendine, a beautiful Cherokee Indian woman in North Carolina who told me she loved me at first sight.

AMERICAN INDIAN STUDIES PROGRAM GUIDE

Bachelor of Arts in American Indian Studies

Master of Arts in American Indian Studies

Doctor of Education in American

Indian Higher Education

PURPOSE, MISSION STATEMENT, PROGRAM OBJECTIVES

COURSE OBJECTIVES

STUDENT EVALUATION FORM
COURSE EVALUATION FORM
PROGRAM EVALUATION FORM

POST DOCTORAL RESEARCH PROJECT

Lone Wolf
Dr Byron Lee Blackwell, JD, Ed. D

Copyright © 2002, 2014 by Dr. Byron Lee Blackwell, JD, Ed.D.

All rights reserved. No part of this publication may be reproduced, distributed, or transmitted in any form or by any means, including photocopying, recording, or other electronic or mechanical methods, without the prior written permission of the publisher, except in the case of brief quotations embodied in critical reviews and certain other noncommercial uses permitted by copyright law. For permission requests, write to the publisher, addressed "Attention: Permissions Coordinator," at the address below.

BookWhirl Publishing
PO Box 9031, Green Bay
WI 54308-9031, USA
www.bookwhirl.com

Ordering Information:
Quantity sales. Special discounts are available on quantity purchases by corporations, associations, and others. For details, contact the publisher at the address above.

Printed in the United States of America

Library of Congress Control Number:		2014932956
ISBN:	Hardback	978-1-61856-502-0
	Paperback	978-1-61856-498-6
	Pdf	978-1-61856-499-3
	ePub	978-1-61856-500-6
	Kindle	978-1-61856-501-3

Disclaimer

This publication is designed to provide accurate and personal experience information in regard to the subject matter covered. It is sold with the understanding that the author, contributors, publisher are not engaged in rendering counseling or other professional services. If counseling advice or other expert assistance is required, the services of a competent professional person should be sought out.

AMERICAN INDIAN STUDIES PROGRAM
PROGRAM DEVELOPMENT

Purpose Mission, Program Objectives

The purpose of the mission statement is to guide the academic leadership of a college or university in determining what educational programs are appropriate for the institution's curriculum by clearly identifying the department or school's overall purpose. A written statement of purpose helps to maintain stability and continuity. In creating a philosophical framework for an American Indian Studies program the following criteria has been established.

Purpose of an American Indian Studies Program

The future direction for American Indian education is self-determination so American Indians can control their own educational systems, and their own political, social and spiritual institutions so that the alarmingly high dropout rate of Indian students can be retarded. The purpose of the American Indian Studies Program is to create future leaders for Indian communities.

Mission Statement

A mission statement is a written statement of purpose that serves as the foundation on which the department or university serves, and as the foundation on which the department builds and justifies the grounds for its existence within the university.

Mission Statement for an American Indian Studies Program

The American Indian Studies Program is designed to present a conceptual framework for students to gain knowledge of a spiritual/ecological/ holistic way of life that has existed for thousands of years in Native North America. The tribal life ways of Native peoples from pre-contact times through the contemporary area allows students to experience tribal histories, ancient religions, various art forms, musical styles and media as an integral element of American Indian cultural expression. The foundation of American Indian Studies programs is Indian cultural and spiritual values regarding the ecological caretaking of mother earth, and vocational/technical skills they so can began using these skills in the service of their Indian communities early in their college careers.

Program Goals

Goal One: It is an objective of _____ college/university to implement a two-year associate of arts degree in American Indian Studies or a three year bachelor of arts degree in American Indian Studies.

Goal Two: It is an objective of _____ college/university to provide liberal arts courses in American Indian Studies that are transferable to four year universities.

Goal Three: It is an objective of _____ college/university to provide students with opportunities to learn the Cherokee language, history and culture.

Goal Four: It is an objective of _____ college/university to increase student understanding and comprehension of American Indian bodies of knowledge in the past as well as the contemporary era.

Goal Five: It is an objective of _____ college/university to provide students with life long skills such as competency in interpersonal relations, self discipline, problem solving and technical knowledge.

AMERICAN INDIAN STUDIES PROGRAM GUIDE

Table of Contents

Part One: Bachelor of Arts in American Indian Studies 1
    Section A: American Indian Program (Minor and Major) 1
    Section B: AMERICAN INDIAN STUDIES DIAGNOSIS TEST 4
    Section C: American Indian Studies Courses 7
    Section D: Course Implementation Plan 86
    Section E: Student Evaluation Form 87
    Section F: Course Evaluation Plan 88
    Section G: Program Evaluation 95

Part Two: Master of Arts in American Indian Studies 96
    Section A: American Indian Studies Graduate Program 96
    Section B: American Indian Studies Courses 100
    Section C: Course Implementation Plan 116
    Section D: Student Evaluation Form 117
    Section E: Course Evaluation Plan 118
    Section F: Program Evaluation 122

Part Three: Doctor of Education in American Indian Higher Education 123
    Section A: American Indian Doctoral Program in Education 123
    Section B: Doctoral of Education Courses 129
    Section C: Course Implementation Plan 153
    Section D: Student Evaluation Form 155
    Section E: Course Evaluation Plan 156
    Section F: Doctoral Evaluation Plan 164
    Section G: Grand Vision Action Plan 165

Section A: American Indian Program (Minor and Major)

Foundation of American Indian Studies

There are six courses or pillars that make up the foundation of American Indian Studies Programs in most universities including <u>Introduction to American Indian Studies</u>. Most other courses in American Indian Studies are offshoots of these six main courses: (a) Introduction to American Indian Studies, (b) The North American Indian, (c) American Indian History, (d) American Indian Law and Federal Policy, (e) American Indian Literature, (f) American Indian Religion and Philosophy, and (g) American Indian Education. Since these courses are the foundation of American Indian Studies they are required courses for the minor in American Indian Studies for a total of 21 units plus three electives for a total of 30 units.

(Minor and Major)

The major in American Indian Studies requires 39 units plus an culminating project or Senior Thesis. In addition to the 21 units required for the minor in American Indian Studies another 12 units are required for the major in American Indian Studies for a total of 33 required units plus another six units as electives and a Senior Thesis. The four required courses for the major in American Indian Studies in addition to the 21 for the minor in American Indian Studies are: <u>Contemporary American Indian History 110</u>, <u>Contemporary American Indian Legal Policy 112</u>, <u>American Indian Democracy 113</u>, and <u>Indian Treaties (1778-1888) 124</u> or <u>Cherokee Treaties 125</u> for a total of 12 units plus two electives.

Electives for both the minor and major in American Indian Studies are: <u>American Indian Science 222</u>, <u>American Indian Women 111</u>, <u>American Indian Mythology 1111</u>, <u>American Indian Culture 1112</u>, <u>American Indian Art 134</u>, <u>American Indian Music 135</u>. There are also three Special Study courses, an Independent Study, and a Directed Reading course.

Special Study In American Indian Studies: 1-3 units.

Student will sign a contract with the instructor to write a brief oral report on a topic in American Indian Studies.

Special Study In American Indian Studies: 1-3 units.

The student will sign a contract with the instructor to write several brief essays on a topic in American Indian Studies, and give an oral report.

Directed Reading In American Indian Studies:

This is a three unit independent course. The student will sign a contract with the instructor to write a research paper on a topic in American Indian Studies, and deliver an oral report on the research paper at the end of the semester with an outline of the oral report and the research paper.

Senior Thesis:

The senior thesis is the culminating project for the major in American Indian Studies. The student will sign a contract with the instructor. A major research paper or project will be turned in to the instructor along with an outline of the senior thesis and an oral report in an American Indian Studies class to be decided by the instructor.

This appendix describes teaching objectives, student learning outcomes, a description of each course, and the textbooks for each course along with course requirements.

Although courses for an entire American Indian Studies Program have been developed with course schedules none have calendar dates. This is because each instructor want to set their own dates for quizzes, exams, etc. The author of this American Indian Studies Guide developed course schedules for the courses he specializes in. The course schedules for the other courses will be developed by the instructor who teaches those courses because of academic freedom concerns. Finally, although books for supplemental reading are not required texts unless the instructor wishes to use them as required texts, they can be useful to students writing research papers.

A. I. S. 1A.	Introduction to American Indian Studies	3 units
A. I. S. 1B.	The North American Indian	3 units
A. I. S. 2A.	American Indian Science	3 units
A. I. S. 2B.	American Indian History	3 units
A. I. S. 3A.	American Indian Law and Federal Policy	3 units
A. I. S. 3B.	American Indian Women	3 units
A. I. S. 4A.	American Indian Religion and Philosophy	3 units
A. I. S. 4B.	American Indian Literature	3 units
A. I. S. 5A.	Contemporary American Indian History	3 units
A. I. S. 5B.	American Indian Education	3 units
A. I. S. 6A.	Contemporary American Indian Legal Policy	3 units
A. I. S. 6B.	Indian Treaties (1778-1888)	3 units
A. I. S. 7A.	American Indian Democracy	3 units
A. I. S. 7B.	Cherokee Treaties	3 units
A. I. S. 8A.	American Indian Mythology	3 units
A. I. S. 8B.	American Indian Culture	3 units
A. I. S. 9A.	American Indian Art	3 units
A. I. S. 9B.	American Indian Music	3 units
A. I. S. 10A.	Independent Study	1-3 units
A. I. S. 10B.	Special Study	1-3 units
A. I. S. 11A.	Directed Reading	1-3 units

Senior Thesis

Section B: AMERICAN INDIAN STUDIES DIAGNOSIS TEST

1). American Indian creation stories coincide with the archeological record.

   True _____   False _____

2). King Phillip's wife and son were sold into slavery in the West Indies after the King Phillip War.

   True _____   False _____

3). The French and Indian War is often referred to as:
   (A) King William's War
   (B) Great War for Empire
   (C) Queen Ann's War

4). The Formative Years was the period of:
   (A) 1871-1928
   (B) 1789
   (C) 1492-1532

5). Beginning with the adoption of the U. S. Constitution and concluding with the passage of the statute that brought an end to treaty-making comprise the:
   (A) Allotments and Assimilation era
   (B) Formative Years
   (C) Indian Reorganization
   (D) Self-Determination

6). The period of Self-Determination was between:
   (A) 1961-Present
   (B) 1943-1961
   (C) 1991-1996

7). Religion and ritual is involved in hunting, fishing, gathering, social and political organization, technology, warfare, and art in Indian spirituality.

True _____   False _____

8). American Indian sacred sites are sacred lakes, hot springs, and mountains.

True _____   False _____

9). The history of Indian education began with the Spanish conquest who wanted to convert the indigenous people to Catholicism.

True _____   False _____

10). The Carlisle Indian School was headed by:
(A) Richard Henry Pratt
(B) Reverent John Elliot

ANSWER KEY

1). True
2). True
3). Great War for Empire
4). B
5). B
6). A
7). True
8). True
9). True
10). Richard Henry Pratt

Section C: American Indian Studies Courses

INTRODUCTION TO AMERICAN INDIAN STUDIES 1A

Instructor: Dr. Byron Lee Blackwell, JD, Ed. D
Office: To be announced
Hours: To be announced
Phone: To be announced

Course Description: American Indian Studies is an interdisciplinary curriculum. There are six courses that make up the foundation of American Indian Studies. These six courses are: The North American Indian, American Indian History, American Indian Law and Federal Policy, American Indian Religion and Philosophy, American Indian Literature, and the History of American Indian Education. This course will employ lecture, discussion, assigned readings, films, and videos, as well as guest speakers from the American Indian community. By studying Indian world views, and cultural history pre-contact and during the conquest period students will gain an insight into problems faced by contemporary American Indians in modern day America.

Prerequisite: Students will be required to take an diagnostic test in order to assess students' present knowledge of Indian culture.

Text: <u>A Student Study Guide To An Introduction To American Indian Studies</u> by Byron Lee Blackwell, JD, Ed. D. This study guide will be made available to you by the author.

<u>The Native American Almanac: A Portrait of Native America Today</u> by Arlene Hirschfelder and Martha Dreip de Montano, Prentice-Hall General Reference, New York, 1993.

Course Objectives: Since American Indian Studies is an historical discipline, the historical method of developing the course was utilized in order to orient students to field of American Indian Studies. This course is an introductory course that will prepare students for more advanced courses in American Indian Studies. It is the purpose of this course to provide students with a brief survey or summary of the six main courses that make up the core or foundation of American Indian Studies Programs.

<u>Learning Experiences and Instructional Methods:</u> This course will employ lecture, discussion, assigned readings, films, and video tapes, as well as guest speakers from the American Indian community. By studying Indian world views, and cultural history pre-contact and during the conquest period students will gain an insight into problems faced by contemporary Indians in modern day America.

<u>Goal Statement:</u> Since American Indian Studies is an historical discipline, the historical method of developing the course was utilized in order to orient students to the field of American Indian Studies. This course is an introductory course that will prepare students for more advanced study in the discipline of American Indian Studies. It is the purpose of this course to provide students with a brief survey or summary of the six main courses that make up the foundation of American Indian Studies programs. This course will provide students with the opportunity to apply problem solving skills in understanding principles and concepts in the discipline of American Indian Studies.

<u>Learning Outcomes:</u> Upon completion of this introductory course students will have gained an understanding of pre-contact and post-contact Indian history, cultural world view, religion, literature, Indian law and federal policy, and Indian education. Furthermore, upon completion of this course students will have demonstrated the ability to communicate effectively and to critically analyze various issues in American Indian Studies such as manifest destiny.

<u>Course Requirements:</u> You are responsible for all assigned readings, lectures, discussions, and films and presentations of guest speakers, and map of Turtle Island (to be discussed). All papers must be typewritten and doubled-spaced and turned in on time.

Policies and Procedures:

There will be graded quizzes in order to help students' assess their process in the class. There will be a mid term and a final examination as well as a term paper and a map of Turtle Island will be turned in to the instructor. The student will identify on the map of Turtle Island where all the various Indian nations originated.

Evaluation and Grading:
Oral Presentation   10%
Mid-term Exam   30%
Research Paper   20%
Final Exam   30%
Class Attendance and Participation   10%

A = 90 to 100
B = 80 to 89
C = 70 to 79
D = 60 to 69
F = Below 60

I = Incomplete: The student must make every attempt to complete the course requirements within the allotted time. If for unavoidable reasons the student cannot complete the course work within the time lines of the course calendar, the instructor, at his discretion, may give the student an incomplete. To receive this grade the student must contact the instructor on a timely basis before the end of the semester.

LECTURE TOPIC	READING ASSIGNMENT
Chapter One	**PAGES**

Unit One: The North American Indian 5
Genesis: Ancient Indian America 5
Section One: Pangaea 7
Section Two: Pre-Contact America 10
Section Three: Lithic Period B Paleo-Indians 10
Section Four: Clovis, Folsum, and Plano Culture 11

Chapter Two
Ancient Civilizations 12

Chapter Three 15
The Mound Builders
Section One: Adena 15
Section Two: Hopewell 16
Section Three: The Temple Mound Builders 16

Chapter Four
Culture Areas 18
Section One: The Arctic Culture Area 18
Section Two: The Subarctic Culture Area 19
Section Three: The Northeast Culture Area 19
Section Four: The Southeast Culture Area 20
Section Five: The Great Plains Culture Area 21
Section Six: The Southwest Culture Area 22
Section Seven: The Great Basin Culture Area 23
Section Eight: The Plateau Culture Area 24
Section Nine: The Northwest Culture Area 25
Section Ten: The California Culture Area 26
Section Eleven: The Meso-American and Circum-Cum-
Carribean Area 27

Unit Two: American Indian History

The Invasion of the Americas 31
Section One: Columbus and the annihilation of the West Indies...............31
Chapter Two: Indian Wars...40
Section One: The Invasion of the Southeast 42
Section Two: The Invasion of the Northeast..44
Section Three: The French and Indian War 48
Section Four: The Revolutionary War 52
Section Five: Wars in the Old Northwest 55
Section Six: Wars of Indian Removal 61
Section Seven: Wars in the West and Far West..68
Section Eight: Indian War in Canada 70
Section Nine: The Massacre at Wounded Knee..77

Unit Three: A Legal History of Federal Indian Policy 88
Section One: Pre-Constitutional Precedents 88
Section Two: The Formative Years 90
Section Three: Allotments and Assimilation 92
Section Four: Termination...95
Section Five: Self-Termination...96

MIDTERM EXAMINATION

Unit Four: American Indian Religion and Philosophy..................93
Section One: Pre-Contact Religious Experience.....................................104
Section Two: Sacred Sites 106
Section Three: Post-Contact Religious Practice 108
Section Four: Post-Contact Religious Movements 109

Unit Five: American Indian Literature...115
Section One: Oral Literature 115
Section Two: Poetry...118
Section Three: Oratory 122
Section Four: American Indian Authors 125

Unit Six: American Indian Education 131
Section One: A History of Indian Education 131
Section Two: Colonial Education 138
Section Three: Mission Education 140
Section Four: The New Deal Area 141
Section Five: The Termination Area 144
Section Six: Self-Determination and Indian Education 147
Section Seven: Traditional Indian Education in America 149

FINAL EXAMINATION

THE NORTH AMERICAN INDIAN 1B

Instructor: To be announced

Office: To be announced

Hours: To be announced

Phone: To be announced

Course Description: This course covers the history, culture, and tribal locations of Indian peoples in North and Middle America from ancient times to the present era, and provides students with an awareness of relationships between Indian tribes living in specific regions as well as their similarities and differences.

Text: Atlas of the North American Indian. Carl Waldman. (1985) Facts On File Publications: New York, NY.

Encyclopedia of Native American Tribes. Carl Waldman. Facts On File Publications: New York, NY.

Exploring Ancient Native America: An Archaeological Guide. (1994). David Hurst Thomas. Macmillan: USA.

Supplemental Reading:

Native America: Portrait of the Peoples. Duane Champagne. (1994).

Visible Ink Express, Detroit, Michigan.

Course Objectives: It is the purpose of this course to trace the location and migrations of Indian tribes and cultures, and to depict the patterns of Indian lifeways and regional culture areas, means of subsistence, methods of transportation, types of shelter, clothing, arts and crafts, religious practices, kinship customs, language groups, as well as the topography (physiography), vegetation, and climate of ancient North America as well as chronicle the Indian wars against the European invaders.

Learning Experiences and Instructional Methods: This course will employ lecture, discussion, assigned readings, films and video tapes, as well as guest speakers from the American Indian community. The Atlas of the American

Indian covers the entire span of Indian history from prehistory post-contact to the present era of contemporary American Indians. American Indian

Studies encompass the fields of archaeology, anthropology, sociology, geography, religion, politics, etc.

Learning Outcomes: Students will explore and gain insight into Ancient Indians, Ancient Civilizations, Indian Lifeways, Indians and Explorers, Indian Wars, Indian Land Cessions, and Contemporary Indians.

Course Requirements: You are responsible for all assigned readings, lectures, discussions, and films and presentations of guest speakers, and map of Turtle Island (to be discussed). All papers must be typewritten and double-spaced and turned in on time.

Evaluation and grading:

Oral Presentation	10%	A = 91 to 100
Mid-term Exam	30%	B = 81 to 90
Research Paper	20%	C = 71 to 80
Final Exam	30%	D = 59 to 70
Class Attendance and Participation	10%	F = Below 60
		I = Incomplete

Atlas Of The North American Indian

The First Americans
Waldman: 1-45

Cultural Evolution
Waldman: 46-56

Religion and Spirituality
Waldman: 57-62

Indian Wars
Waldman: 86-164

Encyclopedia of Native American Tribes

Alphabetical List of Tribes and Peoples: 1-264

Glossary: 265-274

Further Reading: 275-278

MIDTERM EXAMINATION

Exploring Ancient Native America: An Archaeological Guide.

Chapter One: The Global Prologue 1

Genesis: Where We Came From: Some Native American Perspectives

Chapter Two: The First Americans 9

Chapter Three: Spreading Out Across America 49

Chapter Four: Agriculture Imperatives in the American Southwest 89

Chapter Five: Harvesting the Eastern Woodlands 124

Chapter Six: Mississippian Transformation 151

Chapter Seven: Colliding Worlds: Old and New? 183

Chapter Eight: Epilogue: An Enduring Encounter 231

Appendix 245

FINAL EXAMINATION

AMERICAN INDIAN HISTORY 2B

Instructor: Dr. Byron Lee Blackwell, JD, Ed. D

Office: To be announced

Hours: To be announced

Phone: To be announced

Course Description: This course covers American Indian history from the invasion of Christopher Columbus to contemporary times.

Text: The Devastation of the Indies: A Brief Account. (1992). The John Hopkins University Press: Baltimore and London.

A Student Study Guide To An Introduction to American Indian Studies. (1988). Byron Lee Blackwell. California State University San Bernardino. (pp.31-81).

Chronicle Of The Indian Wars. (1993). Prentice-Hall General Reference: New York.

Supplemental Reading:

The Tainos: Rise and Decline of the People Who greeted Columbus. (1992). Irving Rouse. Yale University Press: New Haven & London.

In Defense Of The Indians. (Bartolome de Las Casas). Translated and edited by Stafford Poole, CM.. Northern Illinois University Press: Dekalb.

Course Objectives: It is the purpose of this course to narrate the invasion of America from the Native American point of view, and to tell the truth about the so-called discoverer of America.

Learning Experiences and Instructional Methods: This course will employ lecture, discussion, assigned readings, films and video tapes, as well as guest speakers from the American Indian community. The Chronicle of the Indian Wars narrates the true history of the European invasion of America.

<u>Learning Outcomes</u>: Students will learn the truth about Columbus in the annihilation of the West Indies, and the European war for the North American continent in the dispossession of the original inhabitants of North America.

<u>Course Requirements</u>: You are responsible for all assigned readings, lectures, discussions, and films and video tapes and presentations of guest speakers, and map of Turtle Island (to be discussed). All papers must be typewritten and double-spaced and be turned in on time.

<u>Evaluation and grading</u>:

Oral Presentation	10%
Mid-term	30%
Term Paper	20%
Final Exam	30%
Class Attendance and Participation	10%

The Devastation of the Indies pp.27-132.

The Invasion of the Americas. Dr. Blackwell, 31-77.

Columbus and the Annihilation of the West Indies, pp. 27-132.

Axelrod, Chronicle of the Indian Wars.

Chapter 1 B 15

Chapter 1	Black Legend, Red Men: New Spain	1
Chapter 2	"To Subdue the Wilde Salvages:" Jamestown and the Southern Settlements (1607-1671)	10
Chapter 3	Trouble in New Canaan: The Pequot War (1634-1638)	14
Chapter 4	New England Bleeds: King Philip's War (1675-1676)	23
Chapter 5	Trade and Tyranny: The Dutch-Indian Wars (1626-1664)	38
Chapter 6	Iroquoian Imperialism: The Beaver Wars (1638-1684)	41
Chapter 7	Clients, Allies, Enemies, and a Demagogue: The Indian War Of 1675-1676	46
Chapter 8	Old World Enmities, New World Battles: The Wars of King William and Queen Anne (1688-1713)	51
Chapter 9	Desperate Resistance: The Tuscarora and Yamassee Wars (1710-1716)	59
Chapter 10	An Ear and an Empire: The Fox Resistance, King George's War, and the Chickasaw Resistance (1712-1748)	63
Chapter 11	Paths of Glory: The Period of the French and Indian War (1749-1763)	70

Chapter 12	Coda and Prelude: The Epoch of Pontiac's Rebellion, the Paxton Riots, and Lord Dunmore's War (1760-1774)	95
Chapter 13	White War, Red Blood, the Revolutionary Period (1774-1784)	101
Chapter 14	After the Revolution: Little Turtle's War (1786-1795)	123
Chapter 15	Forlorn Prophecy: The Period of Tecumseh and the War of 1812 (1805-1814)	130

MIDTERM EXAMINATION

Chapter 16	Wars of the Removal: The South (1812-1858)	137
Chapter 17	Wars of the Removal: The Old Northwest (1812-1833)	148
Chapter 18	The Wars for the West: Overture (1840s-1850s)	155
Chapter 19	Early Wars in the Far West (1850-1859)	171
Chapter 20	On the Eve of Civil War (1851-1860)	176
Chapter 21	Blue, Grey, and Red: The Apache Uprising and Navajo War (1861-1864)	183
Chapter 22	Blue, Grey, and Red: The Santee Sioux Uprising, the Shoshone War, and the Cheyenne-Arapaho War	190
Chapter 23	Wars on the Plains (1866-1869)	200
Chapter 24	The Fate of "Conquest by Kindness": The Snake War, the Modoc War, and the Red River War (1866-1875)	211

| Chapter 25 | The Northern Plains and the Northwest: The Sioux War for the Black Hills and the Pursuit of the Nez Pierces (1876-1881) | 221 |

| Chapter 26 | Wars Against the Bannocks, Sheepeaters, and Utes (1878-1879) | 226 |

| Chapter 27 | The Apache Epoch (1870-1886) | 240 |

Epilogue: Ghost Dance and Wounded Knee 248

FINAL EXAMINATION

AMERICAN INDIAN LAW AND FEDERAL POLICY 3A

Instructor: Dr. Byron Lee Blackwell, JD, Ed. D

Office: To be announced

Hours: To be announced

Phone: To be announced

Course Description: American Indian jurisprudence refers to that body of law created by treaties, executive orders, statutes, court decisions and administrative rulings that define and implement the political and legal relationship between the United States and the various Indian nations. The doctrinal foundations in federal Indian law is anomalous in United States jurisprudence. This course is on the legal history of Indian law which can be traced back to 1532 when Francisco de Victoria made the first formal exposition as to the respective rights of the aboriginal inhabitants in the Western Hemisphere. American Indian jurisprudence can be traced to these early sources which are derived from legal precedents in international law developed by the renowned Spanish jurist, Francisco de Victoria, the Father of modern international law. In the Western United States since Indian common laws are shared by many tribes there is a comparative law of Indian common law in tribal courts. Indian social norms, both substantive and procedural, which are specific to some tribes, are common to many others are examined in this course.

Text: An Activity Guide to A Legal History of Federal Indian Policy by Byron Lee Blackwell, JD, Ed. D.

The Rights of Indians and Tribes. (1992). ((2nd Ed.). Steven Pevar. Southern Illinois Press: Carbondale and Edwardsville.

Supplemental Reading:

American Indian Law in a Nut Shell. (1981). (2nd Ed.). William C. Canaby, Jr., Professor of law: Arizona State University.

Indian Common Law: The Indian Common Law: The Role Of Custom In American Indian Tribal Courts by Robert D. Cooter & Wolfgang Fikentscher.

The American Journal of Comparative Law, Volume XLVI, Summer 1998, Number 3.

<u>Course Objectives</u>: The objective of this course is to help students broaden their knowledge and understanding of the legal history of Indian law and federal policy that has historically shaped the political, legal, and economic relationship between the various American Indian nations and the federal and state governments.

<u>Learning Experiences and Instructional Methods</u>: This course will employ lecture, discussion, assigned readings, films and video tapes, as well as guest speakers from the American Indian community. Students will gain an insight into how history aids the legal scholar in tracing development of various legal doctrines and statutory provisions.

<u>Learning Outcomes</u>: Upon completion of this survey course students will have gained an understanding of how federal Indian policy derived from early Spanish law was developed by Spanish jurists. Within an historical perspective during the Pre-Constitutional E a of Discovery, Conquest, and treaty-making when the United States came into existence, and during the Formative Years, Allotments and Assimilation, Termination, and Self-Determination, students will gain an insight into how history aids the legal scholar in tracing the development of various doctrines and statutory provisions. Finally, upon completion of this course students will understand how historical support concerning tribal history and culture brought into evidence regarding negotiation and ratification of treaties aids courts in the adjudication of legal disputes.

<u>Course Requirements</u>: You are responsible for all assigned readings, lectures, discussions, and films and presentations of guest speakers, and map of Turtle Island (to be discussed). All papers must be typewritten and double-spaced and turned in on time.

<u>Assessment</u>: The degree to which the stated course objectives have been achieved will be determined by annual department assessment of the specific course outcomes. Learning outcomes will be assessed through quizzes, midterms and final examinations as well as term papers. Quizzes will assess students' ability to identify terms, ideas, and concepts. Midterms will focus on the students' ability to identify terms, ideas, and concepts through definition,

multiple choice, and specific word definition. Final examinations will assess students' ability to synthesize information and draw logical conclusions through comparison and analysis.

Evaluation and grading:

Oral Presentation	10%
Mid-term Exam	30%
Research Paper	20%
Final Exam	30%
Class Attendance and Participation	10%

AMERICAN INDIAN LAW AND FEDERAL POLICY

A Legal History of Federal Indian Policy

Unit One - AMERICAN INDIAN JURISPRUDENCE

American Indians In Historical Perspective 4
Pre-Constitutional Precedents (1532-1789) 7
Discovery, Conquest, and Treaty-Making 9
The Doctrine of Discovery 11
Conquest 13
Treat-Making 15

Unit Two - FEDERAL INDIAN LAW

A History of Indian Legal Policy 28
The Formative Years (1789-1871) 28
Allotments and Assimilation (1871-1928) 34
Indian Reorganization (1928-1942) 36
Termination (1943-1961) 37
Self-Determination (1961-Present) 38

MIDTERM EXAMINATION

Unit Three - AMERICAN INDIAN LAW

Hunting, Fishing, and Gathering Rights 49
American Indian Spiritual/Natural Law 49
Sacred, Original Instructions 49
The Creator's Founding Prescription 52
Indian Aboriginal Rights 53

Unit Four - AMERICAN INDIAN COMMON LAW
    Substantive Indian Common Law 507-564
  A. Land
  B. Repossession
  C. Inheritance
  D. Environment
  E. Family Law
  F. Contracts
  G. Crimes
  H. Conflict of Laws
FINAL EXAMINATION

AMERICAN INDIAN RELIGION AND PHILOSOPHY 4A

Instructor: To be announced
Office: To be announced
Hours: To be announced
Phone: To be announced

Course Description: This course is an introduction or survey of American Indian religion and Philosophy.

Text: Shamanic Healing and Ritual Drama: Health and Medicine in Native North American Religious Traditions. Abe Hulkrantz. (1992). Crossroads Publishing Company: New York: NY.

Yuwipi; Vision & Experience in Oglala, by William K. Powers. (1982). University of Nebraska Press: Lincoln and London.

Black Elk Speaks by John G. Neihart(1972). Washington Square Press: New York; NY.

American Indian Ecology. (1983) Donald J. Hughes. El Paso: Texas University Press: The University of Texas at El Paso.

Supplemental Reading:

Indian Healing: Shamanic Ceremonialism in the Pacific Northwest Today. (1986). Wolfgang G. Jilek. Canadian Cataloging in Publication Data. ISBN 0-88839120-X.

Offering Smoke: The Sacred Pipe and Native American Religions. The University of Idaho Press: Moscow, Idaho.

Course Objectives: The objective of this course is to help students gain an insight into Indian philosophy of living in spiritual harmony with the Natural World.

Learning Experiences and Instructional Methods: This course will employ lecture, discussion, assigned readings, films and video tapes, as well as guest speakers from the American Indian community. Students will gain an understanding of an holistic and reverent way of life that existed for thousands of years before the arrival of Europeans.

<u>Learning Outcomes</u>: Upon completion of this course students will understand that in American Indian religion that all things are dependent upon each other in order to maintain harmony and balance in the universe, and why each individual part of the ecosystem in the biosphere of earth, air, water climate, soil, plants, terrain and animals is delicate and must be kept in ecological balance.

Students will be able to describe pre-contact religious experience, post-contact religious experience, and post-contact religious movements of Indian people with the arrival of Europeans.

Students will also have an understanding of the Northern Hunting Tradition as well as the Southern Agrarian Tradition in American Indian religion.

<u>Course Requirements:</u> You are responsible for all assigned readings, lectures, discussions, and films and presentations of guest speakers. All papers must be typewritten and double-spaced and turned in on time.

<u>Evaluation and grading:</u>

Oral Presentation	10%
Term Paper	20%
Mid-term	30%
Final Exam	30%
Class Attendance and Participation	10%

A = 91 to 100

B = 81 to 90

C = 71 to 80

D = 60 to 70

F = Below 60

I = Incomplete

Shamanic Healing and Ritual Drama: Health and Medicine in Native North American Religions

Chapter One: The Cultural And Religious Setting 9

Chapter Two: Traditional Medicine In The Northeast 23

The Care of the Sick 25

Health, Well-Being, and the Causes of Disease 28

Doctors and Diviners 33

The Shaking Tent Performance 37

Midewiwin as a Doctors' Organization 39

Chapter Three: Traditional Medicine On The Northwest Coast ... 43

Health, Good Living, and Passages of Life among the Tlingit ... 47

The Nature of Disease 52

The Tlingit Shaman and His Healing Practices 54

The Healed Healer among the Coast Salish 61

The Spirit Canoe Curing Ceremony 65

Chapter Four: Traditional Medicine On The Plains 71

The Eastern Shoshone 72

Shoshone Passages of Life 74

Shoshone Ideas of Health and Well-Being 78

Causes of Disease 80

The Shoshone Medicine Man 83

Individual and Collective Aspects of Curing 87

Methods of Nonprofessional Folk Medicine 94

Curing among the Arapaho 95

The Arapaho Spirit Lodge 96

The Pawnee: The Blessing of the Animal Lodges 101

Chapter Five: Traditional Medicine In The Southeast 105

The Mythical Introduction of Diseases 107
The Immediate Causes of Disease 108
The Cherokee Doctor 109
The Treatment of Diseases 111
Chapter Six: Traditional Medicine In The Southwest 113
The Zuni Religious system 115
Collective Healing among the Zuni: The Medicine Societies 117
Zuni Ways of Curing 121
Zuni Symbolism of Ritual Curing 123
The Navajo World 125
Navajo Themes of Morality, Philosophy, and Health 128
Cosmological Healing among the Navajo 130
The Blessing Ceremony 131
The Holyway Ceremonies 133
The Evilway Ceremonies 135
The Pima and Papago of the Southwestern Deserts 136
Different Diseases for Native Americans and Whites 138
Chapter Seven: Medicine In New Religions 141
Peyote Curing 142
The Sweat Lodge Movement 146

Chapter Eight: Transcultural Medicine Relations: The Interaction
Between Native And Euro American Curing Methods 149
Indian Criticism and Tolerance Of Euroamerican Medicine 151
The Expansion of Native American Medicine into White Society 155
Conclusion 157
A Field of Diffculties 157
The Concepts and Practices of Native Medicine 158
The General Setting of Medical Beliefs and Practices 164

MID-TERM EXAMINATION

Yuwipi: Vision and Experience in Oglala Ritual

Introduction 1
Prelude 5
Sacred Stones 11
The Sweat Lodge: Inside 19
The Vision Quest: On the Hill 33
Preparing for the Sing 38
The Vision Talk 45
Calling the Spirits 53
The Curing 61
The Feast 69
The Vision Quest: Off the Hill 73
The Sweat Lodge: Outside 80
Postlude 84

FINAL EXAMINATION

AMERICAN INDIAN LITERATURE 4B

Instructor: To be announced

Office: To be announced

Hours: To be announced

Phone: To be announced

Course Description: This course on American Indian Literature is an anthology of American Indian literature by Indians on Indian subjects. This course covers traditional Indian literature which was primarily oral, consisted of tales, songs, and oratory, and mainstream Indian literature, written in English by Indians in one of the standard American genres, fiction, poetry, biography, and history.

Text: American Indian Literature: An Anthology. (1991) Alan R. Velie. (Ed.). University of Oklahoma Press: Norman.

Supplemental Reading:

Lame Deer: Seeker of Visions by Lame Deer, John Fire and Erodes, Richard. Pocket Books, a Simon and Schuster Division of Gulf and Western Corporation: New York.

Spider Woman's Granddaughters. (1989). Paula Gunn Allen. Boston: Blacon Press.

Course Objectives: The objective of this course is to present two types of Native American literature: traditional and mainstream American Indian literature.

Learning Experiences and Instructional Methods: This course will utilize lecture, discussion, assigned readings, films and video tapes, as well as guest speakers from the American Indian community. Students will study selected works from the post-contact Delaware epic Walam Olum and the origin myth of the Acoma Pueblo, through the oratory of the early contact period, as well as songs and stories of contemporary American Indians.

Learning Outcomes: Upon completion of this introductory course students will have gained an appreciation and understanding of both traditional and mainstream Indian literature.

Course Requirements: You are responsible for all assigned readings, lectures, discussions, and films and presentations of guest speakers. All papers must be typewritten and double-spaced and turned in on time.

Evaluation and grading:

Oral Presentation	10%
Term Paper	20%
Mid-term	30%
Final Exam	30%
Class Attendance and Participation	10%

A = 91 to 100
B = 81 to 90
C = 71 to 80
D = 60 to 70
I = Incomplete

American Indian Literature: An Anthology

Introduction 3

TALES

The Origin Myth of Acoma 14
Three Menomini Tales 27
    The Man Who Transgressed a taboo 27
    A Warrior's Heart 29
    The Jealous Ghost 31
High Horse's Courting 33
Awl and Her Son's Son 38
The Winnebago Trickster Cycle 44

SONGS

Chippewa Songs 77
    My Love Has Departed 78
    I Can Charm the Man 79
    Why Should I Be Jealous? 79
    If I Am Beaten 79
    I Am as Brave as Other Men 79
    Come, Let Us Drink 80
    The Man Who Stayed at Home 80
    Scalp Song 80
    A Song of Indecision 80
    You Desire Vainly 81
    He is Gone 81
    Love Song 81
    One Wind 81
    The Nature of the Village 81
    With Dauntless Courage 81
Teton Sioux Songs 82
    Opening Prayer of the Sun Dance 83
    Wakan tanka Hears Me 84
    I Have Conquered Them 84
    Song of the Strong Heart Society 84
    Watch Your Horses 84
    You Have No Horses 84
The Earth Only Endures 84

    Song. Concerning a Message from Washington 85
    Mandan and Hidatsa Songs 86
        The Corn Is My Pleasure 86
        He Stared at Me 86
        Take Me to the Sioux 87
        I Will Go 87
        Comrades, Sleep On 87
        Disguised as a Buffalo 87
        We Made Fire 88
        Kiowa "49" Songs 89
        Walam Olum 92
Oratory
Red Jacket
    Speech to Missionary Cram 136
    Speech to Mr. Richardson 141
    Defense of the Seneca Way of Life 141
    Speech to Governor Ogden 143
Pontiac's Allegory
    The Master of Life 145
Tecumseh
    Plea to the Choctaws and the Chickasaws 148
Memoirs
John G. Neihardt
    From Black Elk Speaks 155
John Lame Deer and Richard Erdoes
    From Lame Deer, Seeker of Visions 177
N. Scott Momaday
    From The Way to Rainy Mountain 204
Maurice Kenny
    Corn Planter 213
    Aiionwatha 213
    Sometimes . . . Injustice 214
    Mama Failed to Kill the Rat 214
    The Last Word 215
    Misbegotten Sonnet 216
    Land 217

Saranac Lake, NY 219
Heard Poem 219
After the Reading 220
Carter Revard 221
Wazhazhe Grandmother 221
Support Your Local Police DogOratory 223
Driving in Oklahoma 224
N. Scott Momaday 226
Simile 227
The Bear 227
Before an Old Painting of the Crucifixion 228
Angle of Geese 229
The Fear of Bo-Talee 229
The Great Filmore Street Buffalo Drive 229
Paula Gunn Allen 231
Powwow 79, Durango 231
Crow Ambush 232
Los Angeles, 1980 233
Hoop Dancer 235
James Welch 236
Major Fox 237
Getting Things Straight 237
Harlem, Montana: Just Off the Reservation 238
D-Y Bar 238
Arizona Highways 239
The Man from Washington 240
In the American Express Line 241
Plea to Those Who Matter 241
Grandma's Man 241
Simon Ortiz 243
A Barroom Fragment 243
Washyuma Motor Hotel 243
The Significance of a veteran's Day 244
To & Fro 245
Geary Hobson 246
Deer Hunting 246

    Lonnie Krammer..248
    A Discussion about Indian Affairs...248
    For My Brother and Sister Southwestern Indian Poets.....................249
    Buffalo Poem #1...250
    Central Highlands, Vietnam, 1968...250
Rayna Green 252
    Another Dying Chieftain 252
    Road Hazard 253
    Old Indian Trick..253
    Coosaponakeeta (Mary Mathews Musgrove Bosomsworth), Leader
        of the Creeks, (1700-1763)..254
Gus Palmer, Jr...254
    Frieze..256
    Message to Spring, or, The Choctaw Virgin Moon 256
    For Palo and Francesa, Lovers, In Cold 256
    For Theodore Roethke: 1908-1962 257
    The Poignant Beast..258
    Stone Carvers..258
    Language and Other Redemptive Things..258
    Creek 259
    Waiting...260
    An Eclipse 261
    Legend People 261
Lance Henson..263
    cheyenne winter...264
    extinction 264
    flock..265
    bay poem 265
    impressions of the peyote ritual 266
    oklahoma twilights, I..268
    counting losses in October 268
    dream of home..268
    for soft dresser...269
Charlotte DeClue 270
    Mmmmm. . . . Whiteman's Powwow 270
    Young Wife 270
    (for Lisa and those Northern girls) 272

    Out on the "run" 273
    Diaectic 273
    Separation 274
    Hookin' Honkies 274

Linda Hogan
    turtle 274
    Celebration: Birth of a colt 276
    Heritage 277
    Coyote 278
    Mosquitoes 279
    All Winter 280
    The New Apartment: Minneapolis 281
    Wall Songs 282
    The Truth Is 284

Joy Harjo 287
    Anchorage 287
    night out 287
    What I Should Have Said 288
    Alive 289

nila northSun 291
    up & out 291
    nevada 292
    barrel-racer cowboy chaser 293
    the paper 293
    be careful 294
    I was thinking about death again 294
    another one bites the dust 295

Richard Aitson 297
    The Sun Is Blue 297
    Winter 298
    Old Man Poem 298
    Walk 298

Diane Burns 300
    Gadoshkibos 300
    Big Fun 301
    Booze 'n' LoozingB Part III 302

Louise Erdrich 304
    A Love Medicine 304
    Family Reunion 305
    Captivity 306
    The Strange People 308
    The Butcher's Wife 309
    Here Is a Good for Step-and-Half Waleski 310
    Christ's Twin 310
    Mary Magdalene 311

Fiction

N. Scott Momaday
    From House of Dawn 315

James Welch
    From Winter in the Blood 320
    From The Trickster of Liberty 339

Louise Erdrich
    From Love Medicine 348

LeAnne Howe
    Moccasins Don't Have High Heels 361
    The Red Wars 367

FINAL EXAMINATION

AMERICAN INDIAN EDUCATION 5B

A. Semester, year: To be announced.

Instructor: To be announced.

Office: To be announced.

Hours: To be announced.

B. Course Description: In historical perspective, there are six periods in the history of Indian education that reflect federal policy regarding Indian education in the United States. These are the Pre-Constitutional Precedents during the Pre-Revolutionary Era from 1532 to 1789, the Formative years from 1789 to 1871, Allotments and Assimilation from 1871 to 1928, Indian Reorganization from 1918 to 1942, Termination from 1943 to 1961, and Self-Determination from 1961 to the present.

C. Course Requirements: You are responsible for all assigned readings, lectures, discussions, and films and presentations of guest speakers. All papers must be typewritten and double-spaced and turned in on time.

D. Text: Handbook On A History Of Indian Education In America. (1988). Dr. Byron Lee Blackwell. California State University San Bernardino.

Supplemental Reading:

Indian Education In America. (1991) Vine Deloria, Jr. American Indian Science & Engineering Society: Boulder, CO.

II. Course Goals and Outcomes:

Goal Statement:

The objective of this course is to show how the field of Indian education has a historical, as well as a contemporary dimension in Indian educational policy in the United States of America. Another objective of this course is to show how the antecedent roots of Indian education in America can be traced to early missionary efforts to indoctrinate Native societies, thereby destroying the ability of these societies to resist conquest and colonization.

A. Outcome Statement:

Upon completion of this course students will have an understanding of pre-contact and post-contact Indian education in America. Furthermore, students will have an understanding of traditional Indian education which began with the extended family and tribal Elders which was a clan directive, culminating in an understanding of Indian common law in tribal courts which is based upon customs among many tribes.

IV. ASSESSMENT:

The degree to which the stated goal outcomes have been achieved will be determined by annual departmental assessment of the specific course outcomes. Student learning outcomes will be assessed through quizzes, midterms and final examinations as well as term p pers. Quizzes will assess students' ability to identify concepts. Midterms will focus on the students' ability to identify terms, ideas, and concepts through definition, multiple choice, and specific word definition. Final examinations will assess students to synthesize information and draw logical conclusions through comparison and analysis.

V. POLICIES AND PROCEDURES:

A. Grading: There will be graded quizzes in order to help students' assess their process in the class. There will be a midterm and a final exam as well as a term paper.

B. <u>Evaluation and grading</u>:

Quizzes	No Grade
Oral Report	25%
Term Paper	25%
Midterm	25%
Final Exam	25%

A = 91 to 100
B = 81 to 90
C = 71 to 80
D = 60 to 70
F = Below 60

I = Incomplete: The student must make every attempt to complete the course assignments within the allotted time. If for unavoidable reasons the student cannot complete the course work within the time lines of the course calendar, the instructor, at his discretion, may give the student an incomplete. To receive this grade the student must contact the instructor on a timely basis before the end of the quarter/semester.

LECTURE TOPIC	READING
ASSIGNMENT	PAGES

Chapter One (1492-1776)
American Indians in Historical Perspective 3
Section A. A History of Indian Education 3
Section B. Colonial Education 26
Section C. Mission Education 31

Chapter Two (1779-1871)
The Formative Years 37
Section A. The Treaty Years (1778-1871) 37
Section B. Mission Education in the Treaty Years 38
Section C. Western Removal 51
Section D. Treaty Education 53

Chapter Three (1871-1928)
Allotments and Assimilation 75
Section A. Tribally Controlled Education: 1819-1915) 77
Section B. Government Controlled Education: (1867-1924) 88
Section C. Mission Schools 96
Section D. Government Boarding Schools 99

Chapter Four (1924-1942)
Indian Reorganization 102
Section A. The Meriam Report 102
Section B. The Indian New Deal 105

MIDTERM EXAMINATION

Chapter Five (1943-1961)
Termination 108
Section A. The Public Schools 112

Chapter Six (1961-Present)
Self-Determination 115
Section A. The Kennedy Report 117

Section B. Tribally Controlled Colleges 119

Chapter Seven: Traditional Indian Education In America
Section A. American Indian Metaphysics1 123
Section B. Traditional Indian Technology 128
Section C. Prologue 134

FINAL EXAMINATION

AMERICAN INDIAN SCIENCE 2A

Instructor: To be announced

Office: To be announced

Hours: To be announced

Phone: To be announced

Course Description: This course is a survey course on Indian science from American Indian math to archery to the construction of tepees to American Indian medicine to American Indian ecology.

Text: The Native American Sweat Lodge: History and Legends. (1993) Joseph Bruchac. The Crossing Press: Freedom, CA.

Indian Archery. (1980). Reginald & Gladys Laubin. University of Oklahoma Press: Norman.

The Indian Tipi: Its History, Construction And Use. (1971). Reginald & Gladys Laubin. Ballantine Books: New York.

Supplemental Reading:

American Indian Ecology. (1983). Donald J. Hughes. Texas University Press: The University of Texas at El Paso.

North American Sign Language. (1990). Karen Loptak Watt: New York.

Wampum Belts. Tehanentorens. (N.D.). Six Nations Museum Onchiota, New York.

American Indian Medicine. (1970). Virgil J. Vogel. University of Oklahoma Press: Norman.

Native American Mathematics. Michael P. Class, ed. (1986). University of Texas: Austin.

Course Objectives: The purpose of the course is to show that American Indians were skilled in astrology, mathematics, ecology, medicine, pharmacology, archery and the healing powers of the sweat lodge.

Learning Experiences and Instructional Methods: This course will employ lecture, discussion, assigned readings, films and videotape, as well as guest speakers from the Indian community.

Learning Outcomes: Students will gain an appreciation for the scientific wisdom as well as spiritual wisdom of the original people of America.

Course Requirements: You are responsible for all readings, lectures, discussions, films and presentations by guest speakers. All papers must be typewritten and double-spaced and turned in on time.

Evaluation and Grading:

Oral Report	10%
Term Paper	20%
Mid-term	30%
Final Exam	30%
Class Attendance and Participation	10%

The Native American Sweat Lodge: History and Legends

The Sweat Lodge 1

Historical Survey 9
    The Basic Types of Sweats 11
    Early European Sweat Baths 14
    Early Descriptions of Native American Sweats 17
    The Repression of the Sweat Lodge 25

The Parts Of The Lodge 29
    The Poles 30
    The Covering 33
    The Stones 36
    The Pipe 39

Creation 43
    Noogami's Arrival (Micmac) 48
    The Creation of the Sweat Lodge (Dineh [Navajo]) 50
    The Giver (Joshua) 52
    Earth Namer (Maidu) 57

The Lodge Of Testing 59
    The Bow Wrapped in Bark (Huron) 62
    The Hero Twins (Dineh [Navajo]) 65
    Me'jo and The Bear (Naspkapi) 67
    The Beaver Stick (Blackfeet) 78
    The Sweat Lodge Without a Bucket (Watlala) 81

When Trickster Enters The Lodge 83
    Wolverine and Bear (Passamaquoddy) 85
    How Coyote Made the Seasons (Nez Pierce) 88
    Coyote and Deer Spirit (Yakima) 91
    Coyote and Gray Giant (Dineh [Navajo]) 94
    Coyote and the Navajo (Hopi) 98
    A Dog for the Sweat Lodge (Cheyenne) 103

The Healing Lodge   105
    First Man and the Cedar Bough Lodge (Santee) 108
    The Coming of Medicines (Creek) 109
    Stone Boy (Lakota) 111

Scar Face (Blackfoot) 116
Weetucks Brings the Sweat (Wampanoag) 121
The Blanket of Men's Eyes (Seneca) 124
Turtle Man (Cheyenne) 131

MID-TERM EXAMINATION

American Indian Archery
Chapter One: Introduction 1
Chapter Two: History 11
Chapter Three: Comparisons of Bows 19
Chapter Four: Bow Making and Sinewed Bows 53
Chapter Five: Horn Bows 73
Chapter Six: Strings 105
Chapter Seven: Arrows 111
Chapter Eight: Quivers 127
Chapter Nine: Shooting 133
Chapter Ten: Medicine Bows 151
Chapter Eleven: Indian Crossbows 157
Chapter Twelve: Blowguns, Stone Bows, and Harps 163

AMERICAN INDIAN WOMEN 3B

Instructor: To be announced

Office: To be announced

Hours: To be announced

Phone: To be announced

Course Description: This course is an examination of American Indian women's concepts of spirituality, culture, community, politics, womanhood through native life ways including Cherokee women.

Course Objectives: The objective of this course of this course is to present the native life ways of Indian women.

Learning Experiences and Instructional Methods: This course will utilize lecture, discussion, assigned readings, films and video tapes, as well as guest speakers from the American Indian community especially Indian women.

Learning Outcomes: Students will learn about native life ways through American Indian women's concepts of spirituality, culture, community politics and womanhood.

Course Requirements: You are responsible for all readings, lectures, discussions, films and presentations by Native American women guest speakers. All papers must be typewritten and double-spaced and turned in on time.

Text: Cherokee Women: Gender and Culture Change, 1700-1835. (1998). Theda Perdue. University of Nebraska Press: Lincoln and London.

Sacajawea. (1982). Harold P. Howard. University of Oklahoma Press: Norman.

Pocahontas. (1976). Grace Steele Woodward. University Of Oklahoma Press: Norman.

Supplemental Reading:

Apache: The Sacred Path of Womanhood. Hihn Annerino. (1988). Marlowe and Company: New York.

No Turning Back: A true story of a Hopi Indian girl's struggle to bridge the gap between the World of her People and the World of the White Man. (1964). Albuquerque: University of New Mexico Press.

Spider woman's Granddaughters: Tales and Contemporary Writing by Native American Woman. (1989). Paula Gunn-Allen. Boston: Blacon Press.

Waterlilly. (1988). Ella Cara Deloria. Lincoln: University of Nebraska Press.

Evaluation and Grading:

Oral Report	10%
Term Paper	20%
Mid-Term	30%
Final Examination	30%
Class Participation	10%

Cherokee Women: Gender and Culture Change, 1700-1835. (1998).

Part One: A Woman's World
    1. Construction Gender 17
    2. Defining Community 38

Part Two: Contact
    3. Trade 65
    4. War 86

Part Three: "Civilization"
    5. A Changing Way of Life 115
    6. Women in the Early Cherokee Republic 135
    7. Selu Meets Eve 159

Part Four: Conclusion 185

Pocahontas

The Powhattans 8
The Invaders 41
The Beginning of Jamestown 51
The Rescue 63
Negotiations 74
Powhattan's Coronation 84
The Contest Quickens 92
The Starving Time 111
A Second Chance 118
Signs of Success 128
The Abduction and Conversion 151
The Marriage 160
A Matter of Money 168
The Visit to England 174
Gravesend 184
An Epilogue 187

Sacajawea

The Lewis and Clark Expedition

Chapter One: The Expedition Sets Out 3
Chapter Two: The Journals and Diaries 11
Chapter Three: Sacajawea Comes to Visit 15
Chapter Four: Leaving the Mandans 21
Chapter Five: The Rescue 29
Chapter Six: Portaging the Falls 35
Chapter Seven: Sacajawea Returns to Home Country 43
Chapter Eight: Meeting the Shoshones 49
Chapter Nine: Across the Divide to the Columbia 61
Chapter Ten: Pass the Cascades of the Columbia 73
Chapter Eleven: Camping on the Columbia 81
Chapter Twelve: Winter at Fort Clatsop 87
Chapter Thirteen: The Walla Wallas 95
Chapter Fourteen: The Nez Pierces 101
Chapter Fifteen: Recrossing the Bitterroot Mountains 107
Chapter Sixteen: The Party Divides 111
Chapter Seventeen: Lewis Explores the Marias River 115
Chapter Eighteen: A Skirmish with the Indians 121
Chapter Nineteen: The Mouth of the Yellowstone 127
Chapter Twenty: Down to St. Louis 133
Chapter Twenty One: The Expedition Ends 139

Part Two: Sacajawea's Later Life

Chapter Twenty Two: Sacajawea C What was She Like? 147
Chapter Twenty Three: At Fort Manuel 155
Chapter Twenty Four: Toussaint Charbonneau 163
Chapter Twenty Five: Jean Baptiste Charbonneau 169
Chapter Twenty Six: The Two Versions 175

CONTEMPORARY AMERICAN INDIAN HISTORY 5A

Instructor: Dr. Byron Lee Blackwell, JD, Ed. D.

Office: To be announced

Hours: To be announced

Phone: To be announced

Course Description: This course examines political and social issues of contemporary American Indians such as land, water, civil and tribal rights as well as events in the past that shape Indian policy in the modern era.

Text: The State of Native America: Genocide, Colonialism, and Resistance. (Jaimes, Annette M. (Ed.). South End Press: Boston.

Exiled In The Land Of The Free: Democracy, Indian Nations and the U.S. Constitution. (1992). Oren R. Lyns and John C. Mohawk. Five Rings Corporation. Clear Light Publishers: Santa Fe.

Indian Country. (1984). Peter Matthiessen. The Viking Press: New York, NY.

Supplemental Reading:

Wounded Knee 1973: A Personal Account. (1991). Stanley David Lyman. University of Nebraska Press: Lincoln and London.

Bury My Heart At Wounded Knee. (1981). Dee Brown. Washington Square Press: New York.

Course Objectives: It is the objective of this course to examine modern political and social issues such as land, water, civil and tribal rights that arise from U.S.-Indian relations in the past which affect Indian communities in the contemporary era.

Learning Experiences and Instructional Methods: This course will utilize lecture, discussion, assigned readings, films and video tapes, as well as guest speakers from the American Indian community. Students will gain an insight into the historical and attitudinal differences between Indian nations and the U.S. regarding land, water, civil and tribal rights.

Learning Outcomes: Students will learn how the political, legal, and economic policies of the United States of the previous centuries affect Indian rights in the 20th century.

Course Requirements: You are responsible for all assigned readings, lectures, discussions, and films and presentations of guest speakers including a short work project in the Indian community. All papers must be typewritten and double-spaced and turned in on time.

Evaluation and Grading:

Oral Report	10%
Work Project	20%
Mid-Term Exam	30%
Final Exam	30%
Class Attendance and Participation	10%

The State Of Native America: Genocide, Colonization, and Resistance

Preface: The State of Native North America

Introduction: Sand Creek: The Morning After 1

Table: Key Indian Laws and Cases 13

Chapter I: The Demography of Native North America: A Question of American Indian Survival 23

Chapter II: International Law and Politics: Toward a Right to Self-Determination for Indigenous Peoples 55

Chapter III: Self-Determination and Subordination: The Past, Present, and Future of American Indian Governance 87

Chapter IV: Federal Indian Identification Policy: A Usurpation of Indigenous Sovereignty in North America 123

Chapter V: The Earth is Our Mother: Struggles for American Indian land and Liberation in the Contemporary United States 139

Chapter VI: American Indian Water Rights: The Blood of Life in Native North America 189

Chapter VII: In Usual and Accustomed Places: Contemporary American Indian Fishing Rights Struggles 217

Chapter VIII: Native North America: The Political Economy of Radioactive Colonialism 241

Chapter IX: Trouble in High Places: Erosion of American Indian Rights to Religious Freedom in the United States 267

Chapter X: A Warrior Caged: The Continuing Struggle of Leonard Peltier 291

Chapter XI: American Indian Women: At the Center of Indigenous Resistance in North America 311

Chapter XII: Patriots and Pawns: State Use of American Indians in the Military and the Process of Nativization in the United States 345

Chapter XIII: American Indian Education in the United States: Indoctrination for Subordination to Colonialism 371

Chapter XIV: The Great Pretenders: Further Reflections on White Shamanism 403

Chapter XV: Cowboys and...Notes on Art, Literature, and American Indians in the Modern American Mind 423

Epilogue: Looking for Columbus: Thoughts on the Past, Present and Future of Humanity 439

Exiled In The Land Of The Free: Democracy, Indian Nations and the U.S. Constitution

Introduction 1

Chapter One: The American Indian in the Past 13

Chapter Two: Indians and Democracy: No One Ever Told Us 43

Chapter Three: American Indian Influences on the America of the Founding Fathers 73

Chapter Four: Perspectives on American Indian Sovereignty and International Law, 26000 to 1776 125

Chapter Five: United States-Indian Relations: The Constitution Basis 189

Chapter Six: Iroquois Political Theory and the Roots of American Democracy 227

Chapter Seven: The Application of the Constitution to American Indians 281

Chapter Eight: Congress Plenary Power, and the American Indian, 1870 to 1992 317

Indian Country

Chapter One: Native Earth 1
Chapter Two: The Long River 15
Chapter Three: Mesas 65
Chapter Four: Lost Eloheh 103
Chapter Five: Akwesasne 127
Chapter Six: The High Country 165
Chapter Seven: Black Hills 201
Chapter Eight: At The Western Gate 221
Chapter Nine: East If Mount Shasta 239
Chapter Ten: Great Basin 259
Chapter Eleven: Four Corners 291
Chapter Twelve: To Big Mountain 313

CONTEMPORARY AMERICAN INDIAN LEGAL POLICY 6A

Instructor: Dr. Byron Lee Blackwell, JD, Ed. D.

Office: To be announced

Hours: To be announced

Phone: To be announced

Course Description: This course examines political, legal and social issues such as American Indian religious freedom and water rights of American Indian policy in the later half of the twentieth country. This course also examines some of the key Indian laws and cases in the past that shapes Indian legal policy in the contemporary era.

Text: Handbook of American Indian Religious Freedom. (1991). Christopher Vecesey. The Crossroad Publishing Company: New York, NY.

American Indian Water Rights and the Limits of Law. (1991). Lloyd Burton. University Press of Kansas.

American Indian Policy In The Twentieth Century. (1992). Edited by Vine Deloria, Jr. University of Oklahoma Press: Norman and London.

Key Indian Laws and Cases. This supplement will be provided to you by the instructor.

Supplemental Reading:

American Indian Law: In a Nutshell. (191981). William C. Canby. Professor of Law. Arizona State University.

American Indians: Answers to Today's Questions. (1993). Jack Utter. National Woodlands Publishing Company: Lake Ann, Michigan.

Course Objectives: It is the objective of this course to examine modern political, legal and social issues of American Indian policy on land, water, civil and tribal rights that arise from U.S.-Indian relations in the past which affect Indian communities in the contemporary era as well as critically analyze key Indian laws and cases.

Learning Experiences and Instructional Methods: This course will employ lecture, discussion, assigned readings, films, videotapes as well as legal scholars and guest speakers from the American Indian community. Students will gain an insight into the historical and attitudinal differences between Indian nations and the U.S. regarding land, water, civil and tribal rights.

Learning Outcomes: Students will learn how the political, legal, and economic policies of the United States of the previous centuries affect Indian rights in the contemporary era.

Course Requirements: You are responsible for all assigned readings, lectures, discussions, and films and presentations of guest speakers. All papers must be typewritten and double-spaced and turned in on time.

Evaluation and Grading:

Quizzes	No Grade
Oral Report	10%
Research Paper	20%
Midterm Exam	30%
Final Examination	30%
Class Attendance and Participation	10%

Handbook of American Indian Religious Freedom

Prologue

Chapter One: A Legal Analysis of the American Indian
   Religious Freedom Act 27

Chapter Two: Peyote and the Law 44

Chapter Three: Repatriation, Reburial, and Religious Rights 63

Chapter Four: Sacred Sites and Public Lands 81

Chapter Five: Protection of American Indian Sacred Geography 100

Chapter Six: Law and the Limits of Liberty 116

Epilogue 134

American Indian Water Rights And The Limits Of Law

Preface ix

Chapter 1: Reflections in a Glass Bead 1

Chapter 2: The Development of American Indian Water Rights 6

Chapter 3: Legal Issues and Dispute-Managing Methods in
   Contemporary Water Rights Conflicts 35

Chapter 4: The Peril and Promise of Negotiation: a Closer Look 63

Chapter 5: Groundwater Rights, Planning, and Bargaining in
   South Central Arizona 87

Chapter 6: Conclusion: Improving the Prospects for Negotiated
   Settlements 124

AMERICAN INDIAN DEMOCRACY 7A

Instructor: Dr. Byron Lee Blackwell, JD, Ed. D

Office: To be announced

Hours: To be announced

Phone: To be announced

Course Description: American democracy was not born in ancient Greece or Rome. American democracy is derived from Indian democracy, and the U.S. Constitution came from the Iroquois Indian Constitution, The Great Law of Peace. Deganawidah the Great Peacemaker who gave his people their constitution, the Great Law of Peace in 950 A.D., is the true founding father of the U.S. Constitution.

Text: Iroquois Confederacy of Nations. Hearing before the Select Committee on Indian Affairs. Select Committee On Indian Affairs. United States Senate. One Hundred Congress. First Session on Senate Congressional Resolution 76.

Indian Roots of American Democracy. Special Constitution Bicentennial Edition, 1988. Published by the Northeast Indian Quarterly, Cornell University.

The Birth of Frontier Democracy From an Eagle's Eye View: The Great Law of Peace to the Constitution of the United States of America. Book published at Akwesasne Notes, Mohawk Nation, New York.

Wampum Belts: George Morgan, Native Americans and Revolutionary Diplomacy. (1990). Gregory Schaaf. Fulcrum Publishing: Golden, Colorado.

Supplemental Reading:

Forgotten Founders: Benjamin Franklin, the Iroquois, and the Rationale for the American Revolution. (1982). Bruce Johansen. Gambit Publishers: Ofipswich, Massachusetts.

Debating Democracy: Native American Legacy of Freedom. (1998). Bruce Johansen. Clear Light Publishers: Santa Fe, New Mexico.

Course Objectives: It is the objective of this course to critically analyze the birth of the United States by laying side by side articles of the Iroquois Constitution the Great Law Of Peace with the United States Constitution to prove that Deganawidah the Great Peacemaker is the true founding father of the United States Constitution.

Learning Experiences and Instructional Methods: This course will employ lecture, discussion, assigned readings, films and videotapes as well as guest speakers from the American Indian community.

Learning Outcomes: Students will learn to examine and critically analyze legal as well as historical documents pertaining to the birth of the United States of America.

Course Requirements: You are responsibly for all assigned readings, lectures, discussions, and films and presentations of guest speakers from the American Indian community. All papers must be typewritten and turned in on time.

Evaluation and Grading:

Quizzes	No Grade
Oral Report	10%
Research Paper	20%
Midterm Exam	30%
Final Exam	30%
Class Attendance and Participation	10%

Iroquois Confederacy Of Nations: Hearing Before The Select Committee On Indian Affairs United States Senate.

The Birth of Frontier Democracy from an Eagle's Eye View: The Great Law of Peace to The Constitution of the United States of America PP. 56-137.

Indian Roots of Democracy

Forward xi
Introduction xii

Section I   **HAUDENOSAUNEE SPEAKERS**

Words That Come Before All Else 2
    Thanksgiving Address
Everything Has To Be In Balance 4
Men Who Are Of The Good Mind 8
The Indian Way Is A Thinking Tradition 13
Land Of The Free/Home Of The Brave 18
The Great Law Takes A Long Time To Learn 21

Section II   **ACADEMIC SPEAKERS**

Colonial History: 300 Years Of Cultural History 26
It Is Time To Take Away The Veil 28
The Price Of American Liberty Is Paid By Indian Lands 35
Indian Thought Was Often In Their Minds 40
The Iroquois Had Democracy Before We Did 44
Discovery Of Morgan Papers Adds To The Evidence 49

Section III   **LEGAL SCHOLARS**

On The Historical Quality Of The Nation-to-Nation Relationship .. 54
A Clear Statement from Congress Is Needed On Indian Rights 57
Indian Rights Deserve International Protection 61

Section IV   **Roots Of The Women's Line**

Mother Of Nations - The Peace Queen 68
Interview with Peter Jemison 70
Her Word Was Law: Excerpts from Parker 71

APPENDICES

Appendix A: Senate Resolution 74
Appendix B: Glossary 76

<u>Wampum Belts: George Morgan, Native Americans, and Revolutionary Diplomacy</u>

Introduction: "The Discovery" xv

Chapter One: Liberty and Justice for All: The Dream vs. Reality 1

Chapter Two: Menachk-sink: The Establishment of the First
    U.S. Indian Agency Fort Pitt 25

Chapter Three: Dark Clouds over the Revolutionary Frontier
    British, American, and Indian Intrigues 47

Chapter Four: Black Robes in the Pasture of Light: The
    Christian Indian Mission 71

Chapter Five: Balance of Power: The Courtship of Indian
    Nations Early in the Revolution 87

Chapter Six: Brother Tamanneend"s Mission to the Lenni Lenape 111

Chapter Seven: The White Deer's Mission to the Shawnee 127

Chapter Eight: The Council House and the Mingo Nation 143

Chapter Nine: The 1776 U.S. Indian Peace Treaty 161

Chapter Ten: "The Right to Life, Liberty and the Pursuit of
    Happiness" 197

AMERICAN INDIAN MYTHOLOGY 8A

Instructor: Dr. Byron Lee Blackwell
Office: To be announced
Hours: To be announced
Phone: To be announced

Course Description: Origin myths are important not only for historical and prototypical value but also for religious (spiritual) and archetypical value. Genesis myths are important because they help us to identify the typical, archaic, primitive forms of human behavior. The prototype gives the original structure, the original conception of human conduct. It is a reflection of people's thought processes, and measures human probability, potentiality, and originality. It is important to understand that, when creation myths refer to events as prototypical, the real value is understanding them as archetypical. Archetypes reveal and define form, showing how a truth of the moment has the same structure and meaning as an absolute and eternal one. Myths should therefore be taken seriously because it reveals a reveals a significant unverifiable truth. A myth is a symbolic signpost; it serves as a map of unverifiable truths. Myths deal with metaphysical, absolute truths. The imagery and abstract thought in the symbolism reveal the essential function of the law of nature embodied in the myth. Symbolism is a metaphoric device used by Indians to interpret spiritual reality, and represents the conceptual methodology for analytical interpreting ancient Indian thought.

Text: The Indian Roots. (1989). Dr. Byron Lee Blackwell.

American Indian Genesis. (1989). Dr. Byron Lee Blackwell.

Sproul, Barbara. (1978). Primal Myths: Creating the World. New York: Harper & Row.

Course Objectives: The objective of this course is to employ science from The Indian Roots to prove that American Indian creation stories are based on scientific fact and not savage superstition. This course will show that how ancient Indian philosophers used metaphors and symbolism in myths as a carefully constructed "symbolic cloak" for their abstract thoughts. Furthermore, they employed both the metaphysical (mental) model

(Cherokee), and the physical model (Hopi), in which the Creator was a master craftsman or craftswoman who carves and shapes the environmental landscape.

Learning Outcomes: In order to get as close to the primordial truth as possible as possible, students will analyze the mythical process, as well as examine the mythical events in terms of a mythical signpost, the imagery and abstract thoughts in the symbolism that reflect the laws of nature. Students will understand that the scientific version of how the universe was created and the American Indian version of how the universe are created are essentially the same except ancient Indian philosophers used metaphors and symbolism to describe the same phenomena.

Course Requirements: You are responsibly for assigned readings, lectures, discussions, films and presentations of guest speakers as well as a map of Turtle Island (the Indian name for America). All papers must be typewritten and double-spaced and turned in on time.

Evaluation and Grading:

Oral Report	10%
Term Paper	20%
Midterm	30%
Final Examination	30%
Class Attendance and Participation	10%

The Indian Roots

The Creation of the Earth 1

Turtle Island.. 5
    The Precambrian Era in the Cryptozoic Eon
    Breakup of Turtle Island
    Sacred Book of the Mayas
    Hopi Creation

Super Continent of Pangaea 12
    Late Permian Period in the Paleozoic Era
    Formation of Laurasia, Gondwanaland
    Breakup of Pangaea in the Period and early Mesozoic Era
    Large Asteroid Collides with the Earth
    The Sacred Book of the Mayas

Quaternary Period in the Pleistocene Epoch 17
    Human Beings Appear
    Destruction of the First World by Volcano Fire
    Destruction of the Second World by Glaciers
    Destruction of the Third World by the Great Flood
    Destruction of the Fourth World by Nuclear Fire

Pleistocene Epoch of the Quaternary Period of Cenzoic ("recent life") Era.. 21
    Turtle Island
    Gondwanaland
    Lelauraia
    Lemuria
    Atlantis

Creation of the Earth... 32
    Hot Plume Model
    Cherokee/Seneca Creation Stores
    Hopi Genesis
    Migration in Reverse

American Indian Genesis

The American Indian Genesis 1
    Pleiades Star System (Cherokee)
    Lemuria (Biblical Garden of Eden) (Hopi)
    Turtle Island
    Atlantis (Six Islands of Atlantis) (Cherokee)

The Mythic Foundation of Native American Conduct 7
    Prototype
    Cosmology
    Ontology
    Axiology
    World View
    Ethos
    Ideology
    Archetype
    Ground of Being
    Primary Absolute Reality
    Divine Chaos
    Metaphysical (Mental) Model
    Physical (Shaping) Mod l

The Seneca Creation Genesis 14
    Endless Space
    Eternal Land (the Universe)
    Field Of Plenty (Nebular Hypothesis)
    Breath of Life (Oxygen)
    Chaotic Water Myth (Universe)
    First Sphere (Proto-sun)
    Second Sphere (Moon)
    Third Sphere (Water)
    Etenoha (Mother Earth)
    The Four Sacred Directions
    Yellow (East)
    White (North) Top of the World
    South (Black)
    Red (West)

    Mental Metaphor

The Seneca Genesis 29
    Migration of the First World
    Migration of the Second World
    Migration of the Third World
    Migration of the Four World

Cherokee Genesis (Mental Metaphor) 45
    People of One Fire
    The Sacred Word
    The Sacred Seven
    The Seven Star System (Pleiades)
    The Keepers of the Sacred Fire
    The Fire Keepers of the Sacred Fire

Tsalagi Elo (Cherokee Philosophy) 46
    Creator Being (Mental Metaphor)
    Sign Stimulus
    Light Sound Explosion (Nebular Hypothesis)
    Original Chaos
    Sacrifice Metaphor
    Cherokee Sun (Nebular Hypothesis)
    The Three Elder Fires
    Twelve Vortices of Sound or Spirals of Energy
    Fire (Thought Beings)
    Star Woman
    Dreaming Metaphor
    The Sacred Triangle

Cherokee Creation Genesis 54
The Adawees (Great Angelic Beings)
    Sacred Seven
    Children of the Sun
    Procreation Metaphor
    Dreaming Metaphor
    Sacred Crystals
    Star Maiden
    Brother of the Light Face

Brother of the Dark Face
  Sign Stimulus
  Divine Sacrifice
  Procreation Metaphor
  Forming Metaphor
  Galunlati (Sky Vault)
  American Indian Mythology System
  Symbolism (Metaphorical Device)

Hopi Genesis 72
  Taiowa the Creator
  Sotuknang this Nephew or Son
  Kokyangwuti the Spider Woman
  The Warrior Twins Poqanghoya the Left Son
  Polanqawoya the Right Son
  Creation of Humans from Four Colors

The Creation of the World 76
  Tokpela (Endless Space)
  First World (Tokpela)
  Second World (Tokpa)
  Third World (Kuzkursa)
  Fourth World (Tuwaquachi)
  Masaw the Death Spirit

        Migrations of the American Indian People to the Promised Land
of their Creator 99
  Indian Signature
  Indian Footprints
  Ancient Record
  Indian Supreme Title to Turtle Island (North, Central and South
  America)
  The Great Spirit's Deed
  American Indians the Spiritual Caretakers of Turtle Island
  Sacred Tablets of the Hopi

Comparisons of the Cherokee, Seneca and Hopi Bible 103
  The Book of Revelation in the Holy Bible

INDIAN TREATIES, (1778-1888) 6B

Instructor: Dr. Byron Lee Blackwell, JD, Ed. D

Office: To be announced

Hours: To be announced

Phone: To be announced

Course Description: This is a survey course on the history of Indian treaties from 1778-1888. The theoretical conceptual framework in American Indian jurisprudence is drawn from legal canons derived from principles of international law, political philosophy, and natural law. This course provides a chronological list of all the treaties and agreements the United States made with the Indian nations of America including executive orders, top fifty Indian case laws, statutes, and documents of United States Indian Policy as well as perspectives on international law. Some of this material will be provided by the instructor. The Handbook of Federal Indian Law (1942) by Felix Cohen has laws, statutes and executive orders pertaining to Indian treaties.

Text: A Chronological List Of Treaties and Agreements Made By Indian Tribes With The United States. A Publication of The Institute For The Institute Of Indian Law. Washington, DC. This will be provided to you by the instructor.

Executive Orders Relating to Indian Reservations. (Vol.1.). National Indian Law Library/Native American Rights Fund, Boulder, Colorado. Excerpts will be provided to you by the instructor.

Top Fifty: A Collection of Significant Federal Indian Cases. (1990). National Indian Law Library/Native American Rights Fund. Boulder, Colorado. Cases will be provided to you by the instructor.

Documents of United States Indian Policy. (Second Edition). (1990). Francis Paul Prucha. University of Nebraska Press: Lincoln/London.

Jus Cogens: The Law of Human Rights. Hastings International and Comparative Law Review. Vol. 12, No. 2, Winter 1982. Hastings College of the Law, 1988, pp. 420-521.

Supplemental Reading:

Laws and Treaties. Vol. II. (Treaties). (1904). Charles J. Kappler, LL. M.. Washington: Government Printing Office. This should be in the library.

Handbook of Federal Indian Law. (1942). Felix S. Cohen. United States Government Printing Office: Washington, DC. This treatise has Indian treaties, statutes and executives. This should be in the library.

Handbook of Federal Indian Law. (1982 Edition). Felix S. Cohen. The Michie Company Law Publishers. Charlottesville, 'Virginia. This is the latest version without the treaties.

Atlas of American Indian Affairs. (1990). Francis Paul Prucha. University of Nebraska Press: Lincoln & London.

Charter of the United Nations and Statute of the International Court of Justice. United Nations. New York

Course Objectives: It is the objective of this course to examine documents on United States policy and the executive orders, statutes, and case law pertaining to treaties and agreements the United States made with Indian nations.

Learning Experiences and Instructional Methods: This survey course on treaties will employ lecture, discussion, assigned readings, films and videotapes as well as scholars from the legal community and the Native American community.

Learning Outcomes: Students will learn that continual infringement on treaty rights by statute and execute orders have made a mockery of sacred solemn agreements Indian nations made with the United States in good faith. Students will learn how the United States Supreme Court has circumvented Indian treaty rights by employing the political question doctrine to decline judicial review in cases where the court claims raises issues more properly resolved by the executive or legislative branches of government. However, in international law the doctrine of Jus Cogens is ipso jure, a legal, not a political question. Students will learn how lawyers at the United Nations and the International Court of Justice at the Hague can employ the doctrine of

Jus Cogens to develop legal theories and doctrines to defend human rights of American Indian political prisoners and treaty rights of Indian nations.

<u>Course Requirements</u>: You are responsible for all assigned readings, lectures, discussions, and films and presentations of legal scholars and the Native American community. All papers must be typed and double-spaced and turned in on time.

<u>Evaluation and Grading</u>:

Quizzes	No Grade
Oral Report	20%
Legal Research Paper	20%
Midterm Exam	30%
Final Examination	30%
Class Attendance and Participation	10%

CHEROKEE TREATIES 7B

Instructor: Dr. Byron Lee Blackwell, JD, Ed. D

Office: To be announced

Hours: To be announced

Phone: To be announced

Course Description: This is a survey course on Cherokee treaties beginning with the first Cherokee treaty on November 28, 1785. This treaty was concluded at Hopewell on the Keowee. (Cherokee) (7 Stat. 18) and concluding with the last treaty on April 27. 1868. Cherokee Nation (16 Stat. 727). There were seventeen treaties in all. These legal documents were treaties of peace, exchange of prisoners, sales of land, boundaries, trade, provisions, education, etc.

Text: American Indian Treaties And International Law: Compelling The Doctrine Of Jus Cogens. (Draft) (2002). Dr. Byron Lee Blackwell, Juris Doctor, Education Doctor.

A Chronological List Of Treaties And Agreements Made By Indian Tribes with The United States. A Publication of The Institute for the Development of Indian Law, Inc. (1973).

Executive Orders Relating to Indian Reservations. (Vol. 1). National Indian Law Library/Native American Rights Fund. Boulder, Colorado. Excerpts will be provided to you by the instructor.

Documents of United States Policy. (Second Edition). (1990). Francis Paul Prucha. University of Nebraska Press: Lincoln/London.

Laws and Treaties, Vol. II (Treaties). (1904). Charles J. Kappler, LL. M. Washington: Government Printing Office. This should be in the library.

Handbook of Federal Indian Law. (1942). Felix S. Cohen. United States Government Office: Washington, DC. This treatise has both treaties and laws. This should be in the library.

Handbook of Federal Indian Law. (1982 Edition). The Michie Company Law Publishers: Charlottesville, Virginia. This latest version does not have the treaties.

Jus Cogens: The Law of Human Rights. Hastings International and Comparative Law Review. Vol. 12, No. 2, Winter 11982. Hastings College of the law, 1988, pp. 420-521.

Charter of the United Nations and Statute of the International Court of Justice. United Nations: New York.

Course Objectives: It is the objective of this course to examine documents on United States and the executive orders, statutes and case law pertaining to treaties the United States made with the Cherokee Nation.

Learning Experiences and Instructional Methods: This course on Cherokee treaties will employ lecture, discussion, assigned readings, films and videotapes as well as scholars from the legal community and the Cherokee community.

Learning Outcomes: Students will learn that treaties contain (1) a preamble, (2) terms and conditions, (3) provisions (special conditions, usually referring to something of value, and (4) signatures, seals and marks. Students will learn how execute orders, statutes and case law has infringed on the treaty rights of the Cherokee nation, and how the doctrine of Jus Cogens can be employed at the International Court of Justice at the Hague in order to develop legal theories and doctrines to enforce treaty rights of the Cherokee nation.

American Indian Treaties And International Law: Compelling The Doctrine Of Jus Cogens.

Chapter One: Introduction

Chapter Two: American Indians In Historical Perspective
    Pre-Constitutional Precedents (1532-1789)
    Discovery, Conquest, and Treaty-Making (1828)

Chapter Three: A History Of Indian Legal Policy The Formative Years (1789-1871)
    Allotments and Assimilation (1871-1928)
    Indian Reorganization (1928-1942)
    Termination (1943-1961)
    Self-Determination (1961-Present)

Chapter Four: American Indian Spiritual/Natural Law Hunting, Fishing, and Gathering Rights

Chapter Five: The Doctrine of Jus Cogens

Chapter Six: Conclusion

AMERICAN INDIAN CULTURE 8B

Instructor: Dr. Byron Lee Blackwell, JD, Ed. D.

Office: To be announced

Hours: To be announced

Phone: To be announced

Course Description: American Indian Culture is a survey of American Indian life styles in the United States, and is designed as an introductory course to the basic traditions and customs among North American Indian peoples. In this survey course you will examine Indian world views, indigenous customs and traditions, post contact modifications of life styles, and the contributions that American Indians have made to the rest of the world.

Text: A Basic Call To Consciousness. Akwesane Notes, Ed. (1986). Mohawk Nation. via Rooseveltown, New York.

Sacred Earth: The Spiritual Landscape of Native America. Indian Culture, Inner Traditions International, Ltd. Rochester, Vermont.

Indian Givers: How The Indians Of The Americas Transformed The World. (1988). Crown Publishers, Inc: New York.

Supplemental Reading:

Seeing With a Native Eye: Essay on Native American Religions. (1976). Capps Walter H., ed. Harper & Row: New York.

No Turning Back: A True Account of a Hopi Indian girl's Struggle to bridge the Gap between the World of her people and the World of the White Man. (1964). Polingaysi Qoyawayma. (Elizabeth Q. White). University of New Mexico Press: Albuquerque, New Mexico.

Learning Experiences and Instructional Methods: This course will employ lecture, discussion, assigned readings, films and video tapes, as well as guest speakers from the American community. This course will focus on providing students with a basic understanding of the dynamics Of American Indian culture in the United States.

<u>Learning Outcomes</u>: Students will gain an knowledge of traditional Indian life styles as well the life styles of contemporary American Indians.

<u>Course Requirements</u>: You are responsible for all assigned readings, lectures, discussions, and films and presentations of guest speakers including a short work project in the Indian community.

Evaluation and Grading:

Oral Report	10%
Short Essays	No Credit
Work Project	20%
Midterm Exam	30%
Final Examination	30%
Class Attendance	10%

Basic Call to Consciousness

The Haudenosaunee:
A Nation Since Time Immemorial 1

Thoughts of Peace
The Great Law 7

Deskaheh: An Iroquois Patriot's
Fight for International Recognition 13

Geneva, 1977: A Report On The Hemispheric
Movement of Indigenous Peoples 13

A Basic Call To Consciousness:
The Haudenosaunee Address to the Western World 45

Our Strategy For Survival 74

Sacred Earth: The Spiritual Landscape Of Native America

Part One: Foundations 1
Nature as Theophany 9
Wakan, Orenda, Manitou 14
Timelessness and Time 21
Totemic Revelations 28
Sacred Man and the Great Mystery 35

Part Two: Spiritual Symbolism

Introduction 45
Inscriptions in Stone 48
The Great Horned Serpent 56
The Stone Man 67
The Great Lodge as Microcosmos 74
Initiation and Its Inversions 82

Part Three: Spiritual Landscape

Introduction 89
Language of the Earth, Language of the Sky 91

Celestial Agriculture, Celestial Journey 95
Spiritual Landscape 102
Mountains and Fire, Winds and Waters 113
The Council Fire 119
The Songs of Solitude and Silence 126

Conclusion 139

<u>Indian Givers: How The Indians Of The Americas Transformed The World</u>

Chapter One: Silver and Money Capitalism 1
Chapter Two: Piracy, Slavery, and the Birth of Corporations 21
Chapter Three: The American Indian Path to Industrialization 39
Chapter Four: The Food Revolution 59
Chapter Five: Indian Agricultural Technology 79
Chapter Six: The Culinary Revolution 99
Chapter Seven: Liberty, Anarchism, and the Noble Savage 117
Chapter Eight: The Founding Indian Fathers 133
Chapter Nine: Red Sticks and Revolution 151
Chapter Ten: The Indian Healer 175
Chapter Eleven: The Drug Connection 197
Chapter Twelve: Architecture and Urban Planning 217
Chapter Thirteen: The Pathfinders 217
Chapter Fourteen: When Will America Be Discovered? 267

AMERICAN INDIAN ART 9A

Instructor: To be announced

Office: To be announced

Hours: To be announced

Phone: To be announced

Course Description: This course on American Indian art history is an anthology devoted to twentieth century Native American and First Nation art by bringing together anthropologists, art historians, curators, critics, and distinguished American Indian artists who discuss topics such as sculpture, print making, photographs, as well as performance and conceptual art. This course will discuss the origins of Indian art as well as modern materials used contemporary Indian art.

Text: Native American Art in the Twentieth Century. (1999). W. Jackson Rushing III (Editor). London & New York: Routeledge.

Visions and Voices: Native American Painting from the Philbrook Museum of Art. (1996). Lydia L. Wyckoff (Editor).

The Rock Art of Texas Indians. (1967). W. W. Newcomb, Jr. University of Texas, Austin.

Weaving Arts of the North American Indian. (1993). Frederick J. Dorkstader. New York: Icon Editors as Imprint of Harper Collins Publishers

Course Objectives: The objective of this course is to show how American Indian art preserved the past, and taught future generations of native Americans about their culture and heritage.

Learning Experiences and Instructional Methods: This course is a compendium of diverse discourses on American Indian art history from the theoretical to the spiritual to the aesthetic. New theoretical and critical approaches to American Indian art history are examined such as symbolism and spirituality by having American Indian artists discuss pottery, paintings, sculpture, print making, photographs, performance and conceptual art of the most celebrated American Indian artists.

<u>Learning Outcomes</u>: Students will learn how American Indian art and paintings has its origins in pre-contact pictographs and petrographs painted on or inscribed on decorative pottery, clothing, as record keeping of past history began to take on various materials from the white culture such as pencils and paper inks as well as other commercial materials.

<u>Course Requirements</u>: You are responsible for all assigned readings, lectures, discussions, and films and presentations of guest speakers. All papers must be typewritten and double-spaced and turned in on time.

<u>Evaluation and Grading</u>:

Oral Presentation	10%
Term Paper	20%
Mid-term	30%
Final Exam	30%
Class Attendance and Participation	10%

AMERICAN INDIAN MUSIC 9B

Instructor: To be announced

Office: To be announced

Hours: To be announced

Phone: To be announced

Course Description: History of American Indian musical styles, instruments, tribal dance styles, social and ritual of North American Indian cultures adaption of traditional social music and dance to modern pow wow setting. Students will learn selected songs and dances.

Text: Teton Sioux Music, Francis Densmore.

Indian Dancing and Costume, (GP. Putham). William Powers.

Course Objectives:

1. To study American Indian music and dance as integral elements.

2. To acquire basic skills in methods of analyzing Indian music.

3. To acquire basic ability to distinguish regional music (i.e., Northern, Southern, Southwestern, etc.)

4. To acquire basis skills of retention and singing of Indian songs (i.e., lullabies, love songs, game songs, personal songs, etc.)

5. To learn simple social dances for participation at local pow wows.

6. To develop an appreciation for American Indian music as a non- Western art form.

Learning Experiences and Instructional Methods: Lecture, discussion, films, research and assigned readings will be utilized as instructional aids to supplement student experience and involvement with American Indian music. Authentic musical instruments such as hand drums, rattles, flutes, and whistles will be used by the instructor to demonstrate song accompaniment. Students will be expected to become involved in the "hands on" experience and will:

1. Participate in the performance of selected traditional songs from various tribes, solo and ensemble.

2. Participate in the performance of selected contemporary pow wow songs.

3. Participate in the performance of simple group/social pow wow dances (round dance, two-step, buffalo, and snake dances).

4. Attend at least one Pow Wow to observe and hear special dances (contest and demonstration) and songs that have been incorporated into the modern pow wow.

Learning Outcomes:

1. Be able to distinguish "northern" drum styles from "southern" drum styles.

2. Be able to distinguish hand drums from "kettle" drums.

3. Know which Tribes/regions use flutes.

4. Acquire the knowledge and understanding of ceremonial dance and song: when and why they are performed.

5. Understand the difference religious/sacred, social and personal songs and their relationships to Indian value systems in the past and present.

6. Gain an understanding of the "etiquette" and proper forms of social and ceremonial performances required of participants and observers.

Course Requirements: You are responsible for all assigned readings, lectures, discussions, films, slides, and attendance at pow wows and other cultural events, and participation in dance in class. Grade based on class participation, reading assignments, learning of songs, song identification, several short essays, a term paper, and final exam. Students will one research paper employing ethnos musical approach and basic methods to analyze American Indian music of several tribes from different regions. At least 50% of semester will be devoted to the learning and practice of songs and pow wow social dances.

Evaluation and Grading:

Student Participation and presentations	10%
Research Paper	30%
Short Essays	30%
Final Exam	30%

Section D: Course Implementation Plan

Fall Semester   1ˢᵗ Year
1) Introduction To American Indian Studies A.I.S. 1A
2) The North American Indian A.I.S. 1B
3) American Indian Science 2A

Spring Semester   1ˢᵗ Year
1) American Indian History 2B
2) American Indian Law and Federal Policy 3A
3) American Indian Women 3B

Fall Semester   2ⁿᵈ Year
1) American Indian Religion and Philosophy 4A
2) American Indian Literature 4B
3) Contemporary American Indian History 5A

Spring Semester   2ⁿᵈ Year
1) American Indian Education 5B
2) Contemporary American Indian Legal Policy 6A
3) Indian Treaties (1778-1888) 6B

Fall Semester   3ʳᵈ Year
1) American Indian Democracy 7A
2) Cherokee Treaties 7B
3) American Indian Mythology 8A

Spring Semester   3ʳᵈ Year
1) American Indian Culture 8B
2) American Indian Art 9A
3) American Indian Music 9B

Section E: Student Evaluation Form

Your advice and opinions on the effectiveness of this course will help American Indian Studies improve its courses. Please feel free to address any concerns you have regarding the course content. Your comments will help us to improve the course.

(1) In your opinion did this course meet the objectives stated in the course syllabus?

(2) Did this course meet the stated outcomes for the course?

(3) After completing the course do you feel you are able to communicate effectively and critically analyze various issues in American Indian Studies?

(4) Do you have any other concerns regarding the course content that will help improve the quality of the course?

Section F: Course Evaluation Plan

INTRODUCTION TO AMERICAN INDIAN STUDIES 1A

<u>Course Objectives</u>: It is the purpose of this course to provide students with a brief survey or summary of the six main courses that make up the core or foundation of American Indian Studies programs. This course will provide students with the opportunity to apply problem solving skills in understanding principles and concepts in the discipline of American Indian Studies.

<u>Learning Outcomes</u>: Upon completion of this introductory course students will have gained an understanding of pre-contact and post-contact Indian history, cultural worldview, religion. literature, Indian law and federal policy, and Indian education. Furthermore, upon completion of this course students will have demonstrated the ability to communicate effectively and to critically analyze various issues in American Indian Studies such as manifest destiny.

THE NORTH AMERICAN INDIAN 1B

<u>Course Objectives</u>: It is the purpose of this course to trace the location and migrations of Indian tribes and cultures, and to depict the patterns of Indian lifeways and regional cultural areas, means of subsistence, methods of transportation, types of shelter, clothing, arts and crafts, religious practices, kinship customs, language groups, as well as the topography (physiography), vegetation, and climate of ancient North America as well as chronicle the Indian wars against the European invaders.

<u>Learning Objectives</u>: Students will explore and gain insight into Ancient Indians, Ancient Civilizations, Indian Lifeways, Indians and Explorers, Indian Wars, Indian Land Cessions, and Contemporary Indians.

AMERICAN INDIAN SCIENCE 2A

Course Objectives: This course is a survey course on Indian science from American Indian math to archery to the construction of tipis and sweat lodges to American Indian sign language to wampum belts to American Indian medicine to American Indian ecology.

Learning Outcomes: Students will gain an appreciation for the scientific wisdom as well as spiritual wisdom of the original people of America.

AMERICAN INDIAN HISTORY 2B

Course Objectives: It is the purpose of this course to narrate the invasion of America from the Native American point of view, and to tell the truth about the so-called discover of America.

Learning Outcomes: Students will learn the truth about Columbus in the annihilation of the West Indies, and the European war for the North American continent in the dispossession of the original inhabitants of North America.

AMERICAN INDIAN LAW AND FEDERAL POLICY 3A

Course Objectives: The objective of this course is to help students broaden their knowledge and understanding of the legal history of Indian law and federal policy that has historically shaped the political, legal, and economic relationship between the various American Indian nations and the federal and state governments.

Learning Outcomes: Upon completion of this introduction course students will have gained an understanding of how federal Indian policy derived from early Spanish law was developed by Spanish jurists. Within an historical perspective during the Pre-Constitutional Era of Discovery, Conquest, and Treaty-making when the United States came into existence, and during the Formative Years, Allotments and Assimilation, Termination, and Self-Determination, students will gain an insight into how history aids the legal scholar in tracing the development of various doctrines and statutory provisions, Finally, upon completion of this course students will understand how historical support concerning tribal history and culture brought into evidence regarding negotiation and ratification of treaties aids courts in the adjudication of legal disputes.

AMERICAN INDIAN WOMEN 3B

Course Objectives: The objective of this course is to present the native life ways of Indian women in North America as well as examine the political power of Cherokee Indian women in traditional Indian America.

Learning Outcomes: Students will explore the role of Indian women in traditional Indian societies

AMERICAN INDIAN RELIGION AND PHILOSOPHY 4A

Course Objectives: The objective of this course is to help students gain an insight into Indian philosophy of living in harmony with the Natural World.

Learning Outcomes: Upon completion of this course students will understand that in American Indian religion that all things are dependent upon each other in order to maintain harmony and balance in the universe, and why each individual part of the ecosystem in the biosphere of earth, air, water, climate, soil, plants, terrain and animals is delicate and must be kept in ecological balance with both the spiritual and the natural world.

AMERICAN INDIAN LITERATURE 4B

Course Objectives: The objective of this course is to present two types of Native American literature: traditional and mainstream modern American Indian literature.

Learning Outcomes: Upon completion of this introductory course students will have gained an appreciation and understanding of both traditional and modern Indian literature.

CONTEMPORARY AMERICA INDIAN HISTORY 5A

Course Objectives: It is the objective of this course to examine modern political and social issues such as land, water, civil and tribal rights that arise from U.S.-Indian relations in the past which affect Indian communities in the contemporary era.

Learning Outcomes: Students will learn how the political, legal, and economic policies of the United States of the previous centuries affect Indian rights in the present century.

AMERICAN INDIAN EDUCATION 5B

Course Objectives: The objective of this course is to show how the field of Indian education has a historical, as well as a contemporary dimension in Indian educational policy in the United States of America. Another objective is to show how the antecedent roots of Indian education in America can be traced to early missionary efforts to indoctrinate Native societies, thereby destroying the ability of these societies to resist conquest and colonization.

Learning Outcomes: Upon completion of this course students will have an understanding of pre-contact and post-contact Indian education in America.

CONTEMPORARY AMERICAN INDIAN LEGAL POLICY 6A

Course Objectives: It is the objective of this course to examine modern political and social issues such as land, water, civil and tribal rights that arise from U.S. B Indian relations in the past which shape Indian federal Indian policy in the contemporary era.

Learning Outcomes: Students will how the political, legal and economic policies of the United States in the previous centuries affect Indian rights in the 21st century.

TREATIES (1778-1888) 6B

Course Objectives: It is the objective of this course to examine documents on United States policy and the executive orders, statutes, and case law pertaining to treaties and agreements the United States made with Indian nations.

Learning Outcomes: Students will learn that continual infringement of treaty rights by statute and executive orders have made a mockery of sacred solemn agreements Indian nations made with the United States in good faith. Students will learn how the United States Supreme Court has circumvented Indian treaty rights by employing the political question doctrine to decline judicial review in cases where the court claims raises issues more properly resolved by the executive or legislative branches of government. However, in international law the doctrine of Jus Cogens is ipso jure, a legal, not a political question. Students will learn how lawyers at the United Nations and the International Court of Justice at the Hague an employ the doctrine of Jus Cogens to develop legal theories and doctrines to defend human rights of American Indian political prisoners and treaty rights of Indian nations.

AMERICAN INDIAN MYTHOLOGY 8A

Course Objectives: The objective of this course is to employ science to prove that American Indian creation stories are based on scientific fact and not savage superstition. This course will show how ancient Indian philosophers used metaphors and symbolism in myths as a carefully constructed "symbolic cloak" for their abstract thoughts. Furthermore, they employed both the metaphysical (mental) model (Cherokee), and the physical model (Hopi), in which the Creator is a master craftsman (or craftswoman) who carves and shapes the environmental landscape.

Learning Outcomes: In order to get as close to the primordial truth as possible, students will analyze the mythical process, as well as the mythical events in terms of a mythical signpost, the imagery and abstract thoughts in the symbolism that reflects the laws of nature. Students will understand the scientific version of how the universe was created and the American Indian version of how the universe was created are essentially the same except ancient Indian philosophers employed metaphors and symbolism to describe the same phenomena.

AMERICAN INDIAN CULTURE 8B

<u>Course Objectives</u>: The objective of this course to survey Indian lifestyles in the past and contemporary era as well as examine Indian world views, customs and traditions.

<u>Learning Outcomes</u>: Students will gain a knowledge of traditional Indian lifestyles in the post contact era as well as lifestyles of contemporary American Indians.

AMERICAN INDIAN ART 9A

<u>Course Objectives</u>: The objective of this course is to show how American Indian art preserved the past, and taught future generations about their culture and heritage.

<u>Learning Outcomes</u>: Students will learn how American Indian art and paintings has its origins in pre-contact pictographs and petrographs painted on or inscribed on decorative pottery, clothing, wood and hide objects, and rocky hillsides. Post-contact Indian art and painting that had served as record keeping of past history began to take on various materials from the white culture such as pencils and paper inks as well as commercial materials.

AMERICAN INDIAN MUSIC 9B

<u>Course Objectives</u>:

1. To study American Indian music and dance as integral elements.
2. To acquire basic skills in methods of analyzing Indian music.
3. To acquire basic ability to distinguish regional music. (i.e., Northern, Southern, Southwestern, etc.)
4. To acquire basic skills of retention and singing of Indian songs (i.e., lullabies, love songs, game songs, personal songs, etc.
5. To learn simple social dances for participation at local pow wows.
6. To develop an appreciation for American Indian music as a non-Western art form.

Learning Outcomes:

1. Be able to distinguish "northern" drum styles from "southern" drum styles.
2. Be able to distinguish hand drums from "kettle" drums.
3. Know which Tribes/Regions use flutes.
4. Acquire the knowledge and understanding of ceremonial dance and song: when and why they are performed.
5. Understand the difference between religious/sacred, social and personal songs and their relationships to Indian value systems in the past and present.
6. Gain an understanding of the "etiquette" and proper forms of social and ceremonial performances required of participants and observers.

Section G: Program Evaluation

The American Indian Studies program at _____ college/university will be evaluated by the head of the American Indian Studies department, and by an advisory committee who will determine whether or not the program is achieving its program goals. The advisory committee may be composed of but not limited to committee members from American Indian Studies at Pembroke State University as they have an comprehensive American Indian Studies Program. The American Indian Studies program will be evaluated by five goals by the advisory committee.

Bachelor of Arts in American Indian Studies
Program Goals

Goal One: It is an objective of _____ college/university to implement a two-year associate of arts degree program for the minor in American Indian Studies, and a three year program for the bachelor of arts degree for the major in American Indian Studies.

Goal Two: It is an objective of _____ college to implement liberal arts courses in American Indian Studies that can be transferable to four year universities.

Goal Three: It is the objective of _____ college/university to provide students with the opportunity to learn the Cherokee language, history and culture.

Goal Four: It is an objective of _____ college/university to increase students' understanding and comprehension of American Indian bodies of knowledge.

Goal Five: It is an objective of _____ college/university to provide students with lifelong skills such as competency in interpersonal relations, self- discipline, problem solving and technical knowledge for the 21st century.

Part Two: MASTER OF ARTS IN AMERICAN INDIAN STUDIES

Section A: American Indian Studies Graduate Program

The master of arts curriculum consists of a research methods seminar in American Indian Studies, Theories and Concepts seminar, American Indian Studies Community Internship, American Indian Early Childhood seminar and internship, American Indian Teacher Training Internship, Issues In American Indian Studies, North American Indian seminar. Hunter/Gathers seminar, Cultural Context: Shamanism seminar, Directed Reading seminar, concentrations in the student's field of specialization, and the Masters Thesis which is the culminating work for the master of arts in American Indian Studies. The core seminars will provide breadth of understanding to balance the depth of seminar specializations, and the student's concentration in the student's area of specialization.

Some concentrations the student might consider are American Indian Anthropology, American Indian History, American Indian Law, American Indian Religion and Philosophy, American Indian Literature, American Indian Education, American Indian Democracy, American Indian Tribal Government, American Indian Early Childhood Education. The student will be required to serve an internship in the Indian community, write a practicum propos l, and a practicum report on the internship.

There will be a Certificate in Early Childhood Training. They will be required to serve an teaching internship in a grade school. In order to earn this certificate a student must address early childhood training of American Indian childhood in the past and present (Cherokee or another Indian tribe) in the seminar EdD 810 Teaching American Indian Students, EdD 860 Leadership in American In American Indian Education, and in at least two practicums. There will also be an American Indian Teacher Training program where a masters degree would be awarded certifying graduates to be full time instructors teaching undergraduate courses in American Indian Studies. They will be required to serve teaching internships as an assistant with an American Indian Studies instructor in order to earn an American Indian Teacher Training Program certificate.

Mission Statement

The mission statement for the master of arts degree is to advance American Indian Studies as an interdisciplinary curriculum by cutting edge research projects in Indian law, treaties, anthropology, history, literature, philosophy, Indian democracy, education etc., and by serving as a resource for the Indian community. American Indian bodies of knowledge as an academic discipline are oral traditions, their content and methodology; treaties and treaty rights; literature and philosophy; education; organizational structures of tribal government; Indian law and history; American Indian epistemology, i.e., the origin, development and meaning of American Indian bodies of knowledge; and concerns of contemporary American Indian tribal people.

<u>Masters of Arts Program Objectives</u>: The master of arts student will demonstrate mastery in fulfilling requirements for the degree in American Indian Studies by (a) by advancing American Indian Studies as an academic discipline through scholarly research, (b) learning to investigate the literature in the academic field of American Indian Studies in the student's area of specialization in the concentration chosen, (d) developing applied research and writing skills that are required in core seminars, internships, practicums, the masters proposal, and the masters thesis, providing evidence of being able to conceptualize, organize, analyze, synthesize, and apply judgement to address assignments, issues, problems or situations drawing upon a foundation of knowledge, (e) demonstrating the ability to fulfill the requirements of the Masters of arts program in American Indian Studies.

<u>Master of Arts Student Outcomes</u>: The graduate student should be able to (a) demonstrate competence in developing research and writing skills in assignments, seminars, and the masters thesis, (b) learn to investigate American Indian Studies literature, (c) demonstrating understanding and competence in concepts and theories in the academic discipline of American Indian Studies, and (d) demonstrate the ability to fulfill and complete the requirements for the Master of Arts degree in American Indian Studies.

Required Texts:

A Uniform System of Citation: Forms of Citations and Abbreviations. 12th ed. Cambridge, Mass: Harvard Law Review Assn. Latest edition.

Students will have a choice of two style manuals:

University of Chicago. A Manuel of Style. Chicago: University of Chicago Press, latest edition.

Turabian, Kate L. A. A Manuel for Writers of Term Papers, Thesis, and Dissertations, Chicago: University of Chicago Press, latest edition.

MASTER OF ARTS CURRICULUM

A. I. S.	700	Research Methods in A. I. S.	3 Units
A. I. S.	710	Theories/Concepts in A. I. S.	3 Units
A.I. S.	720	A. I. S. Community Internship	3 Units
A. I. S.	850	Issues in American Indian Studies	3 Units
A. I. S.	880	North American Indian	3 Units
A. I. S.	890	Hunters/Gatherers	3 Units
A. I. S.	900	Cultural Context: Shamanism	3 Units
A. I. S.	910	American Indian Early Childhood Internship in A. I. S.	3 Units
A. I. S.	920	American Indian Teacher Training Internship Project in A. I. S.	3 Units
A. I. S.	930	Directed Reading in A. I. S.	3 Units
A. I. S.	950	Masters Thesis	3 Units

Total Units 33 Units

Section B: American Indian Studies Courses

A. I. S. 700 RESEARCH METHODS IN AMERICAN INDIAN STUDIES

Instructor: To be announced

Office: To be announced

Hours: To be announced

Phone: To be announced

Course Description: This seminar is designed to assist students in gaining the skills for identifying, analyzing, and solving problems in the Indian community through the application of three problem-solving methodologies: research, evaluation, and development. In this seminar specific methods for four different types of community-based research approaches: Needs Assessment, Survey Research, Evaluation, and Cultural Arts.

Seminar Objectives: The concept of community-based research is the future direction of Indian education through self-direction of American Indian communities. The textbook presents four different methods of research that is effective in Indian communities: Needs assessments, survey research, program evaluation, and culture and fine arts. Students will be exposed to concepts related to research design, internal and external validity of research designs, sample selection. reliability and validity of instruments designed for data collection, concepts of descriptive and inferential statistics, and the use of software packages for statistical analysis.

Seminar Outcomes: Upon completion of this seminar students will be able to develop research designs for practicums on development, evaluation, and statistical research methodologies for their practicum reports in the Indian community.

Texts:

Susan Guyette. (1983). <u>Community-Based Research: a Handbook for Native Americans.</u> American Indian Studies Center: University of California, Los Angeles.

Susan Guyette, & Charlotte Heth. (1985). <u>Issues For The Future Of American Indian Studies</u>. American Indian Studies Center. University of California, Los Angeles.

A. I. S. 710 THEORIES/CONCEPTS IN AMERICAN INDIAN STUDIES

Instructor: To be announced

Office: To be announced

Hours: To be announced

Phone: To be announced

Course Description: This seminar examines goals, concepts, and instructional planning in American Indian Studies. Students should understand key events, concepts. and issues from the historical perspective of Native Americans. Students will examine key concepts that govern Native American Indian conduct are prototype and archetype of Native American conduct such as cosmology, ontology, axiology, world view, ethos, ideology, and cultural manifestations of concepts and theories such a rituals, ceremonies, and practice.

Seminar Objectives: Students will understand traditional Indian philosophy of education. bilingual education, how to develop Indian content in social work education through a community-based model, American Indian teacher education, and self-determination as well as Indian cultural world view.

Seminar Outcomes: Students will be able to understand and apply theories and concepts in research projects on American Indian history and culture.

Texts:

Dr Byron Lee Blackwell, JD, EdD. (1989). American Indian Genesis. (Unpublished research).

James A. Banks. (1991, 5th edition.). Teaching Strategies for Ethnic Studies. University of Washington, Seattle: Allyn and Bacon.

Sproul, Barbara. (1978). Primal Myths: Creating the World. New York: Harper & Row.

San Francisco State University
Ethnic Studies Handout

MYTHICAL ANALYSIS OUTLINE

I. WHAT IS THE ESSENCE OF THE CREATION STORY?

From what process did humans result?

What are the implied qualities of human beings?

What are the characteristics of creation?

What are the qualities/characteristics of the "Creator"?

II. THE MYTHICAL BEINGS

What are the features, attributes, qualities of the mythical beings?

III. MYTHICAL SYMBOLS AND SIGNS

Identify the images or symbols found in the myth?

Can any of these be identified as sign stimuli?

Are there behaviors which are evidence of Innate Releasing Mechanism?

IV. MYTHICAL EVENTS

What do the events or drama of the myth imply about interactions or relations?

V. MYTHICAL PLACES

What are the places identified in the myth?

What are the implied relationships between the locations of the mythical places?

VI. WHAT DOES THE MYTH REVEAL ABOUT:

(1) Cosmology (origin and structure)

(2) Ontology (nature of existence)

(3) Axiology (primary characteristics)

(4) World-View (comprehensive items about order)

(5) Ideology (how things should be)

(6) Ethos (set of guiding principles)

VII. WHAT GENERAL IMPLICATION DOES THE MYTH HAVE FOR THOUGHT AND ACTION AS WELL AS THEORIES AND CONCEPTS OF YOUR ETHNIC SPECIALIZATION?

VIII. DOCUMENTATION

Author of the Myth (who wrote/told it/how acquired)

Time period of myth

Era when recorded

Identify source (where published, date, author. exact title)

NAME:
ETHNICITY:
ETHNIC SPECIALIZATION:
FUTURE PROFESSIONAL GOAL:

IDENTIFY AND DESCRIBE THE MYTH

I. WHAT IS THE ESSENCE OF THE CREATION STORY?

II. THE MYTHICAL BEINGS

III. MYTHICAL SYMBOLS AND SIGNS

IV. MYTHICAL EVENTS

V. MYTHICAL PLACES

VI. WHAT DOES THE MYTH REVEAL ABOUT:

VII. WHAT GENERAL IMPLICATION DOES THE MYTH HAVE FOR THOUGHT AND ACTION AS WELL AS THEORIES AND CONCEPTS OF YOUR ETHNIC SPECIALIZATION?

VIII. DOCUMENTATION

San Francisco State University Graduate class handout
Theories and Concepts

Phillip McGee. Ph.D. & Wade W. Nobles. Ph.D.

3

A. I. S. 720 AMERICAN INDIAN STUDIES COMMUNITY INTERNSHIP

Instructor: To be announced

Office: To be announced

Hours: To be announced

Phone: To be announced

Seminar Description: Students will examine different types of research by examining descriptive research, action research, historical, experimental, quasi-experimental, causal-experimental, case study, and developmental, and chose one particular type of research for their internship..

Seminar Objectives: The student will conduct research on a topic/issue/concern by serving an internship in the American Indian community.

Seminar Outcomes: The student will write a proposal, serve an internship in the American Indian community, and write a practicum report on the community-based research.

Texts:

William Carrmack. Brooks. Hill. Phil Lilian, & Linda s. Parker. ((1983). Native American Research Information Service: A Program For Community Development. American Indian Studies Center. University of California. Los Angeles and University of Oklahoma.

A. I. S. 850 ISSUES IN AMERICAN INDIAN STUDIES

Instructor: Dr Byron Lee Blackwell, JD, EdD
Office: To be announced
Hours: To be announced
Phone: To be announced

Seminar Description: This seminar examines the future of American Indian Studies programs across the United States.

Course Objectives: The objective of this seminar is to examine American Indian, issues in higher education. This seminar examines the future of American Indian Studies as an academic discipline.

Seminar Outcomes: The student will analyze issues that will determine the future of American Indian Studies programs as an academic discipline, and write a report on a topic of concern of the student.

Texts:

American Indian Issues in Higher Education. (1980). Contemporary American Indian Issues, No. 3. The Regents of the University of California. American Indian Studies Center. Los Angeles, California.

Multicultural Education And The American Indian. Contemporary American Indian I sues, No. 2. (1979). The Regents of the University of California. American Indian Studies Center. Los Angeles, California.

A. I. S. 880 NORTH AMERICAN INDIAN

Instructor: Dr Byron Lee Blackwell. J.D., Ed.D.
Office: To be announced
Hours: To be announced
Office: to be announced

<u>Seminar Description</u>: This seminar on North American Indians describes ancient Indians, ancient civilizations, Indian life-ways, Indians and explorers, Indian wars, Indian land cessations, and contemporary Indians. This seminar also describes the Northeast Cultural Area, the Southeast Cultural Area, the Southwest Cultural Area, The Great Basin Cultural Area, the Plateau Cultural Area, the Northwest Coast Cultural Area, the California Cultural Area, the Great Plains Cultural Area, the Subarctic Cultural Area, the Arctic Cultural Area, and the Mesoamerican and Circum Caribbean Cultural Area.

<u>Seminar Objectives</u>: This seminar provides an overview of the histories, demography, and culture of hundreds of different Indian tribes as well as languages, subsistence patterns, cultural revolution, and art and technology, shelter, clothing, transportation, religion and spirituality, and social-political organization.

<u>Seminar Outcomes</u>: Student will have an extensive understanding of native life-ways, regional areas, language groups, demography, vegetation, technology, religion and spiritually, history. treaties, law, and education of indigenous people from post-contact to the contemporary era.

<u>Texts</u>:

Carl Waldman. <u>Atlas Of The North American</u>. (1985). Facts On File Publications: New York, New York, Oxford, England.

Duanne Champagne. (1994). <u>Native America: Portrait of the Peoples</u>. Visible Ink Press is a trademark of Gale Research Inc: Detroit, London, and Washington, DC.

Carl Waldman. (1988). <u>Encyclopedia Of Native American Tribes</u>. Facts On File Publications. New York and Oxford.

Arlene Hirschfelder and Martha Kreipe de Montano. (1993). <u>The Native American Almanac: A Portrait Of Native America</u>. Prentice-Hall General Reference: New York, London, Toronto Tokyo, Singapore.

Reader's Digest. <u>Mysteries Of The Ancient Americas: The New World Before Columbus</u>. (1986). The Reader's Digest Association, Inc.: Pleasantville, New York, Montreal.

A. I. S. 890 HUNTERS/GATHERERS

Instructor: To be announced

Office: To be announced

Hours: To be announced

Phone: To be announced

Seminar Description: This seminar describes the religious beliefs, rituals, and myths of the Northern Hunter religious tradition of the Circumpolar Bear Ceremonialism, and the Southern Agrarian tradition of the sacred Corn Mother. The sacred pipe, vision quests. and medicine societies date back extend back to ancient shamanistic practices, and the Sacred Corn Mother generated the source of fertility in plants.

Seminar Objectives: The purpose of this seminar is to d scribe the religious traditions of the northern hunter/gathering tradition, and the southern agrarian tradition.

Seminar Outcomes: Students will understand the hunting and healing rituals of shamans, and a master of animals who protects animals, and the planting, fertility, and harvesting rituals of the agrarian ceremonies devoted to the seasonal cycle of crops.

Texts:

America In 1492: The World of the Indian Peoples Before the Arrival of Columbus. (1991). (Edited by Alvin M. Josephy, Jr.). New York: Vintage Books. A Division of Randon 1 louse. Inc. (Read Northern Hunters by Robins Ridington pages 21-49).

Carl Waldman. (1985). Atlas Of The North American Indian. Facts On File Publications. New York and Oxford. Read pages 1-65.

American In 1492: The World of the Indian Peoples Before the Arrival of Columbus. (1993). (Editor, Alvin M. Josephy, Jr.). Vintage Books. A Division Of Random House, Inc. : New York. (Pages 21-215).

A. I. S. 900 CULTURAL CONTEXT: SHAMANISM

Instructor: To be announced

Office: To be announced

Hours: To be announced

Office: To be announced

Seminar Description: This seminar describes the rituals of Indian shamans or healers from the Shamanic ceremonialism spiritual dancing in the Pacific Northwest to Lakota shamans to the Great Plains in the rituals of the vision quest, the sweat lodge, and Yuwipi, which is a modern curing ritual. This seminar investigates shamanism and the world of the spirits; the shaman as healer; diagnosis and cure; sacred knowledge; and the laws of ecology.

Seminar Objectives: The objective of this seminar is to describe shamanism in several American Indian cultures. Students will learn about the origin of sacred knowledge; the shaman as healer: the spirit world; the laws of ecology; and symbolism in shamanic rituals

Seminar Outcomes: Students will gain an knowledge of the vision quest, sweat lodge, yuwipi, calling the spirits by the shaman, and how the shaman heals.

Texts:

Beck, Peggy, Walters, Anna Lee, and Francisco, Nia. (1992). The Sacred: Ways of Knowledge. Sources of Life. Navajo Community College Press: Tsaile, Arizona.

William K. Powers. (1992). Yuwipi: Vision and Experience in Oglala Ritual. University of Nebraska Press: Lincoln and London.

Lewis, Tomas H. (1990). The Medicine Men: Oglala Sioux Ceremony and Healing. University of Nebraska Press: Lincoln and London.

Harner, Michael. The Way of the Shaman: A Guide to Power and Healing. Bantam Books: Toronto, New York, London, Sydney.

Carl Waldman. (1985). <u>Atlas Of The North American Indian</u>. Facts On File Publications. New York and Oxford. Read pages 57-63.

Wolfgang G. Jilek, MD. <u>Indian Healing: Shamanic Ceremonialism in the Pacific Northwest</u>. Hancock House Publishers Ltd: Washington, DC.

A. I. S. 910 AMERICAN INDIAN EARLY CHILDHOOD INTERNSHIP SEMINAR

Instructor: To be announced

Office: To be announced

Hours: To be announced

Phone: To be announced

Seminar Description: This seminar addresses early childhood training of American Indian children in the past and present.

Seminar Objectives: The objective of this seminar is to describe shamanism in several American Indian cultures. Students will learn about the origin of sacred knowledge; the shaman as healer; the spirit world; the laws of ecology; and symbolism in shamanic rituals.

Seminar Outcomes: Students will gain an knowledge of the vision quest, sweatlodge, yuwipi, calling the spirits by the shaman, and how the shaman heals.

Texts:

Teaching American Indian Students. (1992). (Edited by Jon Reyhner). University of Oklahoma Press: Norman and London.

Cherokee Women: Gender and Culture Change, 1900-1835. (1998). University of Nebraska Press: Lincoln and London.

Swisher, Karen. (May 1991). American Indian/Alaskan Learning Styles: Research and Practice. Eric Digest Abstract.

Deloria, Vine, Jr. (1991). Indian Education In America. Boulder, CO: The American Indian Science & Engineering Society.

A. I. S. 920 AMERICAN INDIAN TEACHER TRAINING INTERNSHIP SEMINAR

Instructor: To be announced

Office: To be announced

Hours: To be announced

Phone: To be announced

Seminar Description: This seminar focuses on training educators on American Indian teaching and learning styles of Indian students from grade school and high school to college.

Seminar Objectives: The objectives of this seminar are to train educators to design instruction to teach Indian students by adapting instruction to Indian culture, and the assumptions, ideologies, strategies involved in the planning and implementing of the American Indian Studies curriculum.

Seminar Outcomes: After the completion of this seminar internship in the native American community educators will be able to serve the needs of the Indian community.

Texts:

Teaching American Indian Students. (1992). (Edited by Jon Reyhner). University of Oklahoma Press: Norman and London.

Swisher, Karen. (May 1991). American Indian/Alaskan Learning Styles: Research and Practice. Eric Digest Abstract.

Wax, M., Wax, R. & Dumant, R., Jr. (1989). Formal Education in an American Indian Community. Prospect Heights, IL: Waveland Press.

Deloria, Vine, Jr. (1991). Indian Education In America. Boulder, CO: The American Indian Science & Engineering Society.

Stein, Wayne J. (1992). Tribally Controlled Colleges: Making Good Medicine. New York: Peter Lang, Publishing, Inc.

A. I. S. 930 DIRECTED READING IN AMERICAN INDIAN STUDIES

Instructor: Dr Byron Lee Blackwell, JD, Ed.D.

Office: To be announced

Hours: To be announced

Phone: To be announced

Seminar Description: This seminar focuses on an topic related to the student's major and/or concentration in American Indian Studies.

Seminar Objectives: The student will write a major research paper on his or her major and/or concentration within the field of American Indian Studies.

Seminar Outcomes: In order to have a concentration within American Indian Studies a student must refer to his/or concentration in at least two core seminars, the Directed Reading seminar, and the masters thesis.

MASTERS THESIS

The masters thesis is the culminating research project for American Indian Studies graduate students.

Section C: Course Implementation Plan

Fall Semester   1st Year

1). A. I. S. 700 Research Methods in American Indian Studies
2). A. I. S. 710 Theories/Concepts in American Indian Studies
3). A. I. S. 720 A. I. S. Community Internship

Spring Semester   1st Year

1). A. I. S. 850 Issues in American Indian Studies
2). A. I. S. 880 North American Indian
3). A. I. S. 890 Hunter/Gatherers

Fall Semester   2nd Year

1). A. I. S. 900 Cultural Context: Shamanism
2). A. I. S. 910 Early Childhood Internship in A. I. S.
3). A. I. S. American Indian Teacher Training Internship in A. I. S.

Spring Semester   2nd Year

1). A. I. S. 930 Directed Reading in A. I. S.
2). A. I. S. 950 Masters Thesis

Section D: Student Evaluation Form

Student Evaluation Form

Your advice and opinions on the effectiveness of this course will help the masters program in American Indian Studies improve its courses. Please feel free to address any concerns you have regarding the course content. Your comments will help us to improve the course.

1). In your opinion did this course meet the objectives stated in the course syllabus?

2). Did this course meet the stated outcomes for the course?

3). After completing the course do you feel you are able to communicate effectively and critically analyze various issues in American Indian Studies?

4). Do you have any other concerns regarding the course content that will help improve the quality of the course?

Section E: Course Evaluation Plan

A. I. S. 700 Research Methods in A. I. S.

<u>Seminar Objectives</u>: The concept of community-based research is the future direction of Indian education through self-direction of American Indian communities. The textbook presents four different methods of research that is effective in Indian communities: Needs assessments, survey research, program evaluation, and culture and fine arts. Students will be exposed to concepts related to research design, internal and external validity of research designs, sample selection, reliability and validity of instruments designed for data collection, concepts of descriptive and inferential statistics, and the use of software packages for statistical analysis.

<u>Seminar Outcomes</u>: Upon completion of this seminar students will be able to develop research designs for practicums on development, evaluation, and statistical research methodologies for their practicum reports in the Indian community.

A. I. S. 710 Theories/Concepts

<u>Seminar Objectives</u>: Students will understand traditional Indian philosophy of education, bilingual education, how to develop Indian content in social work education through a community-based model, American Indian teacher education, and self-determination as well as Indian cultural world view.

<u>Seminar Outcomes</u>: Students will be able to understand and apply theories and concepts in research projects on American Indian history and culture.

A. I. S. 720 A. I. S. Community Internship

<u>Seminar Objectives</u>: The student will conduct research on a topic/issue/concern by serving an internship in the American Indian community.

Seminar Outcomes: The student will write a proposal, serve an internship in the American Indian community, and write a practicum report on the community-based research.

A. I. S. 850 Issues in American Indian Studies

Course Objectives: The objective of this seminar is to examine American Indian issues in higher education. This seminar examines the future of American Indian Studies as an academic discipline.

Seminar Outcomes: The student will analyze issues that will determine the future of American Indian Studies programs as an academic discipline, and write a report on a topic of concern of the student.

A. I. S. 880 North American Indian

Seminar Objectives: This seminar provides an overview of the histories, demography, and culture of hundreds of different Indian tribes as well as languages, subsistence patterns, cultural revolution, and art and technology, shelter, clothing, transportation, religion and spirituality, and social-political organization.

Seminar Outcomes: Student will have an extensive understanding of native life-ways, regional areas, language groups, demography, vegetation, technology, religion and spiritually, history, treaties, law, and education of indigenous people from people post-contact to the contemporary era.

A. I. S. 890 Hunter/Gatherers

Seminar Objectives: The objective of this seminar is to describe shamanism in several American Indian cultures. Students will learn about the origin of sacred knowledge; the shaman as healer; the spirit world; the laws of ecology; and symbolism in shamanic rituals.

Seminar Outcomes: Students will gain an knowledge of the vision quest, sweat lodge, yuwipi, calling the spirits by the shaman, and how the shaman heals.

A. I. S. 900 Cultural Context: Shamanism

Seminar Objectives: The objective of this seminar is to describe shamanism in several American Indian cultures. Students will learn about the origin of sacred knowledge; the shaman as healer; the spirit world; the laws of ecology; and symbolism in shamanic rituals.

Seminar Outcomes: Students will gain an knowledge of the vision quest, sweat lodge, yuwipi, calling the spirits by the shaman, and how the shaman heals.

A. I. S. 910 American Indian Earl Childhood Internship in A. I. S.

Seminar Objectives: The objective of this seminar is to describe shamanism in several American Indian cultures. Students will learn about the origin of sacred knowledge; the shaman as healer; the spirit world; the laws of ecology; and symbolism in shamanic rituals

Seminar Outcomes: Students will gain an knowledge of the vision quest, sweat lodge, yuwipi, calling the spirits by the shaman, and how the shaman heals.

A. I. S. 920 American Indian Teacher Training Internship in A. I. S.

Seminar Objectives: The objectives of this seminar are to train educators to design instruction to teach Indian students by adapting instruction to Indian culture, and the assumptions, ideologies, strategies involved in the planning and implementing of the American Indian Studies curriculum.

Seminar Outcomes: After the completion of this seminar internship in the native American community educators will be able to serve the needs of the Indian community.

A. I. S. 930 Directed Reading In American Indian Studies

Seminar Description: This seminar focuses on an topic related to the student's major and/or concentration in American Indian Studies.

Seminar Objectives: The student will write a major research paper on his or her major and/or concentration within the field of American Indian Studies.

A. I. S. 950 Masters Thesis

Seminar Objectives: The student will write a major research paper on his or her major and/or concentration within the field of American Indian Studies.

Section F: Program Evaluation

The American Indian Studies program at _____ college/university will be evaluated by the head of the American Indian Studies department, and by an advisory committee who will determine whether or not the program is achieving its program goals. The advisory committee may be composed of but not limited to committee members from American Indian Studies at Pembroke State University as they have a comprehensive American Indian Studies Program. The American Indian Studies program will be evaluated by five goals by the advisory committee.

MASTER OF ARTS IN AMERICAN INDIAN STUDIES
Program goals

Goal One: It is an objective of _____ college/university to implement a master of arts degree program in American Indian Studies. .

Goal Two: It is the objective of _____ university to provide students with the opportunity to learn the Cherokee language, history and culture.

Goal Three: It is an objective of _____ college/university to increase students' understanding and comprehension of American Indian bodies of knowledge.

Goal Four: It is an objective of _____ university to offer an American Indian Early Childhood certificate for graduates who wish to teach in kinder garden and grade school.

Goal Five: It is an objective of _____ university to offer an American Indian Teacher Training Program for graduates who wish to teach undergraduate courses in American Indian Studies.

Goal Six: It is an objective of _____ college/university to provide students with lifelong skills such as competency in interpersonal relations, self- discipline, problem solving and technical knowledge for the 21st century.

Part Three: Doctoral of Education in American Indian Higher Education

Section A: American Indian Doctoral Program in Education

DOCTOR OF EDUCATION IN AMERICAN INDIAN EDUCATION

The doctoral program in American Indian Education is an Educational Leadership Program where a doctor of education degree will be awarded to educators and administrators who will be qualified to not only teach graduate courses in American Indian Education, but to take on leadership roles in Indian higher education and administration. The doctoral curriculum consists of core seminars, seminar specializations, concentrations in the students' field of specialization, the comprehensive written examination, and the applied dissertation report. The doctorate in American Indian Education is not based upon scholarly research alone but upon applied research in American Indian Education. The doctoral program in American Indian Education has been designed to focus the student's readings and research reports in the student's chosen area of specialization (Concentration). The concentrations are to be inserted in a paragraph with the name of the concentration above the paragraph in at least two practicums, one seminar specialization, and the applied dissertation.

The core seminars will provide breadth of understanding to balance the depth of seminar specializations, and the student's concentration in the doctoral program. The seminar specializations will prepare students to conduct research in their choice of concentration within the doctoral program. The doctoral program requires the integration of scholarly research with applied research in the American Indian community.

Mission Statement

The mission statement for the doctorate in American Indian Education is to advance American Indian education by serving as a resource for the American Indian community, and by requiring students to apply their knowledge and technical skills in the service of American Indian communities by applied research practicums, and the applied dissertation report, the culminating project for the Doctor of Education degree in American Indian Education.

Doctoral Program in American Indian Education

The foundation of the American Indian doctoral program is Indian spiritual values regarding the ecological caretaking of the earth, and vocational/technical skills so they can begin using these technical and spiritual skills in the service of their Indian communities early in their college careers. Simulated (skills) training courses and experiential public service internships in the Indian community are integrated with practicums that solve problems of immediate concern to the Indian community. Technical skills training and practicum problem-solving internships in the Indian community will help students gain a sensitivity to the moral and ethical issues regarding scientific development. Finally, the American Indian doctoral program integrates and synthesizes liberal arts/technical training with simulated skills training workshops and problem-solving practicums in experiential service internships in the Indian community within a holistic/spiritual/ecological paradigm deeply rooted in Indian traditional culture.

The doctoral program is dedicated to helping students develop professional ethical and moral responsibility in the ecological caretaking of Mother Earth through spiritual ceremonies and technological knowledge in applied research and service to the Indian community. The doctoral program in American Indian education is dedicated to training Indian/non-Indian practitioners in education, administrators, ecology, law, history, treaties, and applied research and practicums for the doctorate in educational leadership for both non-Indian and Indian educators and administrators.

Doctoral Program Objectives:

The doctoral student will demonstrate mastery in fulfilling requirements for the doctoral degree in American Indian Education by (a) learning to investigate the literature of higher education as well as the field of American Indian education, and the student's field of specialization in the concentration chosen, and by demonstrating the ability of being able to relate it to current and future trends and issues in order to solve problems in an educational setting, (b) by developing applied research and writing skills that are required in core seminars, seminar specialization projects, practicums, and the applied dissertation project, and (c) by demonstrating in core seminar work, the specialization projects, and the comprehensive exam, the ability to conceptualize, organize, analyze, synthesize, and apply judgement to address assignments, issues, problems or situations drawing upon a foundation of knowledge, and (d) demonstrating the ability to fulfill the requirements of the Doctoral program in American Indian Education.

Doctoral Program Outcomes:

The graduates in the doctoral program in American Indian Education should be able to (a) demonstrate educational leadership in the American Indian community, who as recognized leading practitioners in their field of specialization, develop innovative advances in doctoral program content and delivery instruction; (b) improve educational practice through applied research practicums in the American Indian community, provide continuing professional training through human resource programs to graduates; and (c) produce graduate practitioners who are recognized internationally as experts in their chosen educational fields and area of concentration in American Indian education; and (d) train students to become department chairs in American Indian Studies.

Doctoral Student Outcomes:

The doctoral student should be able to (a) demonstrate competence in developing applied research and writing skills that are required in core seminar, seminar specializations, practicums and the applied dissertation report, (b) learn to investigate higher education literature in their concentration in their area of specialization, (c) demonstrate understanding and competence in concepts and theories in both higher education and American Indian education, and finally, (d) demonstrate the ability to successfully fulfill and complete the requirements for the Doctor of Education degree in American Indian Education.

The <u>Doctoral Curriculum in American Indian Education</u> consists of:

Core Seminars

Seminar Specializations

Applied Practicums

Comprehensive Examination

Applied Dissertation Report

<u>Core Seminars</u>

<u>EdD 800</u>	<u>Introduction to Doctoral Research Methodologies in American Indian Education</u>
<u>EdD 810</u>	<u>Teaching American Indian Education</u>
<u>EdD 820</u>	<u>Curriculum Development and Program Planning in American Indian Education</u>
<u>EdD 830</u>	<u>Governance and Management</u>
<u>EdD 840</u>	<u>Human Resource Development</u>
<u>EdD 850</u>	<u>Societal Factors Affecting Education</u>
<u>EdD 860</u>	<u>Leadership in American Indian Education</u>
<u>EdD 870</u>	<u>Seminar Specialization One: Emergence of Higher Education in America</u>
<u>EdD 880</u>	<u>Seminar Specialization Two: Politics Law, and Economics of Higher Education</u>
<u>Prac 700</u>	<u>Research Methodology (Statistical) Practicum</u>
<u>Prac 710</u>	<u>Development Methodology Practicum</u>
<u>Prac 720</u>	<u>Evaluation Methodology Practicum</u>
<u>EdD 890</u>	<u>Written Comprehensive Examination</u>
<u>EdD 890</u>	<u>Applied Doctoral Dissertation Report</u>

The core seminars provide breadth of understanding in higher education which balances the depth of the career-oriented perspective of the specialization seminars <u>Emergence of Higher Education</u> and <u>Politics, Law, and Economics of Higher Education</u>. Whereas the core seminars are research papers the practicums are applied research projects. The student must write four practicums. Each methodology (research, evaluation, and development) must be used in three separate practicums. Students will have a choice of which methodology to replicate for the fourth practicum, and have a choice of two or more methodologies for the applied dissertation report.

All of the practicum reports are required to show a relationship to concepts presented in core seminars and specializations. For example, one of the practicums must employ inferential statistics (experimental) and be related to the Research Methodology seminar; one of the practicums must be related to concepts and theories presented in one of the specialization seminars; and the other two practicums can be related to any of the other seminars. Finally, in the student's concentration the report must demonstrate the relationship of the practicum and the dissertation report to the specific concentration. Three approved practicum reports must be met before the student can take the comprehensive examination, and the fourth practicum must be passed before the student can be assigned to a dissertation committee to began the applied dissertation report. The student will be allowed to take the comprehensive examination twice before going on the applied report.

The practicums in the doctoral program are invaluable for preparing students for the applied dissertation report. The applied dissertation process consists of the prospectus, the dissertation proposal, the applied dissertation project, and the dissertation report. Although not required, students are encouraged to served at least one seminar as an assistant to an American Indian Studies instructor. Internships help provide valuable experience which will enhance the education and training provided by the doctoral program.

The student will receive study guides for each course including six study guides developed by Nova Southeastern University that provides guidelines for students to follow in the practicum proposals, practicum reports, dissertation proposals and applied dissertation reports. These study guides are to be used in all of the core seminars and specialization seminars:

1. Guidelines for Form and Style

2. Publication Manual of the American Psychological Association (most recent edition).

3. Learning Activity Packages (LAPS).

4. Research Methodology Guide

5. Guide to the Practicum Process

6. Guide To The Applied Dissertation Process

In addition, along with the textbook for the core seminars and specialization seminars there are study guides to assist the doctoral student in each of core seminars, and the specializations as well as practicum and dissertation study guides from Nova Southeastern University.

Section B: Doctoral of Education Courses

EdD 800 INTRODUCTION TO DOCTORAL RESEARCH METHODOLOGIES IN AMERICAN INDIAN EDUCATION

Instructor: To be announced
Office: To be announced
Hours: To be announced
Phone: To be announced

Course Description: This seminar is designed to assist students in gaining the skills for identifying, analyzing, and solving institutional problems related to their educational concentration through the application of three problem-solving methodologies - research, evaluation, and development. The fourth methodology is employing descriptive statistics through the use of a software package. This course will explain the practicum process which consists of the following: writing the practicum proposal, conducting the study, and writing the report. There are four practicums required. Each methodology (development, evaluation, and research) must be used in three separate practicums, but students have a choice for the fourth practicum. The student will employ several methodologies for the applied dissertation. For the applied dissertation process, there will be a prospectus, a proposal, a project to be developed, and the applied dissertation report. The student will be provided with study guides to research methodologies, practicum proposals and reports, and the applied dissertation report.

Seminar Objectives: The student will be exposed to concepts related to research design, internal and external validity of research designs, sample selection, reliability and validity of instruments designed for data collection, concepts of descriptive and inferential statistics, and the use of software packages for statistical analysis.

Seminar Outcomes: Students will be able to define the problem-solving methodologies (research, development, and evaluation). Students will be able to describe the scientific method (description of problem, formulation of a solution through the statement of purpose, the research question, and the research hypothesis, evaluation of previous research, collection of data, presentation of data, presentation of results, and interpretation, conclusions, and recommendations. The student will apply the three research methodologies in brief reports and recognize the influence of research, evaluation, and development studies on educational policy, practice, and decision making. The scientific method will be employed in the development of the proposal and practicum report for the Research Methodology seminar. Finally, the student will utilize the basic principle of descriptive and inferential statistics through the use of software packages (statistical, word processing, and graphics) in carrying out research, evaluation, and development reports.

Learning Outcomes: Upon completion of this seminar course students will be able to develop research designs for practicums on development, evaluation, and statistical research methods for their practicum reports They will also have gained an understanding of theories and concepts in higher education, research methodologies, the practicum process and the applied dissertation process.

Grading Policies: Seminar grades are given as **Pass, No Pass**, and **Incomplete**. Students who receive "no pass" are given one opportunity to revise the assignment once and resubmit to the instructor. A **Pass** grade indicates that the student has satisfied all seminar projects. A **No Pass** indicates the student has attempted to complete all requirements of the seminar but has failed to meet satisfactory standards, or has not completed all the requirements and has not given sufficient evidence of an effort to complete the assignments. Any student receiving a **No Pass** must repeat the seminar to receive credit. If a second **No Pass** is received, whether for the same seminar or for two different seminars or practicums, the student is terminated from the program. An **Incomplete** grade indicates that the student has failed to complete the seminar requirements, but as a result of consultation with the instructor it is reasonable to expect the student will be able to complete the seminar requirements within allowable time limits.

Absence Policy: Attendance at all sessions is required. Exceptions must be based on an emergency situation, and an agreement with the instructor in respect to alternate assignments. An makeup agreement requires the completion of all assignments relating to the missed session. The assignments must be agreed to upon an early date and turned in on the agreed time line.

Required Text:

Research Methodology: A Study Guide for the Core Seminar. (1998). Grizzle, Grady M., and Ranklin, Gary E. Programs for Higher Education. Nova Southeastern University. This can be order from the University Bookstore.

Isaac, S., & Michael, W. B. (1995). Handbook in research and evaluation. San Diego, CA: E.D.I.T.S.

McMillan, J. H., & Schumacher, S. (1997). Research in education: A conceptual introduction. (4th ed.). New York: Harper Collins College Publishers.

Publication Manual of the American Psychological Association (4th edition). (1994).

Statistical Software. Recommendation: GBSTAT, SPSS, and SYSTAT.

Study guides to be used in each seminar course:

1. Guidelines for Form and Style

2. Publication Manual of the American Psychological Association (most recent edition).

3. Learning Activity Packages (LAPS).

4. Research Methodology Guide.

5. Guide to the Practicum Process.

6. Guide to the Applied Dissertation Process.

<u>Seminar Criteria</u>: Plan a study for each of the three problem-solving methodologies; however, the plan for the research problem-solving methodology must be experimental. Chose three different problems, one for each methodology. Students must demonstrate competency through two in-class quizzes and a take home final examination. Finally, the student will be required to critically analyze an experiential practicum proposal provided by the instructor by evaluating the underlying problem, the purpose of the study, the appropriateness of the problem-solving methodology, and the impact the results could have on educational policy and decision making.

EdD 810 TEACHING AMERICAN INDIAN EDUCATION

Instructor: Dr. Byron Lee Blackwell, JD, Ed.D
Office: To be announced
Hours: To be announced
Phone: To be announced

Seminar Description: In order to retard the high dropout rate of Indian students the educator must bridge the gap between two value systems and cultural world views: the American Indian sacred world view of living in harmony with nature through a deep ecological spiritual connection with the earth, and the western materialistic world view. An understanding of the history of Indian education through federal policy is crucial to understanding why American education in the past has not benefit Indian students. This seminar will examine several teaching and learning styles, including American Indian teaching and learning styles, and explain why the affective learning style is more effective with Indian students.

Seminar Objectives: This seminar course teaches educators how to provide an opportunity for both the dominate culture and the American Indian culture to exist in harmony side by side so that the high dropout rate of Indian students can be retarded. This seminar provides educators with the tools to develop American Indian curriculum by bringing the Indian community into the curriculum development process. The Lakota Indian scholar Dr. Vine Deloria, Jr has noted the Indian theory of relativity is more comprehensive than Einstein's theory of relativity because the Indian concept of the universe has a moral content because the Indian concept of relationship in the universe is both personal and particular. In their caretaking of the natural world American Indians were concerned with the products of their actions than just with the process of their actions.

Learning Outcomes: It is the purpose of this seminar to give educators the tools to empower Indian students through ideologies and strategies in Indian education to keep Indian students in school by adapting instruction and curriculum to Indian culture, and by involving the Indian community in the instructional process. This will be done by Indian students learning both the native language and English, and by applying both to the educational process through a multisensory approach to language instruction in hands-on learning activities. In the Indian culture students use storytelling in the educational process. Storytelling can be used to teach English so Indian students can learn the stories in both English and the native language. Knowledge of American Indian literature should be part of the curriculum as well as teaching in the content areas of social studies, science, and mathematics.

Required Texts:

Teaching American Indian Students. (1998). (Edited by Jon Reyhner). University of Oklahoma Press: Norman and London.

Deloria, Vine, Jr. (1991). Indian Education in America. Vine Deloria, Jr. American Indian Science & Engineering Society: Boulder, Colorado.

Dr Byron Lee Blackwell, JD., Ed.D. (1998). Handbook On The History Of Indian Education In America. This handbook was written for a practicum at Nova Southeastern University.

Swisher, Karen. (May 1991). American Indian/Alaskan Learning Styles: Research and Practice. Eric Diges Abstract.

Deloria, Vine, Jr. Indian education in America. Boulder, CO: The American Indian Science & Engineering Society.

Stein, Wayne J. (1992). Tribally controlled colleges: Making good medicine. New York: Peter Lang, Publishing Inc.

EdD 820 CURRICULUM DEVELOPMENT AND PROGRAM PLANNING

Instructor: Dr Byron Lee Blackwell, JD, Ed. D
Office: To be announced
Hours: To be announced
Phone: To be announced

Seminar Description: This seminar is designed to familiarize the doctoral student with the various theories, principles, and practices related to curriculum development and program planning in American Indian Education. It also includes the study of curricular and instructional design theories, instructional design models, and the implementation and evaluation of instructional design for lesson, course, and academic programs.

Seminar Objectives: It is the objective of this seminar course to include in the course content curriculum, instructional design, and program planning, the foundations of learning and learner characteristics, the history of curriculum and educational philosophy on instructional design, student assessment and program evaluation, and issues and trends in instructional design.

Learning Outcomes: Students are expected to integrate issues and trends from both the past and future in the development of curriculum development and program planning, and integrate technology into the development of curriculum and program planning. Finally, students are expected to employ a systematic process, base upon learning theory, to plan, design, implement, and evaluate instruction in American Indian education.

Required Texts:

Curriculum and Program Planning: A Study Guide for the Core Seminar. (1998). Wratcher, et al. Programs for Higher Education. Nova Southeastern University Bookstore.

How to write and use instructional objectives. (1995). Gronlund, N. E. Englewood Cliffs, NJ: Merril, an imprint of Prentice Hall.

Designing effective instruction. (2nd ed.). New York, NY: Merril, an imprint of Macmillan College Company.

Teaching Tips. (1994). (9th ed.). McKeachie, W. J. Lexington, MA: D.C. Heath & Co.

Videotape - "An Interview With Dr. Jerrold Kemp.@ Nova Bookstore.

Gregorc Style Delineator: A Self-assessment instrument for adults. (1985). Gregorc, A. F. Columbia, CT: Gregorc Associates, Inc. Nova Bookstore.

LSI-IIA Learning-style inventory. Boston. MA: McBer & Company. Nova Bookstore.

EdD 830 GOVERNANCE AND MANAGEMENT

Instructor: To be announced
Office: To be announced
Hours: To be announced
Phone: To be announced

Course Description: This seminar on governance and management examines the internal and external dynamics in a governance process, examines the relationships of various stakeholders in a governance process by explorating a variety of governance models.

Seminar Objectives: Students will distinguish between different models of management and governance, and learn how to become change agents in their organizations by analyzing current issues and trends in all aspects of higher education Students will study governance and management processes, governing charters, external factors such as Foundations, Legislature, Executive Branch, Stockholders/Stakeholders, Organizational Strategy and Policy Development, Alignment, Organizational Effectiveness and Assessment.

Learning Outcomes: Students will distinguish between (a) different models of governance and management, (b) how to become change agents in their organizations by identifying and analyzing issues and trends, (c) rescarching models for examining organizational effectiveness and develop specific measures for outcomes assessments through analyzing the impact of external agencies, accreditation organizations, and (d) by addressing decision-making; policy and procedures in the governing process; by examining the mission, vision, values, ethics, and take responsibility for planning, and development of the organization.

Required Texts:

Reframing organizations: Artistry, choice, and leadership. Bolman, L. G., & Deal, T. E. (1997). San Francisco, CA: Jossey-Bass Publishers.

Organization and governance in higher education (2nd ed.). Needleham, MA: Ginn Press.

Study Guide for Governance and Management. (August 2001). Nova Southeastern University.

Guidelines for Form and Style. Nova Southeastern University.

Publication Manual of the American Psychological Association (most recent edition).

EdD 840 HUMAN RESOURCES DEVELOPMENT

Instructor: To be announced
Office: To be announced
Hours: To be announced
Phone: To be announced

Course Description: Human resources development focuses on employees in an organization setting; and on stakeholder training, organization development, career development, on employee development to achieve attainment of organizational strategic goals and objectives. It also focuses on organizational structure, strategic planning, technology, organizational culture by improving performance in training, education, career development, organizational development, evaluation, and the return on the organization's investment.

Course Objectives: Students should be able to (a) apply human resources development theory and research to improving organizational performance; formulate data collection methods, be able to interpret data, and communicate findings effectively; (b) develop strategic approach for improving individual or group performance; and (c) facilitate methods for evaluating the impact of human resource development plans.

Learning Outcomes: Human resource development models reveal five phases: (a) vision development, (b) performance and needs analysis of the organization, (c) action plan, (d) implementation, and (d) evaluation. In the study guide for the Human Resources Development seminar from Nova Southeastern University states "the purpose of the HRD vision is to identify the organization's ideal and then to integrate the HRD vision with the organizational vision and the organization's strategic plan. The analysis phase attempts to determine the human performance needs of the organization through an organization audit. Normally, the organizational audit involves collecting data to determine what organizational needs are currently unmet. The next phase is to develop an action plan that builds on the previous stages to evaluate the degree to which the action plan met its objectives, and to use this information to improve upon future actions. Throughout the implementation of these phases, the individuals involved function in a variety of roles: analyst; intervention specialist; change manager; and evaluator." (P. 11).

Required Text:

Rothwell, W. J., Hohne, C. K. & King, S. B. (2000) Human performance improvement; Building practitioner competence. Houston, TX: Gulf. (ISBN 0-88415-404-1)

Landon, D; Whiteside, K.S., & McKenna, M. M. (1999). Intervention resource guide: 50 Performance improvement tools. San Francisco: Jossey-Bass. (ISBN 0-7879-4401-7)

Human Resource Development: A Study Guide for the Core Seminar. Programs for Higher Education. Nova Southeastern University. Nova Bookstore.

EdD 850 SOCIETAL FACTORS AFFECTING EDUCATION

Instructor: To be announced
Office: To be announced
Hours: To be announced
Phone: To be announced

Course Description: This seminar focuses on environmental scanning and futures research by analyzing external societal factors that influence the institution of education. Some key concepts that affect education include economics, control (government, the courts, constituencies, etc.), technological, social, and demographical variables (including race, gender, age, poverty, etc.) and competition. This seminar includes planning for the future, forecasting, theories of change, and change agentry analyzing past and present trends in forecasting and futures research. The seminar approach explores interdependent forces in society that impacts directly and indirectly the institution of education such as legislative action, governing bodies, court decisions, constituency organizations, as well as economic, technological and social-demographic factors.

Course Objectives: Students should be able to (a) understand the interdependence and interrelationship of social factors such as economic, control, technological, and social-demographic that influence the institution of education, (b) understand how control factors such as the Legislature, court decisions, governing bodies, constituencies, (c) understand how application of technology influence educational practice, (c) how to apply past and present trends in futures research through environmental scanning, and (d) how to apply the principals of change agentry in planning models so that a preferred future may be possible.

Learning Outcomes: Student will review current topical literature from the Chronicle of Higher Education, as well as the required readings and select sources related to the topic they are exploring and prepare a literature review. The Institutional Societal Factors Inventory (ISFI) will develop in stages. This project involves environmental scanning and analysis of the impact on educational institutions of selected societal factors, and developing a preferred future by employing change agentry principles for the student's educational institution.

Required Texts:

Judy, R. W., & D'Amico, D. Workplace 2020: Work and the workers in the 21st century. (1997). Indianapolis, IN: Hudson institute.

Kknoke, W. (1997). Bold New World: The essential road map to the 21st century. New York< NY: Kodansha International.

Varcoe, K. D., & Zachary, L. J. (Ed.). (1998). Book of Readings: Societal Factors Affecting Education. Fort Laderdale, FL: Programs for Higher Education, Nova Southeastern University. Nova Bookstore.

After completion of this seminar students should be able to employ the concept of change and change agentry principles, and through the application of change theory use planning models and strategies in their organizations so that a preferred future can be implemented.

EdD 860 LEADERSHIP IN AMERICAN INDIAN EDUCATION

Instructor: Dr Byron Lee Blackwell, JD, EdD
Office: To be announced
Hours: To be announced
Phone: To be announced

Seminar Description: This seminar incorporates an examination of historical and philosophical foundations of leaders skills. It also provides a conceptual framework for leadership research, theories and models for American Indian educators, and is designed to empower emerging American Indian leaders/non-Indians leaders through a learner-designated Leadership Development Action Plan (LDAP), which incorporates change theory, organizational paradigms, as well as transactional and transformational leadership strategies. The processes of a manager are planning and budgeting, organizing and staffing, and controlling and problem-solving, but a visionary leader is involved in the process of establishing direction, aligning people, and motivating people.

This seminar examines philosophical foundations of leader skills such as challenging the process; search f r opportunities, experiment and take risks; inspire a shared vision; envision the future, enlist others; enable others to act, foster collaboration, strengthening others, search for opportunities; model the way, set an example, plan small wins; and encourage the heart by recognizing individual contributions, and celebrate accomplishments of others who have contributed to the achievement of the organizational vision.

Seminar Objectives: Students will study theories and models of modern leadership paradigms, learn how be a change agent in their communities, by interviewing a leader they respect; and designing a Leadership Development Action Plan (LDAP). A leader as entrepreneur is a dreamer who transforms visions into reality. Students are expected to keep working journals as the seminar progresses. This seminar is also designed to train doctoral students for leadership roles for positions such as department chairs.

Learning Outcomes: Students should be able to demonstrate understanding and competence in applying concepts and theories in the Leadership Development Action Plan (LDAP). The student should be able to demonstrate competence by develop vision skills such as expressing a vision, exploring a vision, extending a vision, and expanding a vision as a change agent by (a) developing the need for change; (b) establish change agent relationships; (c) collect data to make a diagnosis; (d) examine alternatives and action goals; (e) implement action; (d) provide reinforcement to stabilize change; and (f) develop mechanisms for ongoing internal adjustment. Students are expected to keep working journals as the seminar progresses, two Pro-Active Reading Reports, and prepare and present a case study and Leadership Development Action Plan (LDAP) during the last class. Finally students will understand the leadership roles and duties of department chairs.

Doctoral students will examine (a) the department chair's roles, powers, and responsibilities; (b) types of departments, divisions, and institutions; (c) leadership roles; (d) delegations and departmental committees; (e) department decision making and bringing about change; (f) setting departmental goals and developing action plans; (g) preparing departmental budgets; (h) assigning faculty activities; and (I) managing curriculum and human resources.

Required Text:

Clark, K. E., & Clark, M. B. (1996). Choosing to lead (2nd ed.). Charlotte, NC: Iron Gate Press.

Hesselbein, F., & Cohen, P. M. (1999). Leader to leader. San Francisco, CA: Jossey-Bass, Publishers.

Goonen, N. M., et al. (2000-2001). Leadership: A Study Guide for the Core Seminar. Nova Southeastern University. Programs for Higher Education. Nova Bookstore.

Tucker, Allan. (1984). Chairing the academic department: Leadership among peers. American Council On Education. Macmillian Publishing Company: New York.

Creswell, et. al. The Academic chairperson's handbook. University of Nebraska Press: Lincoln and London.

EdD 870 SEMINAR SPECIALIZATION ONE: EMERGENCE OF HIGHER EDUCATION IN AMERICA

Instructor: Dr Byron Lee Blackwell, JD, EdD
Office: To be announced
Hours: To be announced
Phone: To be announced

Seminar Description: This seminar specialization on the emergence of American higher education has its roots in European American higher education in America which can be traced back to Medieval, Renaissance, and Reformation periods in Europe to the present era in American higher education. This seminar provides a historical, philosophical and theoretical foundation for the establishment of curriculum, governance, law and economics of higher education policy, and will be offered in the summer only. The emergence of both universities and the rise of community colleges will be examined. American Indian education in the past and present will be also be examined.

Seminar Objectives: Students will demonstrate they understand the following components in the medieval educational setting: organizational structure, methods of instruction, physical nature, methods of evaluation and curriculum, knowledge of both background of scholastic culture and the philosophical bases of continuing liberal arts/vocational controversy today, and how these factors have influence American Indian higher education. Students will also be exposed to American Indian traditional modes of teaching and learning in the past as well today.

Learning Outcomes: By the end of the seminar students should be able to describe the nature of higher education in the various periods of education history in the medieval setting and here in the United States; trace the general themes, trends or elements of the past to contemporary times; and be able to explain and identify how social trends, politics, law and economics have shaped not only higher education in American institutions, but also, how it has influenced American Indian higher education.

Required Texts:

Goodchild, L., L., & Wechsler, H. (Eds.). (1997). <u>ASHE reader on the history of education</u> (2nd ed.). Needham Heights, MA A: Ginn.

Lucas, C. J. (1994). <u>American history: A History</u>. New York, NY: St. Martins Press.

Reyhner, Jon and Eder, Jeanne. (1989). <u>A History of Indian Education</u>. Billings, MT: Native American Studies. Eastern Montana College.

Deloria, Vine, Jr. (1991). <u>Indian Education In America</u>. American Indian Science & Engineering Society.

Students are required to chose one of the two books below depending upon their interest in either a four-year university or a community college.

Cohen, A. M. (1998). <u>The Shaping of American higher education</u>. San Francisco, CA: Jossey Bass.

Witt, A. A., Wattenbarger, J. L., Gollattsscheck, J. F., & Suppiger, J. E. (1994). <u>America's community colleges: The first century</u>. Washington, DC: The Community College Press.

EdD 880 SEMINAR TWO: POLITICS, LAW, AND ECONOMICS OF HIGHER EDUCATION

Instructor: Dr Byron Lee Blackwell, JD, EdD

Office: To be announced

Hours: To be announced

Phone: to be announced

<u>Seminar Description</u>. This seminar applies the concepts, theories, and techniques of political, legal, and economic factors in the study of educational policy through local, state, and federal systems in policy decision-making. This specialization seminar will only be offered during the summer session. In the first area of inquiry (politics) are usually a conflict over compelling interests that involves the allocation of scare resources (economics), and is usually resolved by the intervention of the government (law). The second area of inquiry involves disagreements that develop over the intent and interpretation with concepts of policy and policy formation. The third area of inquiry (economics) when finances are intertwined with national and international economic and political policy-making.

<u>Seminar Objectives</u>: In the first area of inquiry (politics), students are expected to have an (a) understanding how organizational culture, conflict, and communication are integrated ingredients of politics in higher education; (b) by an understanding the importance of an organizational frame for understanding organizational behavior and decision-making; (c) use theoretical models by which policy can be formulated, implemented, and evaluated; (d) and understand the involvement of state and federal government in the establishment of educational policy.

In the second area of inquiry (legal), students are expected to (a) understand the nature and scope and the historical overview of educational law; (b) understand how law functions in the organization and the management of a institution as well as the hierarchical legal framework in colleges and universities; (c) and understand how the legal implications of case law and contract law pertain in the operation of a college or university.

In the third area of inquiry (economics), (a) students are expected to understand the relationships of economic variables to institutional planning and budgeting, and strategies for addressing economic developments; (b) have an understanding of the relationship of staffing, scheduling, budgeting in the operational economics of the higher education enterprise; and (c) understand public economic policy in public and private sectors in the local, state, and national levels.

Learning Outcomes: In the politics area of inquiry (a) students will understand and apply political models in higher education; in the legal area of inquiry (b) understand the function of federal and state courts; and in the economics area of inquiry (c) the strategic guidance model. At the last class students will turn in the final report below.

A DESIGN FOR ANALYSIS OF A CRITICAL POLICY DECISION

1. Introduction and Background

    1.1. Brief description of state issue

    1.2. Brief description of context and setting

2. Analysis

    2.1. Goals of organization relevant to the decision

    2.2. Interplay of goal and forces at the state level

        2.2.1. Political Forces

        2.2.2. Legal Forces

        2.2.3. Economic Forces

        2.2.4. Goals impact of emerging decision on organization's goals

        2.2.5. Condition/status of decision

    2.3. Interplay of goal and forces at the organizational level

        2.3.1. Political Forces

        2.3.2. Legal Forces

        2.3.3. Economic Forces

        2.3.4. Goal impact of emerging decision on organization's goals

3. Summary and Conclusions

    3.1. Condition/status of decision at this time

    3.2. Impact of decision on organization

        3.2.1. In relation to goals identified in 2.1

        3.2.2. Other impacts, if any

    3.3. Concluding observations and comments

Required Text:

Gillett-Karam, et al. (2001). Politics, Law, and Economics of Higher Education. Programs for Higher Education. Nova Southeastern University. Nova Bookstore.

Goonen, N. M., & Blechman, R. S. (1999). Higher Education administration: a guide to legal, ethical, and practical issues. Westport, CT: Greenwood Press.

Nova Southeastern University Class Handout for Politics, Law, and Economics Seminar.

White, Geoffrey (2000). Campus, Inc.: Corporate Power in the Ivory Tower. Amherst, NY: Prometheus Books.

Kaplin, W. A., & Lee, B. A. (1995). The Law of higher education: a comprehensive guide to legal implications of administrative decision-making. (3rd ed.). San Francisco, CA: Jossey-Bass.

Kaplin, W. A. & Lee, B. A. (2000). Year 2000. Cumulative supplement to the Law of higher education, (3rd ed.). Washington, DC: National Association of College and University Attorneys.

Honeyman, D. S., Watte barger, J. L. & Westbrook, K. C. (1996). Struggle to survive: Funding higher education in the next century. Thousand Oaks, CA: Corwin Press, Inc.

Recommended Text:

Lenington, R. L. (1996). Managing higher education as a business. Phoenix, AZ: The Oryx Press.

EdD 890 COMPREHENSIVE EX A MINATION

Eligibility:

The eligibility requirements are: (a) completion of least three practicum projects, (b) all of the core seminar courses, and (c) the two the summer specialization projects; however, all four practicums must be completed being advanced to candidacy before being assigned to a dissertation committee. Students will be allowed two attempts to pass the written comprehensive examination. Students who receive a "no pass" on the first exam will be allowed to retake the examination a second time. Students who satisfactory complete the written comprehensive examination will achieve candidacy, and will be assigned to a dissertation committee composed of three faculty members once all eligibility requirements have been completed.

EdD 890 APPLIED DISSERTATION REPORT

The applied dissertation process is the culminating research project for American Indian education doctoral students. In the Guide To The Applied Dissertation Process the practicums prepare students for the applied dissertation report which (a) require greater breadth, (b) greater depth, (c) extensive review and analysis, relevant research and literature, (d) a more comprehensive synthesis, and (d) a more complex design of a particular methodology or one reflecting multiple methodologies. (p. 10).

The following elements of the applied dissertation process are: (a) prospectus, (b) proposal, (c) dissertation project, and the (d) applied dissertation report. The Guide To The Applied Dissertation Process presents an overview of the applied dissertation process from the prospectus, proposal, and the applied dissertation report.

GUIDE TO THE APPLIED DISSERTATION PROCESS. July 2000. Nova Southeastern University, Center for Innovation in Higher Education and Training Programs for Higher Education. Programs for Higher Education. Nova Bookstore.

Section C: Course Implementation Plan

Fall Semester   1st Year

1). EdD 800 Introduction to Doctoral Research Methodologies in American Indian Education

2). EdD 810 Teaching American Indian Education

Spring Semester   1st Year

1). EdD 820 Curriculum Development and Program Planning in American Indian Education

2). EdD 840 Government and Management

Summer   1st Year

1). EdD 870 Seminar Specialization One: Emergence of Higher Education in America

Fall Semester   2nd Year

1). EdD 840 Human Resource Development

2). EdD 850 Societal Factors Affecting Education

Spring Semester   2nd Year

1). EdD 860 Leadership in American Indian Education

2). EdD 890 Written Comprehensive examination

Summer   2nd Year

1). EdD 880 Seminar Specialization Two: Politics, law, and Economics of Higher Education

Prac 700 Research Methodology (Statistical) Practicum

Prac 710 Development Methodology Practicum

Prac 720 Evaluation Methodology Practicum

EdD 900 Applied Doctoral Dissertation Report

Students may begin working on their practicums after their first semester one practicum at a time. After completing three practicums students may take the written comprehensive examination in the spring and summer terms each year. The student will be allowed to take the written comprehensive examination twice.

Section D: Student Evaluation Form

Student Evaluation Form

Your advice and opinions on the effectiveness of this course will help the masters program in American Indian Studies improve its courses. Please feel free to address any concerns you have regarding the course content. Your comments will help us to improve the course.

1). In your opinion did this course meet the objectives stated in the course syllabus?

2). Did this course meet the stated outcomes for the course?

3). After completing the course do you feel you are able to communicate effectively and critically analyze various issues in American Indian Studies?

4). Do you have any other concerns regarding the course content that will help improve the quality of the course?

Section E: Course Evaluation Plan

EdD 800 INTRODUCTION TO RESEARCH METHODOLOGIES IN AMERICAN INDIAN EDUCATION

<u>Seminar Objectives</u>: The student will be exposed to concepts related to research design, internal and external validity of research designs, sample selection, reliability and validity of instruments designed for data collection, concepts of descriptive and inferential statistics, and the use of software packages for statistical analysis.

<u>Seminar Outcomes</u>: Students will be able to define the problem-solving methodologies (research, development, and evaluation). Students will be able to describe the scientific method (description of problem, formulation of a solution through the statement of purpose, the research question, and the research hypothesis, evaluation of previous research, collection of data. presentation of data, presentation of results, and interpretation, conclusions, and recommendations. The student will apply the three research methodologies in brief reports and recognize the influence of research, evaluation, and development studies on educational policy, practice, and decision making. The scientific method will be employed in the development of the proposal and practicum report for the Research Methodology seminar. Finally, the student will utilize the basic principle of descriptive and inferential statistics through the use of software packages (statistical, word processing, and graphics) in carrying out research, evaluation, and development reports.

<u>Learning Outcomes</u>: Upon completion of this seminar course students will be able to develop research designs for practicums on development, evaluation, and statistical research methods for their practicum reports They will also have gained an understanding of theories and concepts in higher education, research methodologies, the practicum process and the applied dissertation process.

EdD 810 TEACHING AMERICAN INDIAN EDUCATION

Seminar Objectives. This seminar course teaches educators how to provide an opportunity for both the dominate culture and the American Indian culture to exist in harmony side by side so that the high dropout rate of Indian students can be retarded. This seminar provides educators with the tools to develop American Indian curriculum by bringing the Indian community into the curriculum development process. The Indian theory of relativity is more comprehensive than Einstein's theory of relativity because the Indian concept of the universe has a moral content because the Indian concept of relationship in the universe is both personal and particular. In their caretaking of the natural world American Indians were concerned with the products of their actions than just with the process of their actions.

Learning Outcomes: It is the purpose of this seminar to give educators the tools to empower Indian students through ideologies and strategies in Indian education to keep Indian students in school by adapting instruction and curriculum to Indian culture, and by involving the Indian community in the instructional process. This will be done by Indian students learning both the native language and English, and by applying both to the educational process through a multisensory approach to language instruction in hands-on learning activities. In the Indian culture students use storytelling in the educational process. Storytelling can be used to teach English so Indian students can learn the stories in both English and the native language. Knowledge of American Indian literature should be part of the curriculum as well as teaching in the content areas of social studies, science, and mathematics.

EdD 820 CURRICULUM DEVELOPMENT AND PROGRAM PLANNING IN AMERICAN INDIAN EDUCATION

Seminar Objectives: It is the objective of this seminar course to include in the course content curriculum, instructional design, and program planning, the foundations of learning and learner characteristics, the history of curriculum and educational philosophy on instructional design, student assessment and program evaluation, and issues and trends in instructional design.

Learning Outcomes: Students are expected to integrate issues and trends from both the past and future in the development of curriculum development and program planning, and integrate technology into the development of curriculum and program planning. Finally, students are expected to employ a systematic process, base upon learning theory, to plan, design, implement. and evaluate instruction in American Indian education.

EdD 830 GOVERNANCE AND MANAGEMENT

Seminar Objectives: Students will distinguish between different models of management and governance, and learn how to become change agents in their organizations by analyzing current issues and trends in all aspects of higher education Students will study governance and management processes, governing charters, external factors such as Foundations, Legislature, Executive Branch, Stockholders/Stakeholders, Organizational Strategy and Policy Development, Alignment, Organizational Effectiveness and Assessment.

Learning Outcomes: Students will distinguish between (a) different models of governance and management. (b) how to become change agents in their organizations by identifying and analyzing issues and trends, (c) researching models for examining organizational effectiveness and develop specific measures for outcomes assessments through analyzing the impact of external agencies, accreditation organizations, and (d) by addressing decision-making; policy and procedures in the governing process; by examining the mission, vision, values, ethics, and take responsibility for planning, and development of the organization.

EdD 840 HUMAN RESOURCES DEVELOPMENT

Course Objectives: Students should be able to (a) apply human resources development theory and research to improving organizational performance; formulate data collection methods, be able to interpret data, and communicate findings effectively; (b) develop strategic approach for improving individual or group performance; and (c) facilitate methods for evaluating the impact of human resource development plans.

Learning Outcomes: Human resource development models reveal five phases: (a) vision development, (b) performance and needs analysis of the organization, (c) action plan, (d) implementation, and (d) evaluation. In the study guide for the Human Resources Development seminar from Nova Southeastern University states "the purpose of the HRD vision is to identify the organization's ideal and then to integrate the HRD vision with the organizational vision and the organization's strategic plan. The analysis phase attempts to determine the human performance needs of the organization through an organization audit. Normally, the organizational audit involves collecting data to determine what organizational needs are currently unmet. The next phase is to develop an action plan that builds on the previous stages to evaluate the degree to which the action plan met its objectives, and to use this information to improve upon future actions. Throughout the implementation of these phases, the individuals involved function in a variety of roles: analyst; intervention specialist; change manager; and evaluator." (P. 11).

EdD 850 SOCIETAL FACTORS AFFECTING EDUCATION

Course Objectives: Students should be able to (a) understand the interdependence and interrelationship of social factors such as economic, control, technological, and social-demographic that influence the institution of education, (b) understand how control factors such as the Legislature, court decisions, governing bodies, constituencies, (c) understand how application of technology influence educational practice, (c) how to apply past and present trends in futures research through environmental scanning, and (d) how to apply the principals of change agentry in planning models so that a preferred future may be possible.

Learning Outcomes: Student will review current topical literature from the Chronicle of Higher Education, as well as the required readings and select sources related to the topic they are exploring and prepare a literature review. The Institutional Societal Factors Inventory (ISFI) will develop in stages. This project involves environmental scanning and analysis of the impact on educational institutions of selected societal factors, and developing a preferred future by employing change agentry principles for the student's educational institution.

EdD 860 LEADERSHIP IN AMERICAN INDIAN EDUCATION

Seminar Objectives: Students will study theories and models of modern leadership paradigms, learn how be a change agent in their communities, by interviewing a leader they respect; and designing a Leadership Development Action Plan (LDAP). A leader as entrepreneur is a dreamer who transforms visions into reality. Students are expected to keep working journals as the seminar progresses. This seminar is also designed to train doctoral students for leadership roles for positions such as department chairs.

Learning Outcomes: Students should be able to demonstrate understanding and competence in applying concepts and theories in the Leadership Development Action Plan (LDAP). The student should be able to demonstrate competence by develop vision skills such as expressing a vision, exploring a vision. extending a vision, and expanding a vision as a change agent by (a) developing the need for change; (b) establish change agent relationships: (c) collect data to make a diagnosis; (d) examine alternatives and action goals; (e) implement action; (d) provide reinforcement to stabilize change; and (f) develop mechanisms for ongoing internal adjustment . Students are expected to keep working journals as the seminar progresses, two Pro-Active Reading Reports, and prepare and present a case study and Leadership Development Action Plan (LDAP) during the last class. Finally students will understand the leadership roles and duties of department chairs.

EdD 870 SEMINAR SPECIALIZATION ONE: POLITICS, LAW, AND ECONOMICS OF HIGHER EDUCATION

Seminar Objectives: In the first area of inquiry (politics), students are expected to have an (a) understanding how organizational culture, conflict, and communication are integrated ingredients of politics in higher education; (b) by an understanding the importance of an organizational frame for understanding organizational behavior and decision-making; (c) use theoretical models by which policy can be formulated, implemented, and evaluated; (d) and understand the involvement of state and federal government in the establishment of educational policy.

In the second area of inquiry (legal), students are expected to (a) understand the nature and scope and the historical overview of educational law; (b) understand how law functions in the organization and the management of a institution as well as the hierarchical legal framework in colleges and universities; (c) and understand how the legal implications of case law and contract law pertain in the operation of a college or university.

In the third area of inquiry (economics), (a) students are expected to understand the relationships of economic variables to institutional planning and budgeting, and strategies for addressing economic developments;(b) have an understanding of the relationship of staffing, scheduling, budgeting in the operational economics of the higher education enterprise: and (c) understand public economic policy in public and private sectors in the local, state, and national levels.

Learning Outcomes: In the politics area of inquiry (a) students will understand and apply political models in higher education; in the legal area of inquiry (b) understand the function of federal and state courts: and in the economics area of inquiry (c) the strategic-guidance model. At the last class students will turn in the final report below.

EdD 870 SEMINAR SPECIALIZATION ONE: EMERGENCE OF HIGHER EDUCATION IN AMERICA

Seminar Objectives: Students will demonstrate they understand the following components in the medieval educational setting: organizational structure, methods of instruction, physical nature, methods of evaluation and curriculum, knowledge of both background of scholastic culture and the philosophical bases of continuing liberal arts/vocational controversy today, and how these factors have influence American Indian higher education. Students will also be exposed to American Indian traditional modes of teaching and learning in the past as well today.

Learning Outcomes: By the end of the seminar students should be able to describe the nature of higher education in the various periods of education history in the medieval setting and here in the United States; trace the general themes, trends or elements of the past to contemporary times; and be able to explain and identify how social trends, politics, law and economics have shaped not only higher education in American institutions, but also, how it has influenced American Indian higher education.

EdD 880 SEMINAR SPECIALIZATION TWO: POLITICS, LAW, AND ECONOMICS OF HIGHER EDUCATION

Seminar Objectives: In the first area of inquiry (politics), students are expected to have an (a) understanding how organizational culture, conflict, and communication are integrated ingredients of politics in higher education; (b) by an understanding the importance of an organizational frame for understanding organizational behavior and decision-making; (c) use theoretical models by which policy can be formulated, implemented, and evaluated; (d) and understand the involvement of state and federal government in the establishment of educational policy.

In the second area of inquiry (legal), students are expected to (a) understand the nature and scope and the historical overview of educational law; (b) understand how law functions in the organization and the management of a institution as well as the hierarchical legal framework in colleges and universities; (c) and understand how the legal implications of case law and contract law pertain in the operation of a college or university.

In the third area of inquiry (economics), (a) students are expected to understand the relationships of economic variables to institutional planning and budgeting, and strategies for addressing economic developments;(b) have an understanding of the relationship of staffing, scheduling, budgeting in the operational economics of the higher education enterprise; and (c) understand public economic policy in public and private sectors in the local, state, and national levels.

Learning Outcomes: In the politics area of inquiry (a) students will understand and apply political models in higher education; in the legal area of inquiry (b) understand the function of federal and state courts; and in the economics area of inquiry (c) the strategic guidance model. At the last class students will turn in the final report below.

EdD 890 WRITTEN COMPREHENSIVE EXAMINATION

The eligibility requirements are: (a) completion of at least three practicum reports, (b) all of core seminars, and (c) the two summer specializations; however, all four practicums must be completed before being advanced to candidacy for the dissertation committee. Students will be allowed two attempts to pass the written comprehensive examination. Students who receive a "no pass" on the first exam will be allowed to retake the examination a second time. Students who satisfactory pass the written comprehensive examination, and have completed all four practicums will be assigned to a dissertation committee composed of three faculty members once all eligibility requirements have been met.

EdD 890 APPLIED DISSERTATION REPORT

The applied dissertation process is the culminating research project for American Indian education doctoral students. In the <u>Guide To The Applied Dissertation Process</u> the practicums prepare students for the applied dissertation report which (a) require great r breadth, (b) greater depth, (c) extensive review and analysis of relevant of relevant research and literature. (d) a more comprehensive synthesis, and (d) a more complex design of a particular methodology or one reflecting multiple methodologies. (p. 10).

The following elements of the applied dissertation process are: (a) prospectus, (b) proposal, (c) dissertation project, and the (d) applied dissertation report. The <u>Guide To The Applied Dissertation Process</u> presents an overview of the applied dissertation process from the prospectus, proposal, and the applied dissertation report.

Section F: Doctoral Evaluation Plan

The Doctor of Education degree in American Indian Education will be evaluated by faculty from the American Indian Studies Program, and by an advisory committee who will determine whether or not the doctoral program is achieving its program goals. The advisory committee may be composed of but not limited to committee members from Nova Southeastern University. The doctoral program will be evaluated by five goals by the advisory committee.

DOCTORAL OF EDUCATION IN AMERICAN INDIAN EDUCATION

Program goals

Goal One: It is an objective of _____ to implement a Doctor of Education degree in American Indian Higher Education.

Goal Two: It is the Objective of _____ university to provide students with the opportunity to learn the Cherokee language, history and culture.

Goal Three: It is an objective of _____ to increase students' understanding and comprehension of American Indian bodies of knowledge.

Goal Four: It is an objective of _____ university to offer an Educational Leadership program for educators in American Indian higher education and administration.

Goal Five: It is an objective of _____ university to provide students with lifelong skills such as competency in interpersonal relations, self- discipline, problem solving and technical knowledge for the 21st century.

Section G: Grand Vision Action Plan

Vision

A vision is a dream or mental image of a preferred future that spans over a certain period of time such as 5, 10, 15, or 20 years or longer. A visionary leader is a culture builder. He creates an ideal image of the organization and its specific culture, and he defines the organizational philosophy that states the vision and develops programs and policies that put the philosophy into practice within the organization's culture. Finally, the visionary leader leads by example and he creates the organization's symbols, metaphors, logos, myths and rituals through a persuasive communication systems network.

The symbol for the American Indian Studies Program will be the Great Eagle carrying the Sacred Pipe representing the unity of all Indian nations in North, Central and South America by the joining of the South American Condor and the Great Eagle in Central America. The American Indian Studies logos will be the Great Eagle which will represent the American Indian Studies Program. The rituals of the American Indian Studies Program will include the metaphor of the American Indian National Anthem, and the vision of the Indian medicine person or Elder holding an Eagle wing leading a spiritual ceremony praying for our sacred earth mother, while burning sage or sweet grass in the spiritual care-taking of Turtle Island (America).

I have a vision the graduates of the doctoral program in American Indian education will be the instructors for both the masters and the doctoral programs, and they will be required to write books and articles on American Indian culture for publication at _____ university in the Southeast Indian Quarterly or the American Indian Research Journal.

They will have the responsibility for developing an American Indian Ecological Studies Program to train American Indians in environmental engineering so they can return to their Indian communities as ecological consultants whose technical expertise and spiritual ceremonies will be employed in the ecological caretaking of the earth. Indians in the doctoral program will also design programs in Indian law, politics, administration, Indian education, computer technology, and educational leadership. The doctorate in American Indian Education will train Native Americans to be leaders in their Indian communities as change agents in American Indian education.

I am creating a spiritual culture for a masters degree in American Indian Studies/Doctor of Education in American Indian Education. This spiritual culture is a holistic/spiritual/ecological paradigm which is based on Indian spiritual values, symbols, metaphors, logos and images, where cooperation, not competition, is stressed in a supportive atmosphere where power is shared and responsibility is delegated, where teamwork is practiced, where leaders are the servants of the people, the women and the Elders, and the spiritual/medicine people.

It is my vision that I will become a department chair of American Indian Studies in the Southeastern United States near or on the eastern Cherokee homeland. I have a dream that this location will become the mecca of Indian research where Indian scholars will come from North, Central and South America. I have a dream we will have a great computerized research center called the Osceola Research Center to honor the great Seminole chief Osceola who refused to sell his sacred earth mother so his people would have grounds to spread their blankets at a place they call Immokalee (my home).

I have a dream that at the Osceola Research Center we will have an American Indian library called the Sequoah Talking Leaves Library to honor the great Cherokee scribe Sequoyah, who with his talking leaves syllabary taught his people how to read and write in Cherokee. In this library we publish outstanding research of Indian scholars quarterly in a journal called either the <u>American Indian Research Journal</u> or the <u>Southeast Indian Quarterly</u>. I have a dream that once a year in the summer outstanding Indian scholars and researchers will present their research for publication at the Great Peacemakers Conference Hall to honor Degannawidah, the Great Peacemaker who gave the Iroquois Confederacy their constitution , the Great Law Of Peace. which was the forerunner of the United States Constitution.

As a visionary leader in challenging the process, searching for opportunities, experimenting and taking risks, I am performing in the roles of change agent, direction setter, spokesman, and mentor in my leadership as chair of American Indian Studies. I have to be a change agent to reverse the high dropout rate of Indian students from high school and college because the schools they attend do not address educational needs of Indian students or respect Indian culture. I also have the role of direction setter because the future direction of Indian education is self-determination so Indian communities can be involved in the education of their children.

As department chair of American Indian Studies, I will also be a mentor and a role model for Indian students. As a mentor, my leadership must serve the best interest of my students because I must help them by showing them how they can use their education to not only improve their academic performance, but also show them how they can use their technical skills to help their people in their Indian communities. As a role model and mentor, I can lead by example by establishing a code of ethics for my students. The best way to build trust between a leader and followers is to always be truthful and honest because trust is the glue that holds together a vision. Without trust a leader is like a bird without wings.

I have to set policies in motion that will allow Indian people to determine what they want their children to learn in an American Indian Studies Program, but I also have to make sure that while Indian students are studying their own culture and history they are able to get a practical education that will give them the skills to not only support themselves, but also to use these technical skills in the service of their Indian communities. Students will be studying and conducting research on their own culture and history in a supportive atmosphere that will stress cooperation and sharing not competition. However, although we will offer many opportunities and access to higher education to Indian students who have been traditionally denied the opportunity for a college education, they will be required to adhere to high standards of scholarly excellence because they are leading the way for future generations of Indian educators.

As chair of American Indian Studies I will establish a great American Indian Culture Cultural Program where we will show both plays and films that are written, directed, acted, and produced by American Indian actors, directors, playwrights, screen writers, and film-makers. The American Indian Culture Center will host Indian powwows, scripture, arts and crafts, Indian poetry, acting, singing, music and dance on campus that will greatly enhance the cultural educational experience of _____ university students. The American Indian Cultural Center will be housed in a Creative Arts building where Indian plays and films will be shown, and a great American Indian Sculpture Center where American Indian arts and crafts will be displayed. I have a dream, a vision we will have a beautiful building called Tecumseh Hall to honor the great Shawnee warrior, chief, orator, and statesman who dreamed of an Indian state where all Indians would be one nation, one people.

Housed within Tecumseh Hall I have a vision of a great computerized research center called the Osceola Research Center to honor the great Seminole chief Osceola who refused to sell the sacred remains of his beautiful earth mother so his people would have grounds to spread their blankets at a place they called Immokalee (my home). Inside the Osceola Research Center I have a vision of an American Indian library called the Sequoah Talking Leaves Library to honor the great Cherokee scribe Sequoah, who with his Talking Leaves syllabary taught his people how to read and write in Cherokee (Tsalagi), where we will publish outstanding research of Indian scholars quarterly in the <u>American Indian Research Journal</u>, or the <u>Southeast Indian Quarterly</u>. Once a year at the <u>Summer Gathering</u> Institute in July outstanding Indian/non-Indian scholars and researchers will present their research at the Great Peacemaker's Conference at _____ university to honor Degannawidah, the Great Peacemaker who gave the Iroquois Confederacy their constitution, the Great Law of Peace, which was the forerunner of the United States Constitution.

I have a vision, a dream we will have a great American Indian Law Center where we will have housed government documents pertaining to Native nations in the Miccosukee Alligator Law Library. The documents housed will be Indian treaties, executive orders, case law, and statutes. The building that will house the Sequoah Talking Leaves Library, The Osceola Computerized Research Center, and the Miccosukee Alligator Law Library will be called Tecumseh Hall to honor the great Shawnee warrior, chief, orator, and statesman who dreamed of an Indian state where all Indians would be one nation, one people. As department chair of American Indian Studies, I must set goals and develop action plans for the future direction of an American Indian Research Culture Center where Indian scholars will come from North, Central and South America.

Finally, as department chair of American Indian Studies I must set goals and design action plans for the future direction of Indian studies. My short term strategy is to get the American Indian Studies Program started with an undergraduate program. My immediate plan is to get a masters degree in

American Indian studies Program started with an American Indian Teacher Training Program. My long range goal is to establish a College of Native American Studies Program with a dean and assistant dean, a chair of North American Indian Studies, a chair of Central American Indian Studies, and a chair of South American Indian Studies where Indian scholars from North, Central and South America will come to study and conduct research in Native American Studies.

Visionary leaders have a mission, a purpose, a destiny to fulfill. Visionary leaders are dreamers who thrive on fantasy and a creative imagination whose visions seem irrational. They are risk takers who have great confidence in their ability to take risks, and they are intuitive about the needs and inspirations of their people. Nevertheless, although visionary leaders are dreamers who thrive on fantasy and a creative imagination, they are doers, they transform visions into reality. I have always been considered a black sheep who deviated from the norm because I have always been a loner who was unorthodox in speaking, writing, and dress. As a visionary leader, I have always been laughed at for having idealistic aspirations because I have always been a dreamer who thrived on fantasy and a creative imagination, but I have always been a <u>doer</u> who <u>transformed</u> his dreams into reality because I never give up.

However, to be an agent of change, the vision must be different from everyone else's, it must make sense to others, and it must be understandable by using simple metaphor or illustrative analogy that provides vivid images. The visionary leader must live the vision by his own personal example, and he must empower others if he is to transform the vision into reality. In order to transform my vision into reality, mission into action, and philosophy into practice, I am communicating my grand vision given to me in a vision so that together we can co-create that great vision into an organizational vision that everyone shares, both Indian and White for the benefit of both people. Together we can transform this grand vision into reality.

CPSIA information can be obtained at www.ICGtesting.com
Printed in the USA
LVOW13s2204050614

388868LV00006B/164/P

Printed in China

中外语言交流合作中心赠
Donated by Center for Language Education and Cooperation

China Intercontinental Press

By the Production Team of Every Treasure Tells a Story

EVERY TREASURE TELLS A STORY

Season 2

You have a new message from National Treasures. Check it now?

Preface I

With a grand history of more than 5,000 years, the Chinese nation has created a brilliant and gorgeous Chinese civilization which has left behind it a vast number of treasures.

President Xi Jinping stressed that "we need to bring all collections in our museums, all heritage structures across our land and all records in our classics to life. In this way, the Chinese civilization, together with the rich and colorful civilizations created by the people of other countries, will provide mankind with the right spiritual guidance and strong motivation."

China's National Cultural Heritage Administration has always committed itself to the protection of Chinese cultural heritage. With the purpose of passing on the Chinese culture and inheriting the Chinese civilization, it has continuously enhanced the protection of cultural relics, safeguarded the cultural heritage, promoted the rational use of cultural relics, and deepened the international exchange and cooperation in terms of cultural relics. There are 767,000 immovable cultural relics and 108 million items or sets of state-owned cultural relics in museums nationwide, which have a long history and have become a cultural symbol of China in the new era.

Guided by the Publicity Department of the Central Committee of the CPC, the documentary If Treasures Could Talk is a joint production by China Media Group and the National Cultural Heritage Administration. It demonstrates the charm of Chinese cultural relics to millions of audiences around the world with exquisite ideas and TV languages, as well as refined narrative techniques. Some of these cultural relics experienced vicissitudes, witnessing the inheritance and preservation of Chinese culture from generation to generation; some went global, recording the high-level realm of Chinese civilization through friendly exchanges and mutual understanding; and some were profound, embodying the belief of Chinese people in kindness and self-improvement. Those cultural relics, which were laid aside and neglected in the past, have been known to the public at present.

As the old Chinese saying goes, "Although Zhou Kingdom was an ancient state, King Wen, its ruler, believed in the mandate of renovation". Today, the book which shares the same title as the documentary, If Treasures Could Talk, is presented to friends all over the world who love culture, cherish cultural relics, and inherit civilization, with the hope of mutual exchange between Chinese culture and the cultures created by other countries, the integration between ancient civilization and modern civilization, and the eternal inheritance of the treasures of Chinese cultural relics and human civilization.

We look forward to and welcome your presence in museums in China to witness the splendid Chinese cultural relics and learn about the long history of Chinese civilization!

Gu Yucai

Deputy Secretary of Party Committee and Deputy Director of the National Cultural Heritage Administration

Preface II

CCTV-9 of China Media Group is the only national platform for professional documentaries in China, which has released a series of superb documentaries presenting the features of Chinese civilization in recent years, with the purpose of interpreting and spreading Chinese civilization through "innovative expressions, media convergence and world-class images".

The surviving Chinese cultural relics are among the best in the world. Though the relics cannot talk, they contain abundant information. How to find the way most suitable for the relics and the current dissemination characteristics to make the relics "talk" from the perspectives of video art, visual presentation, and information organization and re-dissemination has always been a concern of us. In this regard, If Treasures Could Talk is exactly a significant practice and exploration.

If Treasures Could Talk is a hundred-episode documentary of the national cultural project jointly produced by the Publicity Department of the Central Committee of the CPC, China Media Group and the National Cultural Heritage Administration. It collects 100 symbolic cultural relics in the process of Chinese civilization and integrates them into a 500-min masterpiece, with one major relic in each 5-min episode. Not just a brand-new form of documentary serving as the "video index of Chinese civilization", it is also a creative attempt based on new communication context and means, which re-interprets the relics from the perspective of "indicators of civilization process" and enables the audiences to learn about Chinese civilization through the relics.

If we regard the documentary as the first transformation from the physical cultural relics to images, then the book which shares the same title as the documentary should be the second. The book provides an overview of cultural relics spanning eight thousand years in time and tens of thousands of miles in space, helping the readers to establish an impression on the Chinese civilization based on cultural relics and to get an in-depth knowledge about the specific relics. In the book, the macro history is perfectly combined with the small relics, and the relics are no longer "articles" standing in the museum showcases in solitude, but living civilization messengers walking out of the history, providing the readers with access to the historical context as well as Chinese civilization.

This book is a periodic review of the "video index of Chinese civilization". We would like to, together with our audiences and readers, experience the overwhelming charm of the time-honored civilization, explore the vaster space of Chinese civilization beyond the index, and thus better understand the essence and direction of our present time.

Zhang Ning

China Media Group

Contents

- Preface
- Gold Crown with Eagle Finial - Friend and Foe | 013
- Warring States Gold-inlaid Bronze Ewer - Art of War | 023
- The Chime-bells of Marquis Yi of Zeng - Tunes of Antiquity | 033
- Wood Carved Double Headed Tomb Guardian - Between this World and the Next | 043
- Silk Painting Depicting A Man Riding A Dragon - At Heaven's Call | 055
- The Terracotta Warriors - An Image of Empire | 067
- Rectangular Measuring Vessel of Shang Yang - Measuring Unity | 083
- Qin Bronze Chariots and Horses - The Road to Eternity | 097
- Liye Qin Slips - A Slip in Time | 111
- Jade in Nanyue - A Symbol of Peacefulness | 119
- The General's Tomb - A Will of Granite | 129
- "Five Stars Rise in the East" Brocade Arm Guard - "Five Stars Rising in the East Favor the Middle Kingdom" | 137
- Jade Doorknocker with Four Symbols of the Sky - The Dragon, Tiger, Bird, and Tortoise | 147

157 | The Xiping Stone Classics - Broken Yet Awaiting Reunion

167 | Stone Carving of Confucius Meeting Laozi - Tracing Back the Roots

175 | Changxin Palace Lamp - A Light from the Han Dynasty

185 | Plain Unlined Gauze Gown - Luxury and Grace

197 | The Twenty-Eight Mansions Cosmic Plates and Sundial - Cycles of Time

209 | Lacquer Dish with the Leopard Cat Pattern - The Kittens on the Lacquer Dish

217 | Counting Rods - A System of Numbers

225 | Gold-inlaid Bronze Hill Censer - The Calculation of Clouds

237 | "Forever Forget Me Not" Silver Belt Hook - A Secret Oath Worn Close to the Heart

245 | Gold and Silver Inlay Cloud-patterned Rhinoceros Vessel - The Spirited Beast

255 | Tomb Figurine of A Storyteller - The Show Must Go On Forever

267 | Galloping Bronze Horse - The Celestial Steed

A Dialogue across Time and Space

Gold Crown with Eagle Finial

Friend and Foe

Gold Crown with Eagle Finial

Location: Inner Mongolia Museum
Age: Warring States Period
Texture: gold
Size: 6.7 cm in height, 16.5~16.8 cm in diameter
Weight: 1,211.7 g

This gold crown once accompanied its owner as he galloped over the grassland. The gold crown shows off the highest metal working skills of the northern nomads in the Warring States period. It represents the pride and glory of the grasslands. On the top of the crown is an eagle. Its head, neck and tail are connected with gold wire. When the owner rode on horseback, the eagle rock to and fro, looking like it was about to take off. On the petal-shaped crown, a pattern of four wolves attacking four sheep has been engraved. On the main diadem there is a tense standoff between a tiger and its prey; it might pounce at any time.

The grassland nomads had no written language, so their history was written for them by others. In the records of the Han culture of the central plains, the Xiongnu were once called Xianyun. Xian means dog with a long snout. They were seen as greedy and cruel, often coming south to raid and pillage. However from the perspective of the owner of the eagle finial crown, things might seem quite different.

I wear this golden crown and armor.
The grassland is my kingdom.
The people who plant grain in the south of the grassland
look weak and skinny.
The men of grassland eat meat and drink milk.
We are warriors.
But, in terms of bad years…
Well, they seem to have more than enough food set by…

Inscription of Ji Zibai Plate of the Guo State

Compared to the agriculture civilization in the central plains, the grassland nomads had a totally different take on life. Their ornaments all feature animals; hunting, fighting, or just lying in wait. The Gold Crown with Eagle Finial is at the peak of this competition for survival.

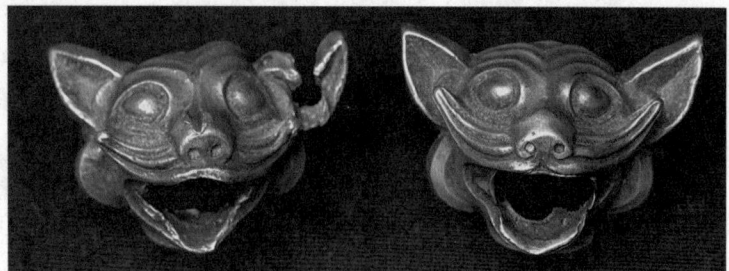
Tiger-head-shaped Silver Ornament

Gold Crown with Eagle Finial   017

Hedgehog-shaped Gold Ornament

Eagle-shaped Gold Ornament

Tiger Biting Cow Gold Plate

Tiger-shaped Gold Plate

Was it ill fortune for the people of the central plains to have such wild northern neighbors? King Wuling of the northern state of Zhao decided to learn from them in the Warring States to form a cavalry army of elite mounted archers. The imitation-driven competitions kicked off. The agriculture civilization of the south that had been on the defensive finally became secure under the Qin and Han dynasties. It fortified the Empire's northern flank with the Great Wall. It not only was the fortress guarding the border, but the frontline in the war against the Xiongnu for the Western Han. However did the endless Wall stop people from communicating with each other? The nomadic ethnic groups wanted silk and grain from the central plains; and people on the central plains wanted the nomad's metalwork, cattle and horses.

The two sides fought with each other one day and made on peace the next. Under Eastern Han Dynasty the southern Xiongnu settled south of Great Wall that the rivals were joined in one huge family.

Today when we look at this golden crown, we can see the shadows of the past rivalries. Two through years in cycles of conflict, division and unity have tempered the steel of the Chinese nation into an un-shatterable crown of unity. It is from this peak that eagle's eye looks down.

The competition of the rivals makes us examine ourselves. Examination leads to understanding. Understanding leads to self-improvement. Thank you, My Friend, My Foe!

The Symbol of Supreme Power

This crown comprises an eagle-shaped top and a gold headband. The eagle stands on a thick, domed, petal-edged golden cap which depicts four wolves in relief each eating a sheep. The wolves, with their claws stretching forward, lie low on the left and right sides of the hemispherical cap, and clenched rear body of the sheep. Looking back with their hollowed horns, the sheep tumble down in front and at back of the cap, struggling with their front legs stretching forward and rear legs on the neck of wolf.

The eagle standing in the center, which is flapping its wings, has a turquoise head and neck. Separated with a golden foil, they are connected to the hollow feathered body with golden wires leading in from the beak, which allows them to be moved to either side. The tail, which is also attached to the body with golden wires, is also movable. Looking down on wolves and sheep from high above, the eagle has an air of supremacy as the king of grassland.

The headband comprises three segments, two in front one at back, all of which bear a twisted rope-like pattern with their respective ends carved into a recumbent tiger, sheep and horse. The two front segments are connected with small tongue-and-groove bars in between, and the lower one joins with the rear segment at ends to form a complete ring.

The crown, as well as other 200 and more gold and silver artifacts, was found in tombs at Aluchaideng, Hanggin Banner, Inner Mongolia, which sits on the Ordos Plateau. Given the quantity and quality of these treasures, the occupant was not likely a common herdsman but rather someone of the privileged class, probably a Chanyu of some tribe as a gold crown with an eagle on the top represents not only wealth but power as well. It's true that Aluchaideng lies at the edge of the Maowusu Desert, where there is nothing but sand. Back in the Warring States

period, however, it was likely an area of wet and fertile land for Hun tribes. Scholars assume that the crown may belong to the chieftain of either Linhu or Baiyang, two tribes which existed here.

The rich presentation of animals and vivid hunting scenes carved on the crown are believed to be a true reflection of the raw nomadic life. Some also presume that it implies how Hun tribes were organized. They believe that the eagle, sheep, wolf, and tiger were tribal totems and that the eagle-centered crown shows that tiger, wolf, horse and sheep tribes were allied under the dominance of the eagle tribe.

Erdos Bronze Ware

Lifelike animal images on the crown blend realism and particularism, showing Erdos aesthetic elements that are closely connected with the bronze culture of northern China, and completely different from that of the Great Central Plain.

Erdos bronze ware, also known as Suiyuan or Northern bronze ware, refers to bronze, gold and silver ware unearthed from northern China. Nurtured by the nomadic culture, most of them were made with animal patterns, realistic and hyperbolic, showing distinguishable vividness. The eagle crown, for example, has a realistic eagle body but an exaggeratedly sharp beak to emphasize its savageness. As for other animals, some parts of them, although hyper-realistically depicted, are crafted so fine to show rich details, such as the huge sheep horns or the horrifying tiger face. These lifelike patterns are typical Erdos bronze ware rendering.

By Wang Yusu

Warring States Gold-inlaid Bronze Ewer

Art of War

Warring States Gold-inlaid Bronze Ewer

Location: Sichuan Museum
Age: The Spring and Autumn and Warring States Periods
Texture: copper
Size: 40.3 cm in height, 13.2 cm in caliber

The intense competition of Warring States period drove many cultural and technological advances. The continual conflict of state versus state was in marked contrast to the ritual order which the Western Zhou sought to enforce.

The images are silent but tell a thousand tales. The gold inlay records the lives of the Warring States aristocracy in the second half of the first millennium BCE. On the top and bottom are mythical creatures.

On the body of the vessel, it's a battlefield. The frequent wars between the vassal states of the Eastern Zhou in the Spring and Autumn Period were about maintain a balance of power between them. The Warring States conflicts were about annihilation and subjugation. The defenders fire arrows and brandish their weapons. Assaulting troops fall from the walls. Men are beheaded. The combat scenes are remarkable. A man holds an enemy head in one hand, and his lifts his weapon high with the other; another headless corpse is on the other side.

The gentle flow of the river is disturbed by combat spilling on to the water. The twin deck war galleys encounter one and other. The soldiers on the upper deck strike out with pole arms; rowers on the lower deck strain at their oars. Men jump into the water and carry on fighting. Drummers at the stern beat out commands.

After the battle comes the victory celebration. Guests stand with glasses in hand, toasting the victorious general in the center of the scene. The surrounds are peopled by musicians.

In war time bows and arrows are deadly weapons. In peacetime they are tools of etiquette. Under the Zhou Dynasty archery became one of the six arts studied by the nobility. The ritual of archery was an important social event. The archers stand in the pavilion and aim at the

target cloth. The shots take flight in order of etiquette. A scorer reports back the results. Spectators gather outside the pavilion.

Hunters shoot at birds in flight using arrows with fine lines attached to bring their prey to earth. The rules forbid the shooting of birds at rest on the ground.

On the upmost layer we see a mulberry field. There is no war here. Men are practicing their archery peacefully and women are picking mulberry leaves. China is the birthplace of silk. The mulberry leaf harvest became a ritual in the calendar.

Today this luxuriant drinking vessel can only be fit to contain those intoxicating memories. The battlefield and the victory celebrations are mute. The mulberry trees will never sprout fresh leaves. But the gold-inlaid ewer from the Warring States period still speaks to us today as loudly as it did to those who feasted with it more than two thousand years ago.

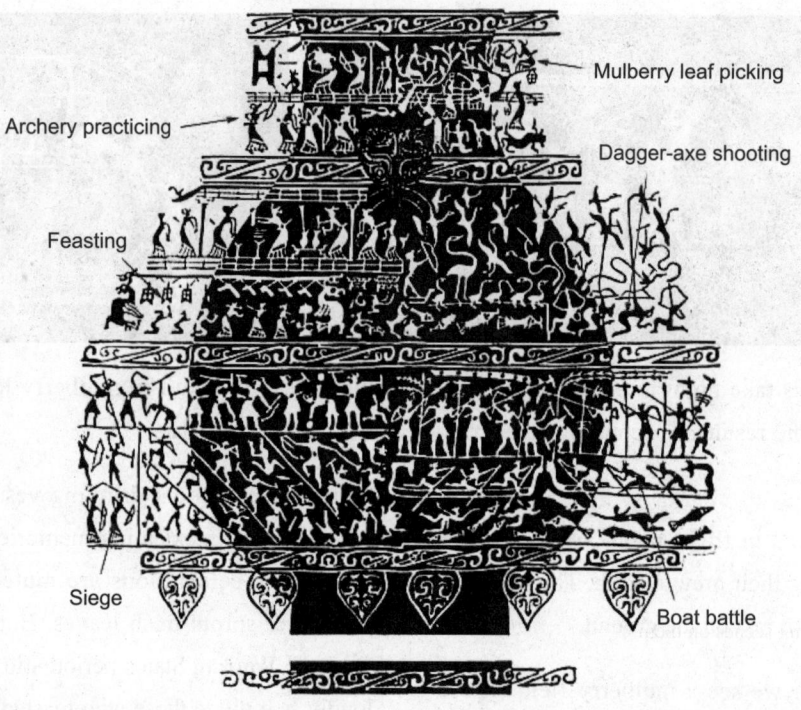

Etiquette in the Ewer

In 1956, during a high school dormitory expansion project at Baihuatan in suburban Chengdu, a group of earth pit tombs from the Warring States period were discovered. The finest piece unearthed is named the Gold-inlaid Bronze Ewer. The body of this ewer, which is 40cm tall and 13.4cm in diameter, is covered with three patterned stripes which divide into ewer into vertical bands. On it are beautiful patterns inlaid with gold and silver, portraying the scenes of battle, feast, music, fishing, and hunting during the Warring States period. This ewer is an important historic relic for the study of social life of this period, and more importantly reflects the rites and music systems at that time.

Sericulture, or silkworm breeding and mulberry leaf picking, is an age-old industry in China. Back in the Shang Dynasty, people had started to make fancy clothes with silk. Silkworm-shaped jade ware were once unearthed in tombs of the Shang and Western Zhou dynasties. All these show that sericulture was closely related to the lives of ancient people. The Han Gilt Bronze Silkworm, collected at the Shaanxi History Museum, is a national Grade 1 cultural relic. This bronze silkworm, life-like in size, has nine abdominal segments, with its head lifting up spinning. The whole piece is vivid and finely made. It is a testimony that as early as the Western Han Dynasty, sericulture had been common. The ancient people

must have been familiar with the physical structure of silkworms to produce such a life-like gilt bronze silkworm.

The uppermost layer of the ewer portrays a group of women picking mulberry leaves. Dressed in long skirts, some women are holding baskets in their hands, some carry baskets on their heads, and others reach out with their hands to pick leaves. Mulberry leaf picking does appear in the portraits of pre-Qin period here and there. In particular, many stone portraits unearthed in Sichuan have mulberry and leave picking scenes on them.

Given the importance of sericulture in ancient China, a system of rites regarding silkworm rearing and mulberry leaf picking developed. Mulberry leaf picking was both a general form of labor and a symbolic rite. Until the Qing Dynasty, silkworm rituals, at which the Queen and concubines picked mulberry leaves to feed silkworms in person, remained an important sacrificial event performed by the imperial harem. Prior to the ritual, the Empress and concubines had to be fast. On the day of the rites day, they picked mulberry leaves with their own hands to feed silkworms.

Empress Xiaoxian Chun Feeds Silkworms by Giuseppe Castiglione of Qing Dynasty (Part)

There are multiple scenes depicting archery on this ewer. Alongside the mulberry leaf picking patterns are scenes of men drawing their bows for shooting. Generally, the drawings of mulberry leaf picking and those of archery are closely associated. Some scholars believe that in ancient times, mulberry offered the raw material to make bows and arrows, so drawings on mulberry leaf picking show the scenes of materials selection and bows and arrows making. In addition, to one side of mulberry leaf picking patterns on the uppermost layer, there are scenes of archery portrayed on the second layer.

According to the *Rites of Zhou*, ancient people worshiped *Gaomei*, the god of marriages and fertility, with archery. The *Book of Rites: Proceedings of Government in the Different Months* records that "The Son of Heaven goes to do so in person, with his queen and help-mates, attended by his nine ladies of honor. Peculiar courtesy is shown to those whom he has (lately) approached. Bow-cases have been brought, and a bow and arrows are given to each before (the altar of) the first match-maker." This is a record of the Son of Heaven bringing his wife and concubines to perform an archery sacrifice to pray for fertility. Moreover, the *Book of Rites: Meaning of the Ceremony of Archery* records that when boys were born, a birth ceremony would be performed at which arrows made of bunch grass were shot into the sky with a bow made of mulberry to symbolize high aspirations.

According to the *Rites of Zhou*, there are six classical arts: Rites, Music, Archery, Charioteering, Calligraphy, and Mathematics. The rite of Archery, as one of these six arts, was originally designed to test people's virtues in archery. During the Warring States period, there were frequent wars between states, so archery became a much valued skill. The archery ceremony of common citizens performed in a pavilion as portrayed on this ewer is a case in point. According to the *Book of Etiquette and Ceremonies*, during such common archery ceremonies, archers were divided into two teams, one competed on the left side, the other the right side. Hitting right at the center was called hitting the "target" (*hu*).

In addition to archery scenes, the second layer of the ewer has scenes of feasting. There were peculiar rules on feasts and music

from the Zhou Dynasty to the Warring States period. Zhou people believed that music could cultivate temperament and foster social harmony. According to the *Book of Rites: King Wen as Son and Heir*, "Music is intended to cultivate the inner man, while rites to polish the external conduct." Therefore, music and rites were closely associated ever since.

Rules on chimes are an integral part of the ritual music system. It can be seen that the chimes on this ewer do not meet the specifications of ritual music. According to the *Book of Rites*, there were peculiar rules on chimes and sounding stones used by emperors, dukes or princes, ministers, high officials, scholars and others. Ministers and high officials were required to place musical instruments on the two sides of their main halls, with sounding stones on the eastern side and chimes the western side. On this bronze ewer, however, chimes and sounding stones are mixed, rather than being placed according to rules. This might be a reflection of propriety disintegration during the Warring States period when the nobility just superficially complied with the rites of Zhou.

Following the mulberry leaf picking, archery rite, feast and music, the third layer of this ewer features the scenes of soldiers fighting hard in battles. During the Warring States period, there were frequent wars between states. Though two states might confront each other in war, both sides would follow certain etiquette, with the courteous exchange of words before the use of force commenced.

The battle scenes portrayed on this ewer reflect the military courtesy at that time. The two sides are holding high their weapons with buoyed morale. In the naval battle as portrayed here, soldiers of both sides are holding high their flags, beating the drums, and shouting aloud to boost morale. Military flags during the Warring States period were called "*pei*" on which are patterns identifying the ranks of nobility. As for drums, there were also rules. There is an old saying goes, "Kings use *Lu* drums, vassals use *Bi* drums and generals use *Jin* drums." People of different ranks mastered different drums. Even if in the event of battle emergencies, the system of rites remained a much-valued aspect.

The *Book of Rites: Summary of the Rules of Propriety* also records that, "Morality, virtue, benevolence, and righteousness would not be complete without rites; and education on good conduct would not do without rites too." On this bronze ewer, we can see not only the various aspects of social life during the Warring States period, but also learn about the importance of rites at that time. As a nation valuing rites, China has historically educated its people with courtesy and rites. Morality, virtue, benevolence, and righteousness rooted in rites have not waned even until today.

By Lian Yongxin

The Chime-bells of Marquis Yi of Zeng

Tunes of Antiquity

The Chime-bells of Marquis Yi of Zeng

Location: Hubei Provincial Museum
Age: Warring States Period
Texture: wood and bronze
Size: 748 cm in length, 265 cm in height

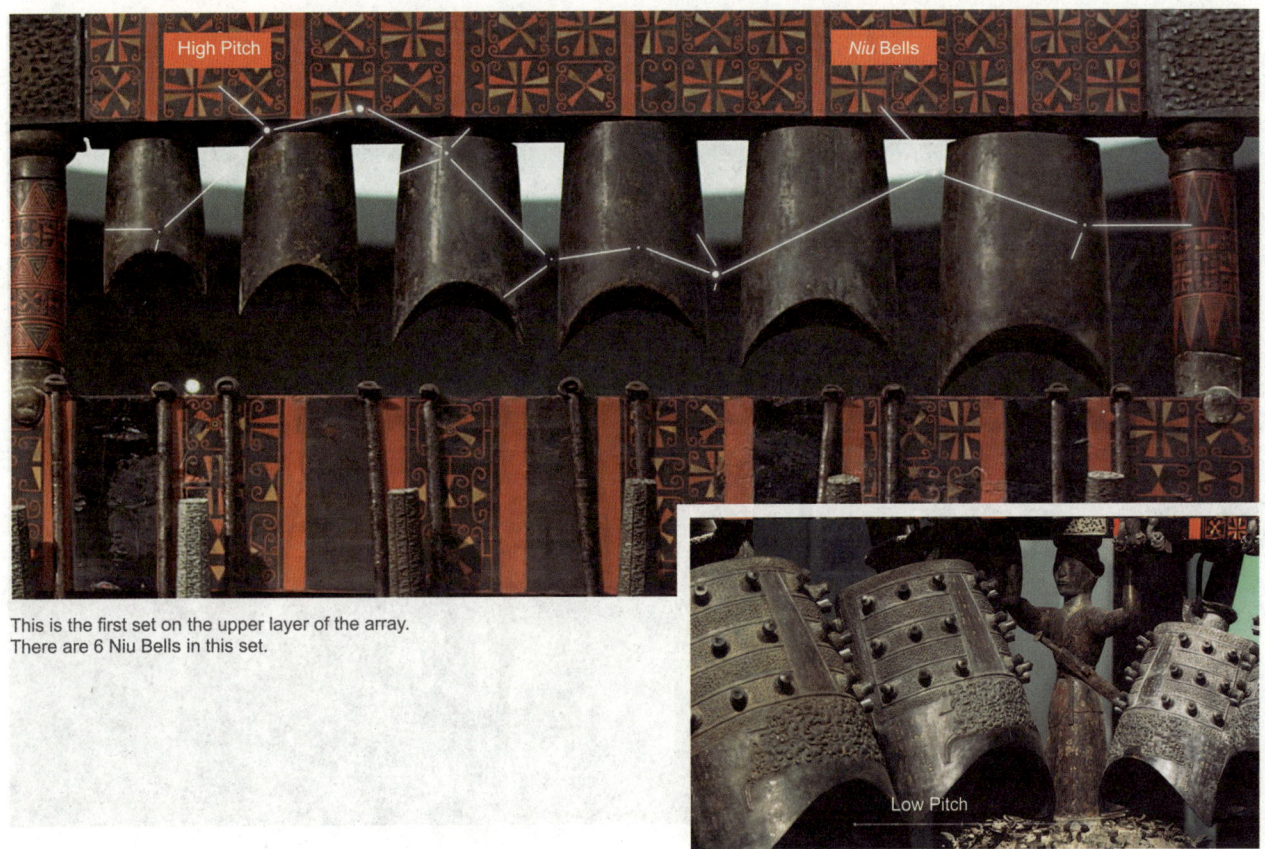

This is the first set on the upper layer of the array.
There are 6 Niu Bells in this set.

This audio was recorded in 1986. The chime-bells were cast in the 4th century BC.

A Recording of the Chime-bells of Marquis Yi of Zeng of 1986

Recorded by Hubei Provincial Museum and China Record Corporation

Recorded on 2:00 a.m., March 29th, 1986 to 6:00 a.m., April 6th, 1986

The temperature is 18°C. The tuning frequency is 440 hertz.

Inscriptions of Musical Temperament

The whole of bells form a complete instrument. Each bell has two different tones. The whole set is composed of 65 chime bells (including *Bo* Bells in the center) and divided into 8 sets over 3 layers. The lowest pitched bell is the 1st bell in Set 1 of the lowest layer - sounded from the front. The highest pitch is the sound of side part of the 1st bell in Set 1 of the upper layer - sounded from the side. The tonal range of the *Yong* Bells covers 5 octaves.

Set 2 of the middle layer is composed of 12 *Yong* Bells with no protrusions.

Niu Bell   Yong Bell   Yong Bells with No Protrusions

Chime-bells of Marquis Yi of Zeng are composed of 64 chime bells and one *Bo* Bell from King of Chu. Except for this *Bo* Bell, each chime bell is inscribed with two different tone names.

Name of Tone

Name of Tone

At 6 am on April 6th, 1986. The recording session concluded.

The tomb of Marquis Yi of Zeng was discovered in 1978. The occupant's name is Yi. He was the ruler of the state Zeng in the Warring States period. The State of Zeng was called the State of Sui in historical records. It was located at today's Suizhou in Hubei Province.

Men of noble characters perform in order, starting with chime bells and ending with chime stones.

——*The Mencius*

Ritual is to regulate the people. Music is to promote harmony.

——*Records of the Grand Historian*

Poems inspire people; rituals build people; music makes people.

——*The Analects of Confucius*

Sound from different instruments should be harmonious, so that the immortals and human beings both like it.

——*Book of Documents*

2018 marks the 40th anniversary of the discovery of the Chime-bells of Marquis Yi of Zeng. We once again thank the archaeologists who recovered these masterpieces for posterity.

The complete set of Chime-bells of Marquis Yi of Zeng

Tunes of Antiquity

With solid evidence, the history of Chinese music can be dated back at least 9,000 years ago. It has been confirmed that the 18 bone flutes unearthed from Jiahu Site in Wuyang County, Henan Province in 1980s were 9,000-year-old artifacts made of bird bones by ancient Chinese.

The earliest musical instrument ensemble know to us was discovered at Taosi Cultural Relics (2,500 BC-1,900 BC) in Shanxi Province, including *tuogu* (a hollow-trunk drum made from the skin of Yangtze alligator), stone chime and clay drum found in tomb No. 3002.

In the age of bronze, approximately the 21st century BC, our ancestors forged a host of bronze musical instruments such as cymbals, *zheng* (bell-shaped instrument), bells and *duo* (bell-shaped large instrument with a clapper). Given its particular musical features, the bell played an important role in the history of music in China. By the material, musical instruments divides into eight categories, namely, metal, stone, string, bamboo, gourd, clay, leather and wooden instruments. *Chime-bells* are metal instrument topping the rank and are the major ones in an ensemble. Large *Chime-bells* hung on 2-3m high and 6-7m long racks prevailing in the Warring

States period evolved from three-in-one cymbal suites. *Chime-bells* were popular before the Qin and Han dynasties. As musical instruments, however, they were something religious used more for showing imperial power.

Excavation of the 2,400-year-old tomb of Marquis Yi of Zeng began in 1978. Totally 125 musical instruments of eight types (*Chime-bells*, *bianqing*, drum, Chinese zither, *se*, *sheng*, *chi* and *paixiao*), as well as more than a thousand of playing tools and accessories were discovered in the tomb. Some of them, such as the ten-stringed violin, *junzhongmu* (a toning tool made of wood), and *chi*, were rare archaeological discoveries of the pre-Qin period.

For the *Chime-bells* of Marquis Yi of Zeng, the longer rack is 748 cm long and 265 cm high while the shorter rack is 335 cm long and 273 cm high. The largest bell is 152.3 cm high, weighing 203.6 kg; and the smallest one is 20.4 cm high, weighing 2.4 kg. *Chime-bells* are hung on two perpendicular wooden racks. The whole set comprises 65 bells, which are hung at three levels and are divided into eight groups. *Niu* Bells are arranged on the top while *Yong* Bells in the middle and lower level, with a *Bo* bell in the middle. As a percussion instrument, a bell gives different tones by striking at different positions. Striking the font middle produces a sound from the front, while a strike to the side produces a sound from the side. While the bronze musical instrument producing two tones with one bell is recognized as a great invention of the pre-Qin period, one should strike the best spot to play music with accurate pitch yet without making typical metallic noise. Teamwork is required to play a complete concerto. Players should move around quickly to find the best spot, and sometimes strike two quite separated bells simultaneously, which is certainly a challenging skill that requires repeated practice to master. As the whole set of two-tone bells covers a wide range, spanning five and a half octaves and including the twelve-tone equal temperament, the *Chime-bells* of Marquis Yi of Zeng are the most magnificent pre-Qin musical bells with the most exquisite forging craftsmanship and the most complete musical characteristics that have ever been found in China. Arguably, its discovery has rewritten the history of music in China and beyond.

Made of bronze, *Chime-bells* are generally played with *bianqing*, another musical instrument made of jade or black stone.

Jiahu Bone Flute

Clay Drum

Bo Bell from King of Chu

The pleasant and crisp chord played with *Chime-bells* and jade chimes was highly appreciated in ancient China. The jade chimes unearthed together with the *Chime-bells* from the Tomb of Marquis Yi are the largest one with the most chime pieces found today. Renowned as "king of chimes", it has 32 chime pieces, each gives a single scale. Results of the restoration research indicate that the whole set of chimes spans three octaves with 12 semitones. Comparing with the bell, the sound of chime is less loud and lasts shorter. However, it is not easy to be covered and becomes clearer, and that's why these to types of instruments are ideal companions for playing a piece of harmonious concerto.

Music knows no borders. As a typical artifact representing the spiritual world and the physical life of ancient Chinese people some 2,400 years ago, the sonorous and enduring sound of Marquis Yi's *Chime-bells* not only reflects the excellent workmanship of musical instruments, but also refreshes the cultural influence of rite and music that has lasted since the Zhou Dynasty.

By Gao Ran

Wood Carved Double Headed Tomb Guardian

Between this World and the Next

Wood Carved Double Headed Tomb Guardian

Location: Jingzhou Museum
Age: Warring States Period
Texture: wood
Size: appr. 170 cm in height

Wood Carved Double Headed Tomb Guardian

The tomb guardian is placed in a tomb to protect its occupant from forces unseen. Eyes stretched wide, tongue protruding, it radiates defiance. But instead of cold hard bronze, it's made of warm soft wood.

The body is decorated in delicate lines of scarlet paint that weave an abstract pattern. Four sets of antlers sprout from the crown, symbolizing the sprouting of new life. Everything about it seems to betray its origins in warm humid south in the ancient State of Chu.

Painted Lacquer Tray with Phoenix Patterns of the Western Han Dynasty

Painted Round-ear Cup with Deformed Bird Patterns of the Warring States Period

Painted Lacquer Shield with Dragon and Phoenix Patterns of the Warring States Period

Lacquer Wood Sacrificial Vessel of the Warring States Period

Chu was the home of mysteries and magic. The State of Chu grew from a small semi-barbarian state on the middle reaches of the Yangtze to a great kingdom that encompassed most of southern China. It always held the image of a wild, passionate and artistic people, in contrast to the more staid and disciplined northerners. Nature and animals feature prominently in their art.

Wood Carved Double Headed Tomb Guardian

A man drives a carriage by a willow tree. Three people are running in front of him. With no perspective it seems they could be suspended in the sky. A pair of wild geese fly over them. Three others look up, seeking signs from the heavens. A yellow dog chases after wild pigs. Spring is coming. Friends whisper together under a tree. Take care! Someone could be listening in.

These tomb goods leave us with a strong feeling of the spirit of the Chu people. It existed as both Chinese and yet still on a plain of its own.

This lacquer coffin was made in early Western Han Dynasty just after 200 BC. Over three hundred sprites are seated among the clouds. This one pushes away from the cloud and sits in mid-air, smiling beatifically. This one

draws an arrow to his bow, aiming into the far distance. This one steals a thermal and lifts a nimbus with its hand. And this one tumbles like an acrobat across the field of heaven. A lonely spirit sings to itself, while far away, another plays the zither.

These spirit guards are the spirit of Chu: playful, skilled and artistic. They reflect the environment of that ancient society. Figures, human, animal, and somewhere in between, fill the scene.

With a single breath, the tomb guardian has held by its post in the airless vault. Neither wood nor horn decayed. It maintains its vigil for us today, from two thousand years to eternity.

Tomb Guardian

Figures of tomb guardians are funerary objects commonly and exclusively seen in tombs of Chu Culture. Most of them are wooden sculptures consisting of a base, an animal body and antlers, and are rare in other cultures of the Warring States period. A large part of tomb guardians has been unearthed in Jiangling, Hubei Province, or Yingdu, the old capital of Chu State. Yingdu, also known as Jinan City, was the center of politics, economy and culture of the state, the most advanced metropolis of southern China during its 400-year history. A host of tomb guardians unearthed here demonstrate that they embodied the most essential "cultural genes" of Chu people.

Most of these guardian figures are found in medium- and large-sized tombs constructed with at least an inner coffin and an outer coffin, a structure designated for someone standing above inferior officials but below higher-ranked members of the aristocracy, according to the strict social-class-based funerary rituals passed down from the Zhou Dynasty. One would never find a piece of such tomb guardian in rough tombs of ordinary folks. Higher-ranked members of the aristocracy were usually buried in larger and more complex tombs with more exquisite tomb guardians, such as this wooden one, which is fully covered with finely crafted patterns,

Single-headed Tomb Guardian

Double-headed Tomb Guardian

Colored Lacquer Jewelry Box

showing intricate details in red, yellow and golden. A reasonable assumption is that the owner must have been a highly respected person in the State of Chu. Nevertheless, his power and superiority did not survive under the wheel of history and this 2,000-year-old tomb guardian is the only object to have survived.

Chu tombs are generally divided into square chambers to mirror real houses of the time. In most cases, only one tomb guardian is found in the head chamber of a tomb, among other bronze ware or potteries. As the safeguard of the tomb and the guide to lead the soul to the heaven, the tomb guardian was an irreplaceable article in the funeral.

Arts of the Western and Eastern Zhou dynasties, regardless their forms, were always based on the ritual system. Unlike their counterparts of the Great Central Plain, the people of Chu nourished by their romantic culture knew how to make those cold, rigid rules aesthetically dynamic. Another example aside from the tomb guardian is the drawing on a color varnished casket unearthed from the Baoshan Tomb. Although the drawing is an ultimate presentation of Chu art, archaeologists argue about the possible scenarios shown. Latest research findings have provided us with yet another romantic interpretation that it relates to a wedding in the Zhou Dynasty.

The occupant in the carriage is a messenger sent by the bridegroom-to-be to propose, and the girl on her knees in front of the carriage is a receiver of the bride's family. They are communicating the views of the couple, completing a necessary process in the marriage ritual of the Zhou Dynasty, when young couples were banned to determine their marriage without the permission of their respective parents and the introduction of a go-between. Pairs of flying swan geese are a sign of a successful proposal. Below them, all ritual steps have been completed, so the couple, as well as their escorts, meets in an open field. The hopping boars and dogs represent vitality and the warm weather of spring. The three girls enjoying the lovely day are depicted again in the last chapter of the drawing, in which they stand beside the bride.

In 278 B.C., Yingdu was taken over by Bai Qi, a well-known general of Qin, and the king of Chu was forced to relocate, marking the decadence of the once potent power. This abundant region embraced new masters as a unified empire was found by Qin Shi Huang, who launched a nation-wide program to unify industrial specifications and Chinese characters. Despite this, some local customs never died and somehow sustained even after the Chu State's demise. Deeply influenced by their culture, the people of Chu

were still accustomed to burying wooden puppets instead of a tomb guardian.

The reign of Qin did not last long before rebellions raised up across the entire country, but mainly in places from the old Chu. Since the beginning of the Western Han Dynasty, the culture of Chu was revitalized. Rulers of Han adopted its rituals and interwove them with the national ritual system. That is why we are able to appreciate the graceful patterns of Chu culture on the varnished coffin at the Mawangdui Tomb.

Although generations of Chu people have passed away, the brilliant culture they created has survived and has finally discovered from under the ground after thousands of years.

By Li Kai

Silk Painting Depicting A Man Riding A Dragon

Silk Painting Depicting A Man Riding A Dragon

Location: Hunan Museum
Age: Warring States Period
Texture: silk
Size: 37.5 cm in length, 28 cm in width

Silk Painting Depicting A Man Riding A Dragon

What becomes of us after death? The Chu people who lived over 2,000 years ago believed that we enter an immortal realm.

Our traveler in time has a solemn look. Dressed in his finery with sword and a gentleman's cap, he rides his dragon mount into eternity. The dragon's raised head and tail give it a boat-like form. This is indeed a voyage into the unknown. The silk painting was made in the Warring States Period and is the earliest such found to date. It was unearthed from Zidanku Tomb at Changsha, Hunan Province. It rested on the boarding between the outer and the inner coffins. It served as a pennant to lead the soul at its earthy farewell. The canopy rises high in the air, to show that the tomb's occupant is wandering the skies. A carp is

Silk Painting Depicting A Man Riding A Dragon

leading the way from below. The dragon is a mythical creature that can pass from this world to the next.

"Oh Soul, come back! The quarters of the world are full of harm…Return to your old abode, your quiet and restful home." The Chu people believed that after passing away, the earthly soul sank into the depths, while the immortal spirit flew to the heavens. The funerary silk paintings placed between inner and outer coffins were intended to guide and protect the wandering spirit so it could return to earth immortal.

The T-shape silk painting was created nearly 200 years later in the Western Han Dynasty. It too was intended as a

guide for the spirit of the departed. It represents the cosmology of the people of Chu towards the end of the first millennium BC. In the painting, life and death are joined in a dynamic cycle like yin and yang. The afterlife is governed by the same rules of time and space as the world we know. The bottom of the silk painting depicts the underworld. In the long darkness of night, a titan stands on a giant turtle, deters the demons and supports the earth above. In the middle, the soul and spirit of the occupant are carried by two dragons and travel through the human world. At the top, the gate to the heaven is wide open. Sun and moon shine together. This is where the voyaging spirit will become immortal. The inner and outer coffins are also painted the views of the nether world.

Although the form of life disappears for a while after death, with the blessing of sacred ritual objects, the balance of *yin* and *yang* can be restored. The soul takes shape again and the life eternal continues in another dimension. The Chu used fantastical and mysterious cultural symbols to illustrate the glorious path leading the dead to another form of life.

Life and death are like day and night. Life and

EVERY TREASURE
TELLS A STORY   062

Red Ground Color Painted Coffin, the Western Han Dynasty

death cannot be reversed by human hand, but like the changing seasons and repeating days, there are currents hidden in nature. The Chu belief in the secrets of life was expressed in their colorful paintings. They did not fear death because they believed that death was not just the end of mortal being, but also the entry into the world of the immortal. Treat the dead as the living. This is a view of life and death that has lived in China for thousands of years. People believed that living as a man and becoming an immortal after death is the way of the universe. And to get between life and death, earth and heaven, one should ride on a dragon.

Silk Paintings and Values of Life and Death during Chu and Han Periods

During the middle years of the Warring States period, the people of Chu started to paint on silk fabrics. In the Chu culture, it was believed that the soul of the deceased would leave their flesh, lingering around outside and being vulnerable, and might sometimes scare his or her descendants. It was therefore necessary to call it back through funeral rites, and lay it to rest in the tomb. This belief is demonstrated in Qu Yuan's "Summoning the Soul" in the *Songs of Chu*. This painting, portraying the tomb occupant, is the summoning banner used to guide him. When the painting was just unearthed, it was supported on the top side with a thin bamboo stick, to which a brown wire was attached for hanging it on a "soul guider" pole held high in front of the coffin as the burial team marched to the tomb site. The silk painting would then have been buried with the coffin, covering it and showing its owner the way to the afterworld.

Five figures can be seen in this silk painting: a man in the center, a dragon boat under him, a bird head beside the dragon head, a crane at the tail of the dragon and a fish beneath. The man, the occupant of the tomb, dresses exactly as depicted in the *Songs of Chu*: a tall hat on his head and a long sword at his waist. The bird, likely a phoenix, and the dragon are creatures that communicate the secular world and the heaven, or at least the people of Chu believed, and serve as the guide of the soul. The crane, signifying longevity, represents the occupant's wish for eternal life. The canopy over them is a symbol of the heaven, indicating the destination of the occupant's soul. While many believe the fish on the lower left is a carp, its connotation has been greatly disputed. Some say it merely shows an aquatic setting; while others assume that it is a soul guider like the dragon and the phoenix. Nevertheless, it is agreed that the theme is "leading the soul to the heaven", reflecting the mysterious spiritual belief of the people of Chu.

Another silk painting showing similar content is of a Lady, Phoenix and Dragon, discovered at Chenjia Mountain near Changsha. This painting was also completed during the Warring

States period, but predates the one depicting a Man Riding a Dragon. The two are regarded as "Twin Jewels of Pre-Qin Painting". As one can see in the top center, a huge phoenix is flapping its wings with its head and tail lifted up, and claws struggling as it attempts to fly. A curled dragon is on its left and a lady stands on the lower right, who is probably the tomb occupant. You may notice something below the lady that resembles a part of crescent moon. Some believe that it is a soul summoning boat. Like the one depicting a Man Riding a Dragon, the purpose of this silk painting was also to call back the soul of its owner and lead her to the heaven.

Originated from the Chu culture, the Han culture shows clear relations with its predecessor. One piece of evidence is the T-shaped Western-Han silk painting discovered in Tomb 1 of Mawangdui, Changsha. It has inherited many features, both in terms of content and form, from silk paintings created during the period of Chu. Bottom up, this painting depicts the underworld, the secular world and the heavenly realm respectively. The lower part of the painting depicts a subterranean scene. A topless giant stands on top of a double dragon-bodied fish, holding up a white platform, i.e. the earth, with a python

Silk Painting Depicting a Woman, a Dragon and a Phoenix, Warring States Period

T-shaped Painting on Silk from Xin Zhui's Tomb, the Western Han Dynasty

creeping between his legs. This part reflects mythology about the underworld. The secular world in the middle section is divided into two parts by a round jade. The lower part shows a funeral and the upper part presents the occupant, who faces towards the west, escorted by her attendants on the way to the heaven. The canopy above them refers to the sky. Two dragons fly up across the jade, guiding the occupant's soul to the heavenly realm on top of the drawing. Two servants stand by the heaven's gate, with their hands clasped, waiting for the occupant's arrival. Above them, two human-bodied holy beasts pull ropes to sound the *duo* bell between them. In the heaven part, you can see a red sun (with a crown in it) on top right, a crescent moon (with a toad and a rabbit in it) on top left, and the snake-bodied god sitting between them, delivering an air of authority and sanctity. This silk painting, being the most complicated and fantastic among other paintings of that time, manifests fanciful mythological figures redolent of the brilliant Chu culture.

In comparison with the silk painting of Mawangdui, the one found at Jinqueshan, Linyi, Shandong Province displays more elements of the Han culture. Instead of containing all three parts from the underground to the sky, this silk painting completed during the middle Western Han Dynasty depicts only the afterworld under the sun, the moon and three mountains of immortals, possibly Penglai, Fangzhang and Yingzhou, the three legendary mountains in the ocean in the tales spread over the State of Qi during the Warring States period. Omitting figures of the Supreme God or other mysterious creatures, this drawing underscores secularity and Han-dynasty Confucianism by showing officials and common folks dancing, weaving, wrestling, or doing other everyday activities.

You may have noticed from the aforementioned four silk paintings that people's imagination about the afterworld was changing from the Warring States period to the Western Han Dynasty. In the beginning, people were quite uncertain about their death so the early painting mirrors only the process of guidance by dragon and phoenix without specifying a destination; the painting by the early Western Han Dynasty, the one found at Mawangdui, tells us that the occupant's soul goes to a place similar with the heaven of Western religions; and the painting discovered at Jinqueshan presents a world with holy mountains and how life looks like out there. This suggests that people had developed a clear perception about the afterworld, and portrayed it in a much more realistic way.

The art of silk painting started to decline somewhere between the final years of the Western Han Dynasty and the Eastern Han Dynasty. Most silk paintings of that time are much less complex, or simply indicate the occupant's name and birthplace, plus a few memorial words. This phenomenon suggests that the ritual of deity worship based on the Chu culture had declined along with the diminishing concept of "summoning the soul to the heaven". As the identity of the tomb occupant was more demonstrated by text, the art of silk painting stepped down from the stage of history.

From its emergence to its end, the art of silk painting shows not only the fusion of cultures, but also the evolution of our ancestors' perception of life and death. The development of the inclusive Han culture, which has absorbed features of the Chu culture, attests to the diversity and comprehensive nature of Chinese civilization. According to the transformation of ancient people's wish for immortality to a more realistic attitude towards the death, we see the development of rational life values. What remains unchanged among all the changes is our aspiration for life and good wishes to those who passed away.

by Wang Yusu

Line Drawing of the Underworld on the T-shaped Painting on Silk

The Terracotta Warriors

An Image of Empire

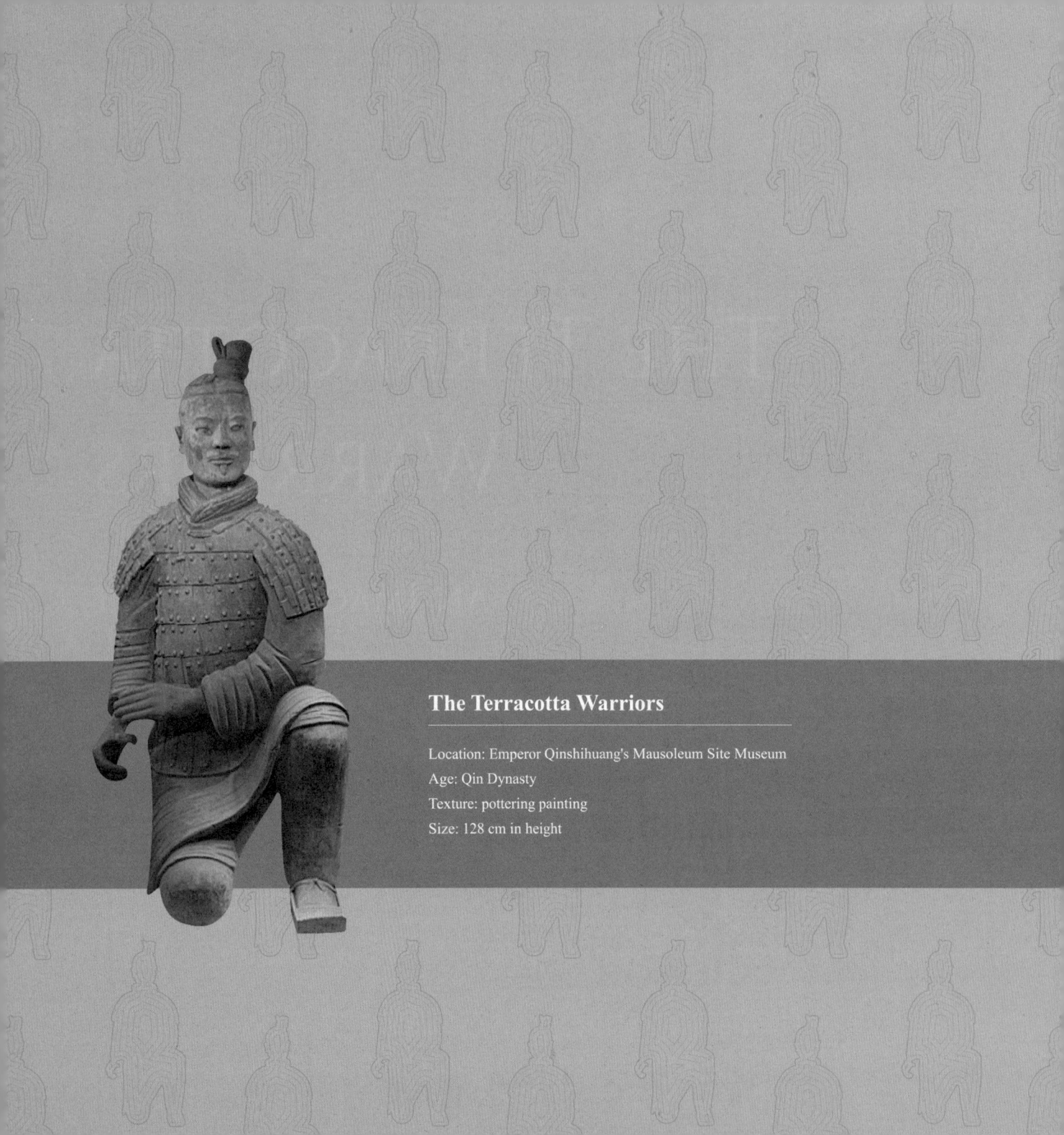

The Terracotta Warriors

Location: Emperor Qinshihuang's Mausoleum Site Museum
Age: Qin Dynasty
Texture: pottering painting
Size: 128 cm in height

The tranquil and ordered scenery belies the extraordinary magnificence of what lies beneath. Below the modest monument lies a tomb; a tomb in which the history of an empire is frozen for all eternity.

It was in 1974 that the first stirrings of an incredible discovery were made. An underground army, part of the vast tomb complex for China's First Emperor, was gradually disinterred. the dust on the mirror was accidentally stirred up. Terracotta Warriors and Horses of the first emperor of Qin at the Lishan Mountains' foot were exposed. The mirror of time allows us to reflect on what this means, then and now. Qin Shi Huang's 7,000 strong immortal army is arrayed in three great pits near his tomb at Lintong in Xi'an, the site of the Qin capital.

160 of these Terracotta Warriors in kneeling posture were excavated at the east end of Pit No.2. They form the vanguard. They are archers, clad in their armour and

hair tied up, ready for battle, holding real weaponry in the hands as they entered the underworld.

This archer is among the most junior rank in the battle array. He is also the epitome of these Qin warriors. His head and back are straight as his legs crossed over each other to form a steady triangle. A posture that provides both a steady platform from which to fight and offers a small target to the enemy. This would have been textbook training drilled into his living comrades.

Our archer's chest and stomach are protected by large sections of plate. The shoulders and waist have smaller pieces allowing him to move and weild his bow.

The raised right foot supports the weight of the entire body. The detailing of his footwear is precise. A thick robust heel and toe for marching, even the tread on the sole has been carefully reproduced to allow him to fight effectively in the netherworld.

The posture, the armor, and the clothing are exact reproductions of actual warriors, their faces, beards and hair all differentiated. Only their weapons of bronze and wood have struggled with the test of time. When they were first discovered and excavated, there was still color in the warriors' apparel and faces. Faces that appeared to

EVERY TREASURE
TELLS A STORY | 074

be so real they might have been alive. These are the faces of the men who united the Warring States into one great Empire, at the behest of their king.

The stars travel across the sky, mountains and rivers stretch over the land, generation come and go but these man-made effigies hold the collidascope of time stopped in their hands. Their power still rules the land, their Emperor still commands.

Above ground the Dynasty of Qin Shi Huang is long gone, superceded by many others, imitators all. Under the surface, in China's heart, these warriors still await command. They are gone, and yet they are here, and in truth, buried for all those centuries, they never left.

Qinshihuang's Mausoleum and Terracotta Warriors

As the unified country was further consolidated and developed, financial and human resources were highly controlled by the centralized government, allowing for sufficient advancement of the art of sculpture. Since the ruler of Qin used this very form of art as a tool to boast of his feats and power, China saw the first flourishing era of its sculpture industry as achievements were made in pottery, stone and bronze sculpture.

These achievements are best proved by the Terracotta Warriors. Soon after his ascendance to the throne at the age of 13 in 246 B.C., the young monarch ordered the construction of his tomb. In 221 B.C., after Qin unified other six states, he deployed around 700,000 workers from across the country to carry on the project and only completed it 36 years later when he died at the age of 50.

A Monument in Qinshihuang's Mausoleum

Located in the northern wing of Mount Li about 5km to the east of Lintong District, Xi'an City, Shaanxi Province, the mausoleum of the founding emperor of China's first feudal empire was built on immeasurable human, material and financial resources. The extent of its luxury and might is unimaginable, and we can only obtain some information from the historical record: the foundation was excavated down to the groundwater level; the stones used were finely crafted and infused with molten copper and tin; internal river beds were filled with mercury; the tomb vault was embedded with night pearls to resemble star constellations; and oil-firing nightlights were provided to symbolize the emperor's longevity. It is no exaggeration to say that the Mausoleum of Qin Shi Huang is a spacious underground palace. Unfortunately, no one has described the precise structure of the palace, which has become a secret buried underground for thousands of years.

The Full View of Pit No.1, Emperor Qinshihuang's Mausoleum Site Museum

A Corner of Pit No.2, Emperor Qinshihuang's Mausoleum Site Museum

Kneeling Terracotta Warrior

From 1974 to 1976, three subsidiary burial pits of large terracotta warriors were discovered successively south of Xiyang Village, Lintong, a location to the east of the Mausoleum, or to the north of the east passage of the Mausoleum. The three pits are similarly structured, accommodating a considerable number of funerary objects. The pit is divided into lanes by parallel earth walls, covered with black brick flooring. Originally, the pit was covered with woods and reeds. There are doorways on each side, which were blocked with standing timbers and sealed with compacted soil after terracotta warriors and horses were put in, forming a closed underground military camp.

The rectangular pit No. 1 measures 230m long x 62m wide, covering an area of 14,000 square meters. A spacious hall is set at the east end, where many full-sized terracotta warriors or horses were found. Based on their density, the total number of warriors or horses is estimated to exceed 6,000. Pits No. 2 and 3 are smaller. The L-shaped pit No.2 measures 124m long x 98m wide, covering an area of about 6,000 square meters, accommodating more than 1,400 warriors or horses. The pit remains under excavation today, we can see traces of ruined woods and some warriors or horses left in their original positions. Shaped like the Chinese character " 凹 ", pit No. 3 is probably a command for the warriors and horses in the other two pits. This pit, measuring 28.8m long x 24.57m wide and covering an area of about 520 square meters, has been severely damaged and a raft of broken figures or models are to be found there.

Terracotta warriors had been arranged underground as per the real military system of Qin. Soldiers are positioned according to their rank and function. In addition to a large number of warriors holding weapons, cavalrymen (holding bridles and bows), chariot drivers, generals (wearing tall hats) are also found in these pits. Kneeling Terracotta Warriors are discovered in the array of heavy-duty infantry at the northeast corner of pit No.2. Keeping the upper body straight, they kneel on the right leg and look forward with hands in a bow-holding position, like they are ready to fire arrows. To truly reflect the military system and tactical plans of Qin, the body and clothing are made life size, even the patterns of their shoes were carefully crafted to resemble the real thing.

In ancient China, funerary sacrifice was commonly accepted and applied. Dummy sacrifice, replacing human sacrifice popular in the Shang Dynasty since the Spring and Autumn and the Warring States periods, prevailed in the Qin and Han dynasties. Most dummies were made of pottery clay, but wooden, stone or bronze models were also found. The Terracotta Warriors, the most famous amongst other masterpieces of the time, features sophisticated craftsmanship. Weighing more than 300kg each, the height of these warriors and horses averages 1.8m, i.e. they were carved individually against the portrait of real soldiers before being fired, showing unique and vivid characters through different hair styles, clothing, shoes, facial expressions and gestures.

By Gao Ran

Rectangular Measuring Vessel of Shang Yang

Measuring Unity

Rectangular Measuring Vessel of Shang Yang

Location: Shanghai Museum
Age: Warring States Period, Qin Dynasty
Texture: bronze ware
Volume: 202.15 ml

Rectangular Measuring Vessel of Shang Yang

085

This mundane looking rectangular bronze pan started a revolution. It's a measuring vessel – a *sheng* – a unit of a little over one fifth of a liter, used for liquids… or grain. The conforming of differing standards into a single unified system was crucial to China's economic development – and political psychology.

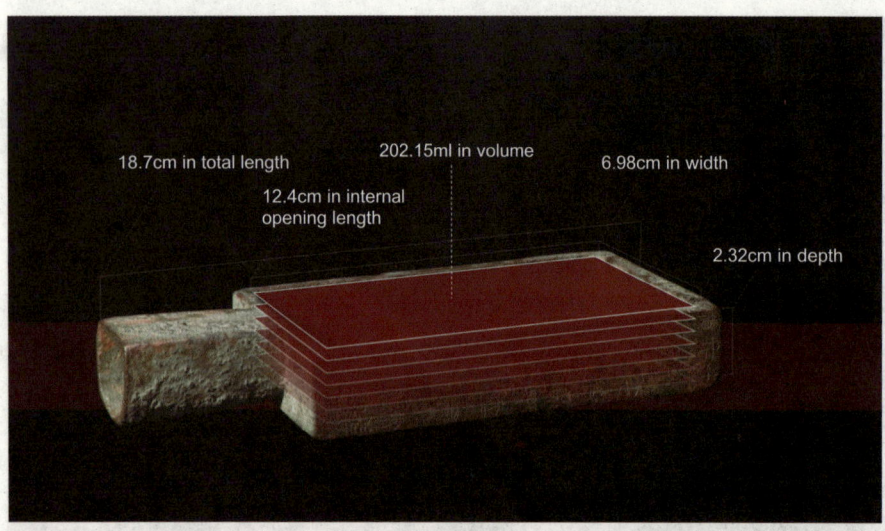

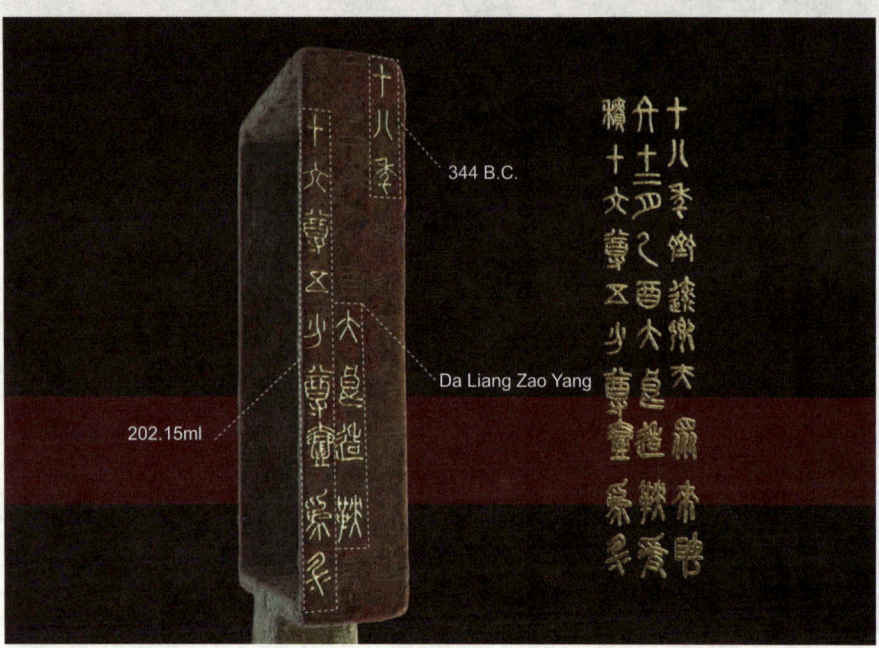

Colored Bone Ruler and Gilt Bronze Ruler

A sheng is a capacity unit as well as a tool for measuring grains. The ancient form of the character "sheng" could be interpreted as a grain of rice sitting on a spoon. Made of solid bronze, the rectangular vessel features abrupt vertical sides and a short handle. On its outer surface, there is a 32-character inscription. Like a birth certificate, it lists its time creation, dimensions and designer's name.

In this case the designer's name is Da Liang Zao Yang, also known to history as Shang Yang. Da Liang Zao was his title as the reforming Chief Minister of the state of Qin. In the fierce competition of the Warring States era, each state sought to introduce a social, political and military system that would gain it an edge over its rivals. Shang Yang believed nothing less than social revolution was required, to enlist the support of the entire populace. The first priority was to win their trust. Legend has it that he erected a 3m high wooden caber outside the capital's south gate, and offered a reward to whoever could move it to the north gate. No one dared try. So he increased the reward, one, two, three, four, five times. Finally someone was tempted and dare move the caber. Shang Yang immediately fulfilled his promise. Shang Yang having demonstrated his trustworthiness, the process of standardizing weights and measures could begin.

The *Du* was used to measure length; the *Liang* was used to measure capacity; the *Heng* was used to measure

Dagui Bronze Weighing Instrument Inscribed with Imperial Edicts of Two Emperors

Melon-ridge-shaped Bronze Weight

Yanke Bronze Measure

Gongdou Pottery Measure

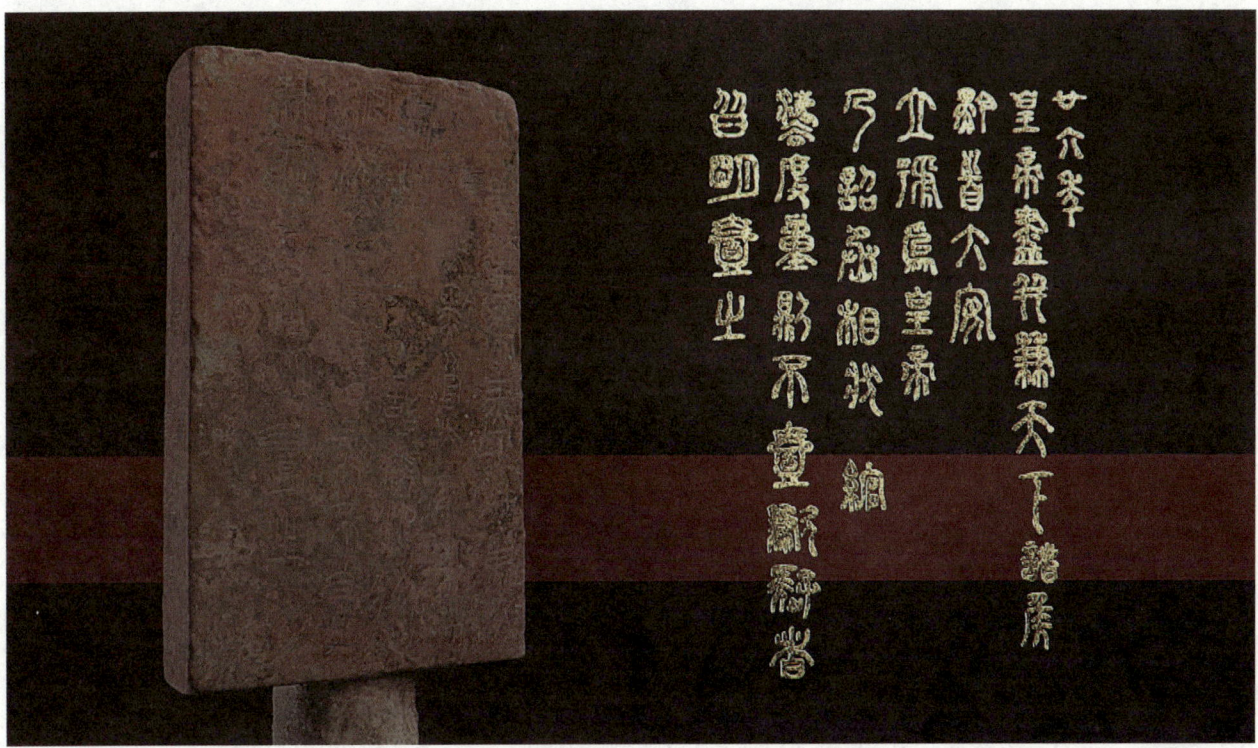

weight. In earlier times weights and measures varied from state to state, and even within an individual state they could be wildly different. Shang Yang clearly defined the Sheng by producing a standard measure for it. A simple measure that revolutionized trade and brought benefits to government and people alike, notably because taxes and tithes were to be paid in grain. Along with other reforms to encourage agriculture and military service, the state of Qin went from strength to strength.

This is the imperial edict that was engraved onto the base of Shang Yang's Measuring Vessel after Qin Shi

Huang unified China. A total of 40 characters. In 221 BC, the king of Qin overcame the last of his rivals to make himself ruler of all China: the First Emperor. A key aspect of the unification was the enforcement of universal standards in weight and measures, as well as in the writing of characters. This has been an essential part of the glue of empire ever since. The general idea of the edict is that now China has been unified, people are leading a settled life, and Du, Liang and Heng have been unified into one standard. Qin Shi Huang's inscription sits two centimeters in distance and 123 years in time from those of Shang Yang, but in so doing the ruler of the civilized world both implicitly and explicitly recognizes his debt to the bygone Chief Minister.

In a state based on military-agricultural system, a peasant household could provide men to serve or grain for taxes, and a unified measure meant a unified system for a unified state. From this, Chinese ancestors living in the vast land have a better understanding of what a unified state is. One measure, one people, one Emperor.

Shang Yang in History

China had designated historiographers very early on to take responsibility for safekeeping, documenting and collating historical records. Among the historical literature which has been passed down to date, most well-known are the Twenty-Four Histories. The *Records of the Grand Historian* by Sima Qian is one of them. This masterpiece documents the Chinese history over more than 3,000 years from the legendary Yellow Emperor period down to the fourth year of the Great Beginning (*Taichu*) calendar of the Emperor Wu of Han. One of the biographies in this book is the *Biography of Lord Shang*.

Lord Shang (*Shangjun*) refers to Shang Yang, while biographies (*liezhuan*) record the life stories of kings, princes, vassals and other representative figures, as well as the biographies of ethnic minorities. The *Records of the Grand Historian* includes 70 biographies, with the *Biography of Lord Shang* being the eighth, between the *Biographies of the Disciples of Zhongni* and the *Biography of Su Qin* in sequence. This is a clear demonstration of the importance of Shang Yang in history.

According to this biography, we are told that Shang Yang was initially named Gongsun Yang, also known as Wei Yang for his origin from a royal clan of the State of Wei. Later he was ascribed in Yushang (his birth place) for his great service in the reform of the Qin, and was also called Shang Yang or Lord Shang.

In his youth, Shang once served as a petty official in the State of Wei. The King of Wei, however, did not put his on any important position for a long period of time. So when he heard that the Duke Xiao of Qin was recruiting men of insights for a reform cause, he went to Qin, where his ideas on building a strong state and military soon won over the trust of the Duke. Shang was later appointed *zuo shuzhang* (the tenth rank of Qin nobility and officialdom), *Da Liang Zao* (also *da liangzao*, the sixteenth rank) and other official titles, and finally masterminded the reform of Qin.

Facing a society of collapse and corruption and incessant wars between vassals, Shang advocated for law as a tool to maintain social order and build a strong and prosperous Qin. In this light, Shang developed a range of laws and decrees, including establishing a mutual supervision and whistle-blowing system under which if one household violated the law, neighboring ten households would be punished by association; if one failed to report a criminal case, he or she would be executed by being cut in two are the waist; people who reported a criminal case might be rewarded in the same way as those who behead enemies; those who fought for personal reasons would be punished to varying degrees according to circumstances; those who were committed to agricultural production and contribute to good harvest and increased output of textile may be exempted from servitude or tax; those of royal lineage without military merits may not be included in the family register, to name just a few. Backed by the Duke Xiao, these laws and decrees were quickly implemented across the state, with impressive results.

Social reform on such a big scale worked well to build a strong Qin soon. However, it also compromised the vested interests of Qin nobility who began to hold grudges towards Shang. After the Duke Xiao died, Shang was accused by Prince Qian of conspiring against the state, ending up being killed in an encirclement. His dead body was carried back to Xianyang, torn asunder by five carts, and exposed to the public as a warning. Nonetheless, Shang's death did not stop the reform in Qin, and his governing ideas lived on and finally paved the way for Qin to unify the Middle Kingdom.

The Seal Script and Its Influences

The text on the Shang Yang Rectangular Measuring Vessel is in seal script, a font style of ancient China. The seal script has its big and small forms, with the big one for bronze and stone drum inscriptions while the small one being the standard script after the Qin annexing the other six states.

The Tortoise Plastron with Inscriptions Showing King of Shang's Inquiry about Fu Lai's Wellbeing

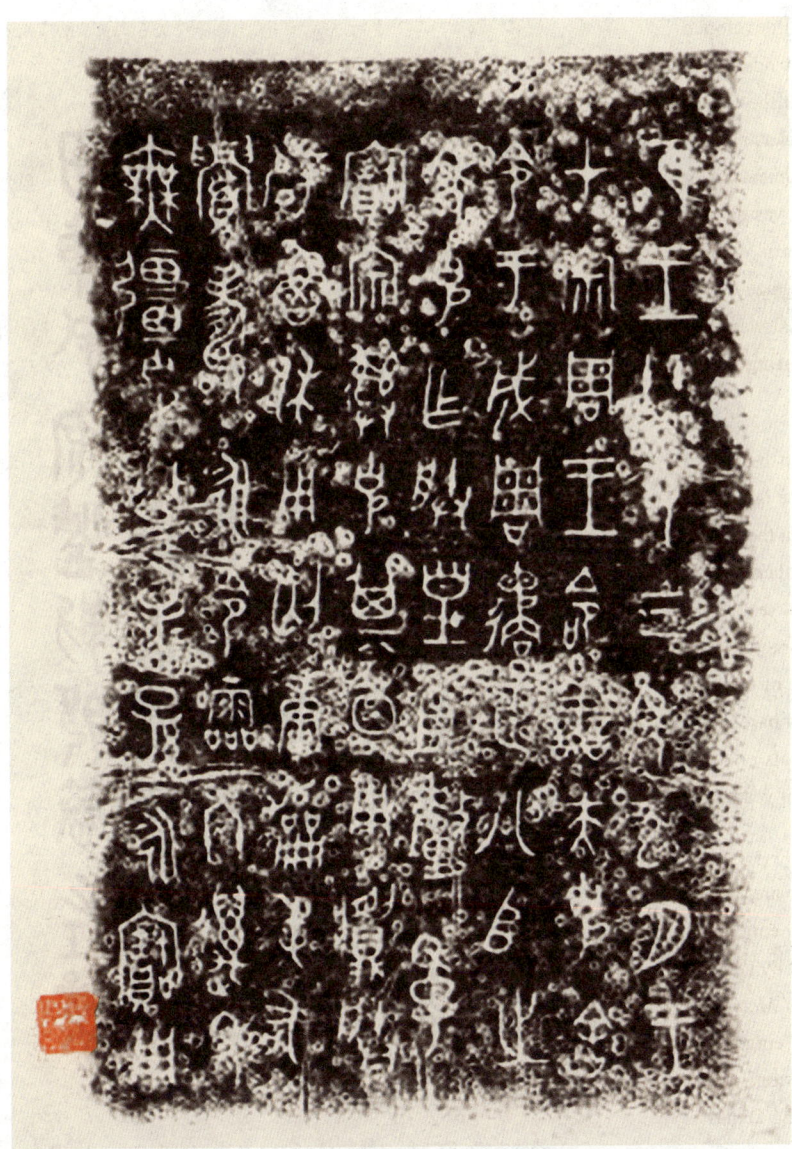

A Rubbing of Inscription on the Xiao Ke *ding*

The birth of the seal script was closely related to the oracle bone script, so named as it was carved or written on tortoise shells and animal bones. It is the earliest written language so far unearthed in China. The Oracle Turtle Shell of the King Wu Ding of Shang Divining the Physical Condition of Fu Lai, collected by the Palace Museum, has such inscriptions on it, with drilled and carved holes on its back that were burned when performing divination. Oracle bone script, discovered in 1899, became an instant hit in the academic community. Scholars including Luo Zhenyu, Wang Guowei, Guo Moruo, Dong Zuobin, Tang Lan and Chen Mengjia all interpreted and studied these inscriptions with remarkable results, enabling us to understand these texts and learn more about the Shang Dynasty. Seen from its number and structural form, oracle bone script represents a rather strict system of writing, characterized by symbolic, denotative, connotative, and pictophonetic elements, though with obvious traces of primary hieroglyph.

With the use of oracle bone script, texts gradually appeared on bronze ware, called bronze script, a type of large seal script. These two are similar in many ways. The majority of scholars believe that bronze script was developed from oracle bone script but was more complex and standardized. The Xiao Ke *ding* (a small food vessel) collected at the Palace Museum has bronze scripts on it, numbering 72 characters in eight rows. These bronze scripts were mainly used to document major historical events while glorifying what ancestors and vassals had achieved. They play a critical role in filling the gap in ancient literature. However, these scripts are difficult to recognize due to various forms of the same character caused by vassal wars and divergence during the Spring and Autumn and Warring States periods.

After annexing the other six states, the Qin began to standardize writing in small seal script, based on the large seal script of the Qin. The Stone Drums of Qin collected at the Palace Museum have inscriptions in Qin large seal script on them, pretty close to those in small seal script. The rise of small seal script was epoch-defining. The structure of Chinese characters was standardized and finalized ever since. The evolution of Chinese characters since then has never departed from this base, with no material changes in structure, locations of radicals or other components. Many characters, developed thousands of years ago, are still in use today.

Scholars began to study inscriptions on bronze ware, stones and other objects very early on, which gave rise to epigraphy. Formed in the Song Dynasty, epigraphy was founded by Ouyang Xiu. The word *jinshi* first appeared in the *Records of Metal and Stone* (*Jinshilu*) by Zhao Mingcheng and the word "epigraphy" (the study of inscriptions on ancient bronzes and stones) was first used by Wang Mingsheng and others in the Qing Dynasty. In the late Qing Dynasty and early Republic of China period,

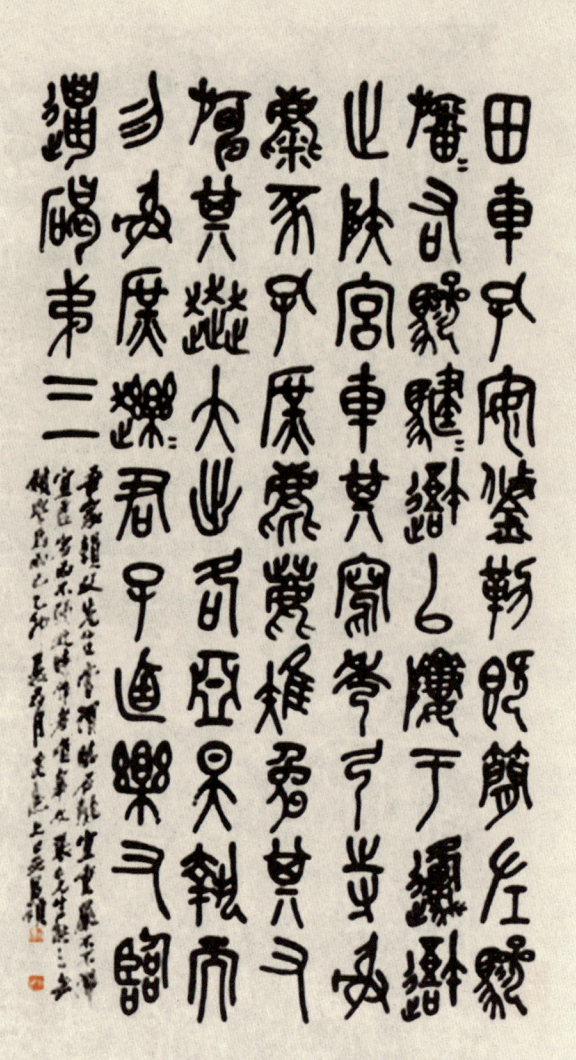

Calligraphic Work Copying the Inscription on the Stone Drum, by Wu Changshuo, Qing Dynasty

Xiao Ke *ding*

epigraphy was extended to include oracle bones and bamboo scrolls newly unearthed, and on to funerary ware and miscellaneous articles, gradually evolving into the predecessor of Chinese archaeology. It is due to the study and interpretation by generations of epigraphers of the historical information carried by bronze and stone inscriptions in seal script that we are able to fill in the gap of historical literature, and renew our understanding of the Shang and Zhou dynasties. Thus, it is obvious that the seal script played an important role in history.

Thanks to the prominence and popularity of epigraphy, many replicas and rubbings of seal script inscriptions were able to survive to date, becoming a unique part of the history of Chinese art. *The Stone-drum Inscriptions Copied by Wu Changshuo* in the Palace Museum collection was one representative piece of calligraphy. Written in 1915 when Wu was already 71 years old, this work boasts thick, unpretentious strokes, with lines of varying width. This is truly a work of high artistic standards that not only reproduces the original inscriptions in every sense but also creates something

Stone Drum of the Qin Dynasty

new with its unique vigor of style and powerful strokes. Moreover, works of calligraphy in seal script by many famous people have survived to this day, including Fu Shan, Qian Dian, Deng Shiru, Wu Dacheng, Zhao Zhiqian, Qi Baishi, Zhang Daqian, Ma Heng and Huang Miaozi. Therefore, we can see clearly that the seal script had a huge impact on the painting circle.

By Bai Wei

Qin Bronze Chariots and Horses

The Road to Eternity

Qin Bronze Chariots and Horses

Location: Emperor Qinshihuang's Mausoleum Site Museum
Age: Qin Dynasty
Texture: bronze
Weight: 1,061 kg

Qin Bronze Chariots and Horses

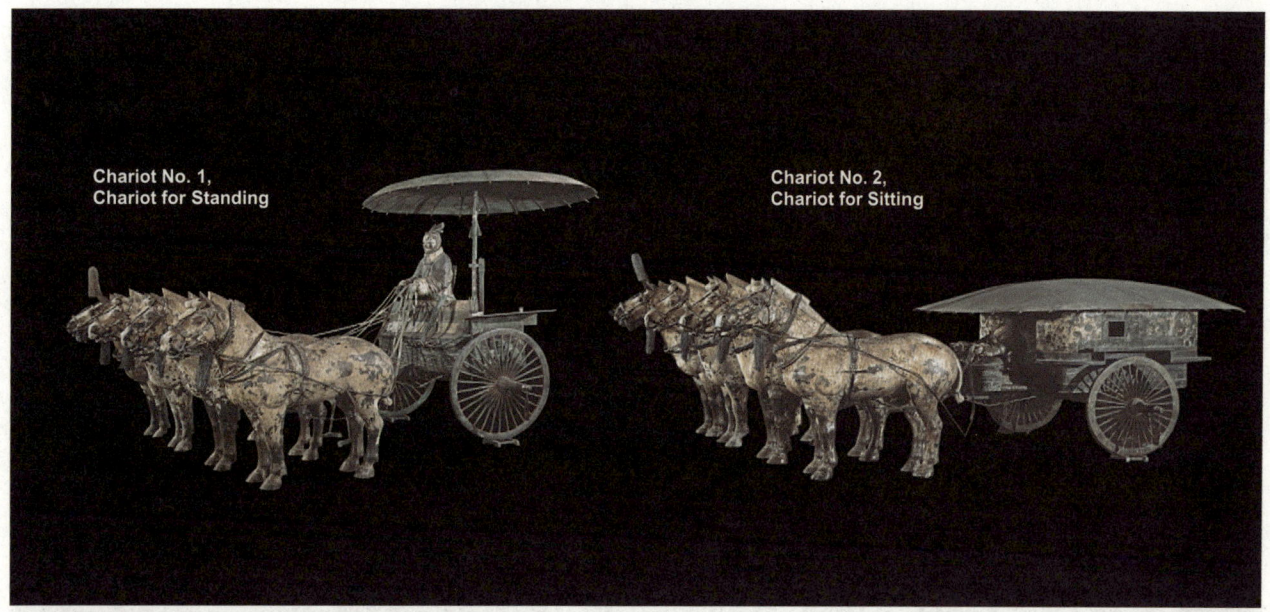

Chariot No. 1, Chariot for Standing

Chariot No. 2, Chariot for Sitting

Not even the mightiest among us can escape death, though China's first emperor, Qin Shi Huang, certainly had elaborate plans to do so.

In the winter of 1980, just west of the great tomb mound at Xi'an that houses the Emperor's final resting place, two bronze models of a horse and chariot team were unearthed.

The first, Chariot No.1, is a high chariot, faithful in every detail to a life-size example, including carriage, four horses, carriage ornaments and a standing driver. The main parts of the model are made of bronze, while the ornaments are made from gold and silver. In many places it is finely painted.

These are the most complete and detailed representations of how the elite aristocracy lived and travelled ever found by archaeologists. The extravagant use of metals is characteristic of a ruler who felt that nothing was beyond his command.

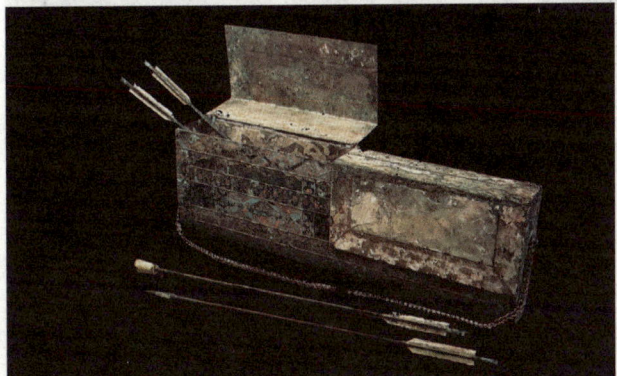
Accessories of Chariot No. 1 - Bronze Arrows and Arrow Container

Chariot No.1 is 152cm tall and 225cm long, a half size scale model of a real chariot. The reduction in size distinguishes the chariot from other funerary objects. But as a model it doesn't lose any detail. It weighs more than a ton and is made of more than 3,000 separate parts. The larger parts were made by hollow casting while the wide or thin pieces are forged metals. The many complex components were split into simple parts, which

were then assembled by hinges, buckles, rivets and rings. The independent parts are precisely matched to each other, indicating the high quality of craftsmanship available to the Qin.

When Ying Zheng, King of the State of Qin established himself as ruler of all China in 221BC, he gave himself a new title, Qin Shi Huang, a title which went further than simply

Hinge
Buckle
Rivet
Ring

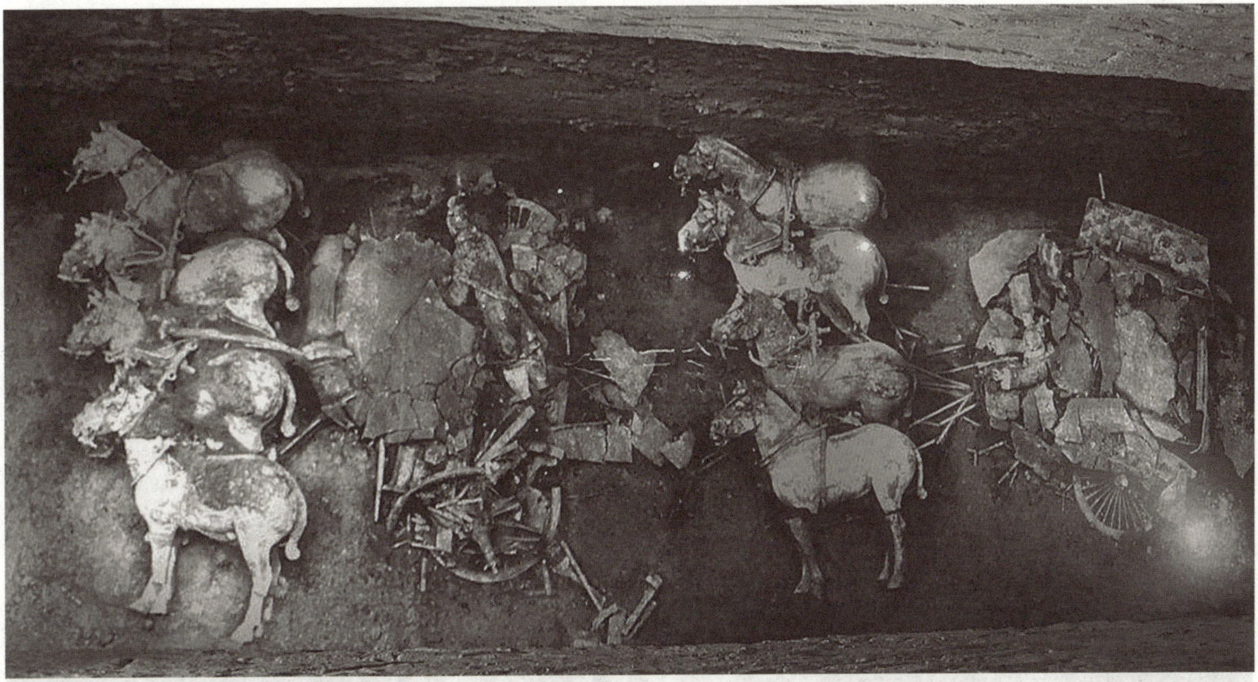

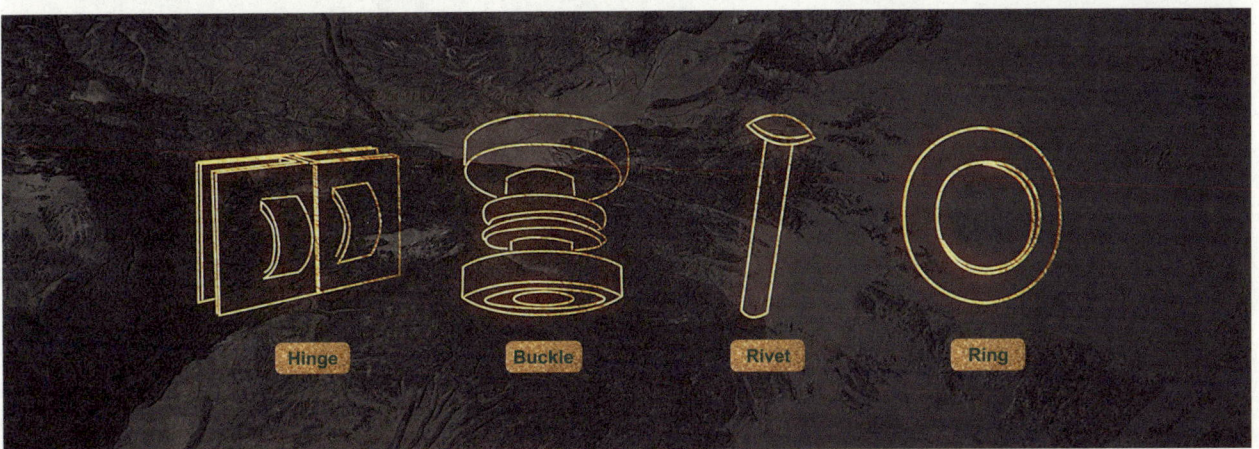

"first emperor" since it implied a unique authority to parlay with heaven. Qin Shi Huang set about unifying his domain by re-organizing its government into commanderies directly responsible to his central government, standardizing the written language and the system of weights and measures, including, even the width of carriage tracks.

Qin Shi Huang made five tours of inspection around his empire. He died in 210BC during the fifth tour, aged 49. His body had to be brought back to the capital secretly, in a closed carriage, with incense burnt to hide the smell of decay.

But his magnificent bronze chariots were there to await him, ready to travel west to the land of the setting sun, and the life eternal.

The Steed Underground

In the winter of 1980, two well-made large painted bronze models of a horse and chariot team were unearthed at the west side of the Mausoleum of Qin Shi Huang. This was another major archaeological discovery following the discovery of the Terracotta Warriors pit here. These two models were discovered in the doorway of a large burial pit, lying one behind the other facing the west, with the front one identified as No. 1 and the rear one as No. 2.

Following excavation, hoisting, moving, cleaning, matching, assembly and restoration, these bronze models have been proved to be the largest and most structurally complex burial chariots and horses with the most intact riding gear and best craftsmanship discovered in China to date. With a gross weight of approximately 1,200kg, each carriage has a cart with two segregated compartments, with the front one for the driver and driven by four horses while the rear one for the owner to ride, designed to segregate the driver from the owner, thus showing the distinguished status of the owner. Except being half of the real size, from overall structure to fine details, these vehicles are identical to real ones. Both are assembled from a large number of ready-cast parts with a highly complex structure, joined and connected by means of casting, welding, buckles and hinges, among other techniques. The chariot doors and windows can still be readily opened or shut. Such life-like details and distinct quality offer a concrete physical example for studying the dress code and transportation in the Qin Dynasty.

The tones of colors painted on both vehicles are rather cold. Painted onto the milky white background is a variety of cloud designs and geometric patterns in red, purple, blue, green, black and yellow colors, which appear solemn, dignified, splendid and elegant.

The Very Moment of Discovery of Qin Bronze Chariots and Horses

These patterns, which are generally outlined, coated, or overlaid on the base color, appear on the vehicle body, driver, horses and ornaments. These patterns generally fall into two categories: cloud or cloudlike patterns which are mainly painted and seldom cast, and geometric patterns in diamond, round, triangular and other shapes, dominated by two sides or quadrilateral continuity diamond patterns. Such crisp, plain and yet elegant patterns, when accompanied by the gold and silver ornaments on the chariots and horses, appear luxurious.

The two chariots, though both among the imperial procession of Qin Shi Huang, are starkly different in their shape, structure and armament. Chariot No. 1 is tall with an umbrella canopy, 225 cm long. Behind the standing driver seat is a compartment for carrying

Patterns on the Outside of the Quiver of Chariot No. 1

cargo and people, called carriage, about 152 cm tall, single shaft and two-wheeled. Its body is structurally more complicated, and its accessories are mostly decorated with neat geometric patterns. The cart is in a rectangular shape, with the front and two sides flanked with boards while a door is opened in the middle of the tail board. In the cart, there is a cross-shape umbrella stand on which is a long bronze umbrella. The round bronze canopy perfectly covers the entire cart and imperial officers, while the driver stands by the chariot, exuding a solemnity and playing a leading and guarding role in the guard of honor. On the top of the front board is a crossbar, known as *shi*, which serves as an armrest and, when necessary, a lookout. Su Xun, a famed writer from the Song Dynasty, named his eldest son Su Shi, later famously known as Su Dongpo, expressing the expectation that his son would be such a horizontal bar that is quiet and reserved yet an indispensable part of a chariot. He also gave his son the courtesy name "Zizhan", to express his hope that Su Shi would think big and aim high on this crossbar.

Patterns on the Inside of the Rear Door of Chariot No. 2

Chariot No. 2, 328.4 cm long and 104.2 cm tall, is bigger with an awning. It is a two-wheeled and single shaft vehicle, with the standing driver seated. There is no armament other than swords carried by the imperial officers. The shape of the carriage describes an inverted T, with a protruding awning on the top, four sides fenced in, and windows on two sides to offer more privacy. Passengers may comfortably sit or lie down in the cart. Therefore, this chariot is called a "canopied sedan chariot". With predominately cloudy patterns, this vehicle offers the comfort of a resting tool. When unearthed, Chariot No. 1 was lying before Chariot No. 2, suggesting that the former was a leading vehicle subordinate to the latter. The *Book of Jin*: Travel and Dress records that, "vehicles on which passengers can sit are called sedan chariots, while those on which passengers can only stand are called standing chariots or high chariots."

The Expressways of the Qin Dynasty—*Chidao*

From Shang Yang's Reform to the period of Emperor Qin Shi Huang's period, the State of Qin took more than one century to annex six other states. The biggest challenge facing Qin then was how to cement the central authority of a feudal country and further crack down on the restoration and separatist forces of slave owner aristocracy. In response, Qin Shi Huang rolled out a range of measures, including establishing a transport system centering on the capital Xianyang. During the Warring States period, each state had their own road systems with varying gauges, which meant that the transport system would hamper military operations in the event of war. In light of this, Qin Shi Huang issued decrees to unify writing and gauges across the country when merging the other six states. From this point on, the Chinese nation adopted "uniform systems of writing and gauge."

Prior to unifying the other six states, there were three roads leading from Xianyang to northwestern border areas: Longxi Commandery, Beidi Commandery and Shangjun Commandery. The territory of Qin originally covered only a corner stretching to the west of Hangu Pass. Following unification, it expanded far beyond the original Qin territory. In 220 B.C., Qin Shi Huang ordered the construction of royal roads or *chidao* with Xianyang at the center, the earliest "state roads" in Chinese history. The building of these highways expanded a transport system with the capital as the hub, changing the original road network. The royal roads were mostly built on existing roads of the six states, so construction advanced rapidly. In the following year, Qin Shi Huang was able to travel via these royal roads to visit various places across the country.

Qin Bronze Chariot No.1

Qin Bronze Chariot No.2

Among the newly built royal roads, there were three trunk lines: one leading directly eastward to the former states of Qi and Yan (today's Hebei Province and Shandong Province), one southward to the former states of Wu and Chu (corresponding to modern areas along the middle and lower reaches of the Yangtze River) and one from Xianyang northward to Yunyang (today's Chunhua County, Shaanxi Province) and on to Jiuyuan County, southwest of Baotou City. With a combined length of about 900km, these roads were built to defend against Xiongnu's aggression. The construction of royal roads adapted to the needs of economic development of a unified nation, including stimulating the exchange of goods, recovering and developing war-torn agricultural production, establishing strong grain bases and developing agriculture and war policy. These roads greatly facilitated transportation from the capital to other places and helped strengthen central control over local governments.

As these trunk lines were centering on Xianyang, like a cobweb in certain areas, if a restoration of power happened anywhere within the former territories of the other six states, the central government could send neighboring troops in place to control these former capitals of states via these royal roads. The building of these roads also showed the boldness and determination of Qin Shi Huang to defend the country against Xiongnu's aggression.

The Qin armed forces were divided into infantry, cavalry and chariot troops, with both land and water components. During the reign by Qin Shi Huang, the army was mainly comprised of infantry, and the cavalry emerged as a separate service and used as a main force in wars annexing other states. The water force played an important role in annexing the State of Chu and attacking Baiyue. These bronze chariots and horses epitomize the grand scene of the Qin Army which traveled and fought far and wide to unify the Chinese nation. Being the fruit of the wisdom and talent of ancient working people, these chariots and horses are of great value to studying the politics, military, technology and art of ancient China.

By Gao Ran

Liye Qin Slips

A Slip in Time

Liye Qin Slips

Location: Liye Qin Slips Museum
Age: Qin Dynasty
Texture: wood
Quantity: over 37,000 pieces

The year is 2018 and another of China's national treasures is about to spill its secrets. Liye Qin Slips are held in their own Liye Qin Slips Museum in Hunan Province. The wooden slips look inconspicuous, but hidden in the blurred characters is huge amount of information. It describes the life of a county under the Qin Dynasty in the late 3rd century BC. In June 2002 the discovery of over 37,400 slips in an ancient well in Liye, Hunan Province excited the world.

"We could barely recognize the characters on the slips. They were burned and soaked so it is hard to restore their original appearance. But through techniques such as multispectral acquisition, we are able to read them clearly."

> A Nanyang household headed by Zheng Bubao with the curtesy title Bugeng, making him a minor aristocrat. His wife is called You. They have a young son called Zaosi.

This is the record of a family that lived 2,200 years ago. The householder was Zheng Bubao and given the title of Bugeng, which exempted him from corvee service. He had a wife called You and their son was called Zaosi. It's an example of early Imperial bureaucracy.

"Does it look like our household registers? I know another slip that looks like our identity cards."

> Wu Sao from Hanshenli in Handan. He has yellow skin, elliptical face and is about 170cm tall.

In 23 characters, it introduces us to Wu Sao from Hanshenli in Handan. With the slip, Wu Sao could avoid his identity being stolen. Officials could also use it as census data. Although Wu's body has long turned to dust, this wooden slip has preserved his appearance for millennia.

After Qin Shi Huang united his empire he imposed a system of prefectures and counties. There were more than 40 prefectures in total. Dongting Prefecture's Qianling County was in all respects, unremarkable amongst them. The officials here were typical bureaucrats of their time. The Liye Qin Slips are the day to day record of their government work. Most of the slips relate to life in the Qin Dynasty after Qin Shi Huang united the Warring States. They cover events and affairs on daily and monthly basis from 221BC to 209BC.

Each slip is the record of an event. It is a model of how the Qin administrative system worked. The over 37,000 pieces of slips are an encyclopedia of county life in the Qin Dynasty. They cover subjects including postal communication, the administrative organization system, trade, arithmetic, daily events and festivals. It is a panorama of the operation of a Qin county under the system of prefectures and counties.

  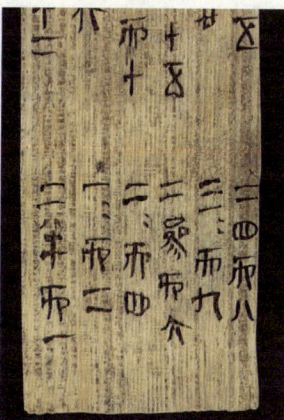  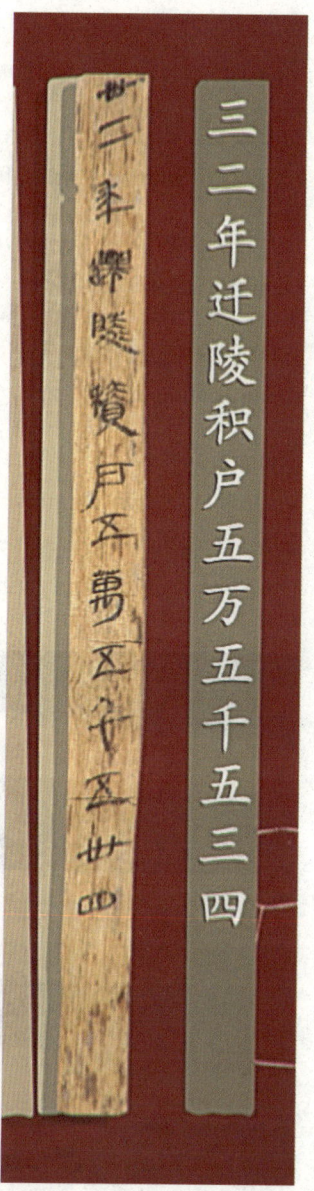

In 219 BC the death rate of corvee service personnel in the county reached an alarming one in seven.

In 215 BC the county's warehouse manager sold the last 15 liters of wine to a man called Cheng.

In the same year there were 55,534 households in Qianling.

And there are even 3 pieces of one of the oldest multiplication tables discovered to date.

There are less than 1,000 words in the official dynastic records about the administrative system and social life under the Qin. However the 200,000 characters of Liye Qin Slips vastly expand on this vacuum.

The lives of the officials and subjects of the early empire live on in these 37,000 slips. They are truly a shining treasure house of history.

The System of Prefectures and Counties on Bamboo Slips

After he swept across states and forged the fragmented territories into one united country, one question most challenged Qin Shi Huang, the first emperor of the united China: how could he achieve stable and sustainable governance, and ensure a long-standing reign for his successors? According to the *Historical Records: Biography of Qin Shi Huang*, his ministers and officials were engaged in fierce debate over this issue. Vetoing most of the views, the emperor finally decided to implement the system of prefectures and counties proposed by Li Si.

The decision made by Qin Shi Huang has posed far-reaching influence not only to his empire, but also to the entire history of China. Archaeologists were not able to find more until the discovery of the Liye Qin Slips, which provided valuable records about circumstances in the Qin Dynasty. The administrative instrument of Qianling County, the Liye Qin Slips much resembles the official documents that public employees are familiar with today. At the base layer of the regime, counties were under the jurisdiction of prefectures and the central government. By studying these ancient slips, we could infer the whole system from this one single instance, and investigate details about the implementation of the system from a microcosmic perspective.

We are able to see functions of the local government of Qianling County by reading these slips. First, it should execute administrative decrees from its superior and receive instruments from the central and prefectural governments; second, it should fulfill its administrative duties and issue local official documents within the county boundary; third, it should report to the central and prefectural governments and accept their audits; and finally, it should review instruments submitted from lower administrative agencies. It can be noticed that local government agencies today perform functions much as their predecessors did in the Qin Dynasty.

Nevertheless, how could the government ensure the sustainability of this administration mode and avoid deviation from the original imperial policies when convenient transportation and communication vehicles commonly seen today were not available in those remote years? One of the tools applied in the Qin Dynasty was the official instrument, which served as a shuttle delivering information between government agencies at all levels.

Standing in front of piles of slips, one could truly be astonished by the enormous volume and strict specifications of these instruments. It is conceivable that officials had to cope with the heavy workload, which must be equal to, if not greater than that of public employees today.

Delivery and receipt of instrument should be recorded, indicating date and time. Furthermore, instruments were circulated as per strict regulations. By "Yi You Xing", the instrument, generally an urgent one, was delivered by postman; by "Yi Ci Xing", the instrument was circulated from one county to another; and by "Bie Shu Chao Song", a copy of the instrument was delivered when the original needed to be kept.

Frequent circulation of official documents and strict work procedure accounted for a large part of the governance in the Qin Dynasty. We have known from the Liye Qin Slips that these official documents were dealt with by assistants to head of the prefecture or county. They were also supported by a group of clerks familiar with the formatting and wording of official documents that link the county to the central government. In the Qin Dynasty, every county government had such a documentation department, which functioned as the center of local political power, where national affairs and local issues were fully communicated. With the help of the instrument delivery system, which acted in the same way as blood capillaries of the human body, Emperor of Qin could manage to extend his power to every corner of the country and control government agencies like arms and fingers.

As indicated above, a small piece of bamboo slip contains a great deal of information about the regime. The writing of each and every character required careful consideration. In his *Inscription about a Crude Dwelling*, the ancient poet Liu Yuxi expressed his joy for he was freed from exhausting desk work. Just by seeing the Liye Qin Slips, we can imagine the fatigue suffered by first-line public servants of the Qin Dynasty when they faced over-elaborated regulations and complex interagency relations.

By Li Kai

Text on slip No.152

Jade in Nanyue

A Symbol of Peacefulness

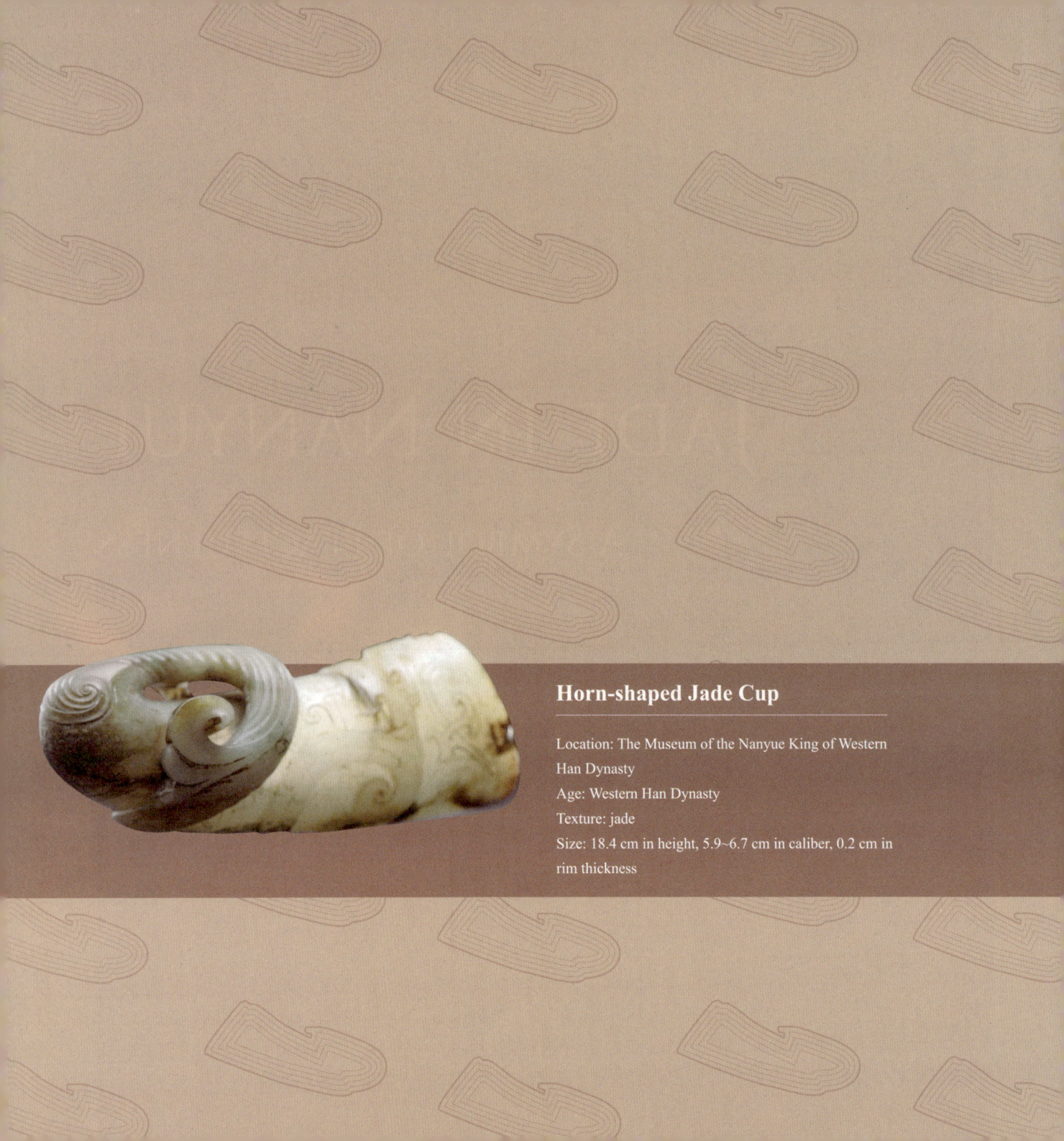

Horn-shaped Jade Cup

Location: The Museum of the Nanyue King of Western Han Dynasty
Age: Western Han Dynasty
Texture: jade
Size: 18.4 cm in height, 5.9~6.7 cm in caliber, 0.2 cm in rim thickness

"Fanyu" Han-style Bronze Tripod from King of Nanyue's Tomb

Rainforests, swamps, mists…This is the land of Nanyue, in China's deep south. 2,000 years ago the first emperor, Qin Shi Huang, saw the potential of this fertile land. Zhao Tuo was sent to take command of the Qin army in the region in 218 BC. Zhao's rule of the region extended from the Qin Dynasty long into the Han Dynasty. According to the *Records of the Grand Historian*, Zhao was the long-lived king in Chinese history, dying in 137BC aged over 100. Zhao Tuo was succeeded by his grandson Zhao Mo. However the independent status established by Zhao Tuo after the Fall of the Qin, was gradually eroded and in 112BC Nanyue was occupied by a Han Army from

Jade Seal of Zhao Mo

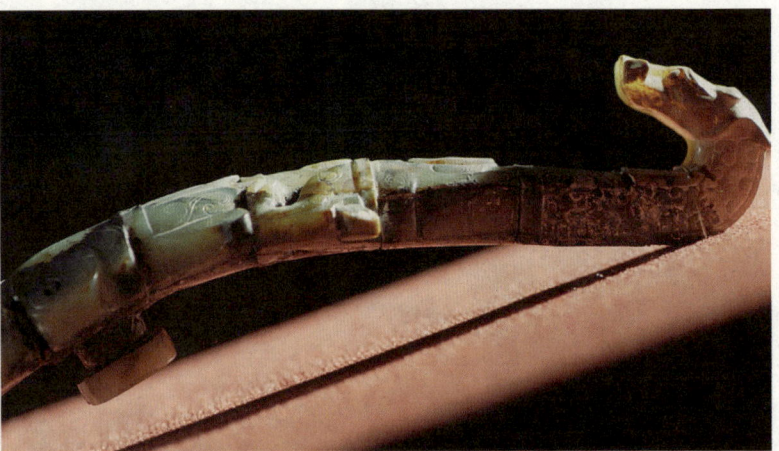
Eight-segment Iron-core Dragon-and-tiger-shaped Jade Belt Hook

Jade Chess Pieces from King of Nanyue's Tomb

the north. In 1983 Zhao Mo's tomb was discovered. Among the grave goods were spectacular jade objects which showcase the artistry of the jade craftsmen of the time.

Jade has a special place in Chinese culture. It represents virtue, or displays an individual's wealth. It can also be a companion in death. In the Han-dynasty jade objects were commonly used in many ways, ranging from ritual objects to ornaments or utensils. They are records of Han history and culture. Although Nanyue was located on the fringe of Han culture, it was founded by a general from the central plains and shared this respect for jade.

Big Jade Disc

Zhao Mo, the King of Nanyue, was no doubt a lover of jade. He drank with jade cups. His belt fastening was made of jade. He wore jade pendants. Even his chess pieces were made of jade.

This jade cup is an imitation of the rhinoceros horn. In ancient China it was believed that the rhinoceros horn could neutralize poisons. The cup's owner must have been a good drinker. Since the cup cannot be stood upright, it must be held, or the contents downed in one gulp. On the outer surface is am image of a mythical Chinese creature, a *Kui*.

Openwork Carved Double-ring Jade Pendant with Dragon and Phoenix Patterns

Tiger-head-shaped Gold Hook and Dragon-shaped Jade Pendant

The image of dragon is common to many jade objects. This is a dragon-shaped jade pendant. This is a jade disc with the dragon design. This is a jade pendant with the image of a dragon and a Chinese phoenix. 2,000 years ago, it was placed on the face of the departed King. Perhaps to help him see clearly in the next world: the dragon in the inner circle is supporting the phoenix outside. They are facing the opposite directions, giving the design a vivacious rhythm.

In life jade reminds the king to be a virtuous. In death, jade brings peace to the soul. Complete jade suits were the most extravagant of these funeral objects. People at the time believed that jade could help keep the soul from

Jade Suit with Silk Threads from King of Nanyue's Tomb

disintegrating and becoming lost. Complete jade suits were the most extravagant of these funeral objects. With 2,291 pieces of jade strung with red silk thread, the suit carried the dream of immortality. Compared with the suits that use gold, silver or bronze thread, Zhao Mo's suit is unique with red silk.

Nanyue, the southern extremity of Qin and Han territory, inherited the traditional jade culture in the central plains, but also absorbed exotic local influences. Jade the beautiful stone. The Chinese character for "jade" is the same as the character for "King" with just one extra dot added. A king might vanish in the river of time. But with jade his writ will last longer. Jade brings peace to the body, to the mind, and to the world. And peace is the pathway to eternity.

Funerary Jade of the Han Dynasty

Extremely deep affection will last not long;

Things start to decline once they reach their apex;

The decent should always be modest and warm like a piece of jade.

from the *Book of Documents*

Jade culture is unique to the Chinese civilization. Over thousands of years our ancestors created countless verses and poetry to eulogize the jade. Do you know about this special type of jade which was not intended to be worn or collected for appreciation, but to be buried with its owner? Such jade ware is known as funerary jade.

The burying of jade had long been a tradition since old times, and this tradition was innovatively revitalized during the Han Dynasty, with the jade burial suit being the most representative. The jade suit was designed only for top royal members and could also be granted to some important officials. Gold-threaded jade suits, among those made of silver, bronze and silk threads, were only prepared for the emperor and his brothers. Restored gold threaded jade suits include the two for Liu Sheng, King Jing of Zhongshan, and his wife Dou Wan (the Western Han Dynasty; and preserved in Mancheng County, Hebei Province), the one for Liu Xing, King Xiao of Zhongshan (the Western Han Dynasty; Dingxian County), and the one for Liu Wu, King of Chu, or his father Liu Yingke, as some argued (the Western Han Dynasty; Xuzhou City, Jiangsu Province), and one for Cao Teng, Cao Cao's grandfather (the Eastern Han Dynasty; Bozhou City, Anhui Province).

In addition to these complete suits, residual pieces of other suits have also been discovered due to the constant and rampant robbing of tombs. Jade masks are another simple form of funerary jade. One of the important reasons for noble members of the Han Dynasty to value jade suit so much is that they believed jade has a magic spiritual power, which concentrates and protects their soul eternally.

Although most people were sure about this power, only a limited number of upper-class members had the privilege to wear jade. Beside the regulations, the cost of more than a thousand of jade pieces and so many gold or silver threads were beyond the common folks, who would turn to jade cicadas, pigs and plugs instead. As the tool for preventing the "essence" from draining out of nine major

Mask Pieces for Wife of Marquis of Jinmu, the Western Zhou Dynasty

Liu Sheng's Jade Suit with Silk Threads

orifices of the human body according to the *Baopuzi*, the finish of jade plugs was rough.

Jade cicada was a type of *fanhan*, something put in the deceased's mouth as if it were food. The *Rites of Zhou* provides clear regulations about *fanhan*: "Peals for king, jade ware for lord, *ji* for grand master, shells for serviceman and grains for ordinary folk". Archaeologists generally find shells, or jade cicadas in cases of Han-dynasty tombs. Highly respected in the Han Dynasty, cicadas were a symbol of purity, pride and spirit communication, and additional connotations were added as time went by. The quality of Han-dynasty jade cicadas, mainly of the raw stone, was closely related to the owner's economic status. This jade cicada was unearthed from Tomb No. 6 at Tushantun, Qingdao. Its glimmering crystalline quality and vivid appearance is evident. What a lovely piece it is.

Jade handles, usually in the shape of a pig, are another form of funerary jade commonly seen during the Han Dynasty in addition to jade cicadas. They were put in the hands of the deceased because they were not supposed to "leave with their hands empty". According to the *Book of Etiquette and Ceremonial*, the handle was wrapped with a piece of red and black fabric, measuring 40 cm long and 17 cm wide, and put in the hands of the deceased before binding it tight with silk ribbons. As explained in the *Shiming*, wo

Jade Pig from Tomb of Jiancaoping, Taiyuan, Shanxi

Jade Cicada from Tomb No. 6 of Tushantun, Qingdao

refers to something put in the hands of the deceased. Jade pigs were popular funerary handles during the Han Dynasty. Among the early domesticated animals, pigs had long been considered as a symbol of wealth. Pig-shaped jade handles were put in the deceased's hands because their descendants hoped they were not leaving empty handed, and could live an affluent life in the afterworld.

Speaking of the funerary jade made during the Han Dynasty, we have no reason to bypass the excellent craftsmanship of the same time. As you can see, these jade cicadas and pigs are fine art works with firm but streamlined profiles; and the *Han Ba Dao*, or "eight cuts", a relatively straightforward carving skill, is what shaped their vivid appearance. Most archaeologists believe that the skill, while there is no way to determine its origin, was so named because the raw stones were carved into masculine shapes with just eight cuts, which is obviously not an accurate number. Generally, funerary jade objects are simply cut to bring out some inherent characteristics of the real thing; and honestly speaking, most of them seem slapdash products. However, it is this slapdashness that in turn highlights their simplicity.

China's society had developed an ever-advanced material culture by the Han Dynasty, when the worth of individuals was recognized and valued along with the development of productivity. People were no longer sacrificed in religious rituals or funerals. Instead, they were more modernistic than people of previous dynasties. Unlike their counterparts before the pre-Qin period, which were basically symbols of rituals and social status, jade objects were crafted to celebrate the real life or express hopes in the Han Dynasty. In fact, tons of ritual jade objects were then reworked for new use. While it is true that the tradition of funerary jade had been passed down, Han people redefined it and made their new choice. The jade not only carried their sincere hopes that the afterlife of the deceased would be as affluent and happy, it also reflected their gratification and affection to the real world.

By Wei Zhen

The General's Tomb

A Will of Granite

The General's Tomb

Location: Maoling Museum
Age: Western Han Dynasty
Texture: stone
Size: 168 cm in length, 190 cm in height

Maoling Mausoleum of Emperor Wu of Han

Tomb of Huo Qubing

Close by the great tomb mausoleum of Emperor Wu of Han is the tomb of the heroic young warrior who served him, the legendary cavalry general, Huo Qubing. Huo's tomb is built in the shape of the Qilian mountains to commemorate his many victories on China's northwest frontier. Huo's tomb is surrounded by an extraordinary collection of carved stone statuary.

EVERY TREASURE TELLS A STORY | 132

Stone Man

A Rearing Horse

A Monster Eating a Goat

The figure of a man, a face wracked with pain or anguish – it could be a piece of modern art ... or something from the pre-historic past.

The fertile land of the Central Plains attracted ferocious predators. This represents a goat being devoured by a beast, just as the Xiongnu horsemen would sweep down from Mongolia and the northwest to pillage China's northern provinces. They were an enemy much to be feared.

This stone steed rears up in defiance. Just like the Han Dynasty was about to in 140 BC, when the 16-year-old Emperor Wu came to the throne and Huo Qubing was born. The Han Dynasty had been founded some 62 years previously and for all those decades had lived with the Xiongnu threat.

A heavy set stone man grapples with a wild bear. This shows the sort of spirit that the teenage general took into battle with him. At the age of 19 Huo Qubing led a lightening campaign in which he defeated 5 Xiongnu tribes in 6 days. Time and again he led his cavalry armies in overrunning Xiongnu forces and capturing their leaders. On one occasion he approached the enemy camp alone and persuaded them to surrender.

A mighty war horse tramples on a supine Xiongnu warrior, lying on his back with arrows in his right hand and a bow in the left hand.

Horse Trampling on Xiongnu Warrior

Man and Bear

Boar

A Rising Horse

Tiger Lying on Its Stomach

Lying Elephant

In 119 BC the 21-year-old Huo Qubing encircled and killed 70,000 Xiongnu warriors. He conducted a series of rituals in the mountains of Eastern Mongolia to symbolize this historic Han victory, before continuing his pursuit of the enemy as far north as Lake Baikal. He had effectively annihilated the Xiongnu clan. After the battle it was said "the Xiongnu fled far away and there was no Xiongnu in the southern desert." The Han Dynasty was freed from their historic pest.

His contemporary, the Grand Historian Sima Qian, said of him "he strengthened the border, resumed lost territory in Hexi Corridor, captured the Qilian Mountains, connected with western areas and defeated the northern nomads." It was to be dazzling but brief appearance on the stage of history. Huo died in 117 BC, aged 23.

The stone statues are silent in the wilderness. These simple rough carvings are quite different from the realistic styles of other generations but are still masterpieces of the Han-dynasty art. The stone is as hard as the will it immortalizes. A life that carved its mark on destiny and was gone in a flash. But the legend lives forever. Huo Qubing, the young warrior with the will of stone.

The Monument of Huo Qubing, the Young General

Huo Qubing was an eminent general during the Western Han Dynasty. As a nephew of Wei Qing, the Great General of the time, Huo engaged in battles against the Hun since the age of 16. He led troops to fight against the enemy at borders on six occasions, winning each of them. Huo was best known for gaining the victory in the Battle of Qilian Mountain. By defeating the main force of Hun army, he guarded the security of northwest Han and, more importantly, cleared the Hexi Corridor, leading to better economic and cultural exchanges between the Han Dynasty and Western Asian countries. To recognize his achievements, Emperor Wu of Han conferred many honorable titles on him. Unfortunately, Huo died when he was only 23. Falling in great grief, Emperor Wu buried Huo in Maoling, his own imperial mausoleum, and built Huo's tomb with a natural boulder, cut into the shape of Qilian Mountain to commemorate Huo's distinguished military achievements. The large stone carvings in front of Huo's tomb are not only monuments to the young hero but also bear valuable stone inscriptions of the Han Dynasty.

According to records, inscribed stone monuments were erected as early as the Qin Dynasty. However, the earliest ones preserved are those from the Western Han Dynasty, i.e. the stone monuments at General Huo's tomb are the earliest and the most complete art of stone inscription in China. Sixteen stone carvings in total have been well preserved: a Hun Intruder Hoofed by a Warhorse, a Recumbent Horse, a Galloping Horse, a Stone Man, a Man and a Bear, a Monster Preying on a Sheep, a Boar, a Lying Tiger, a Recumbent Ox, a Recumbent Elephant, a Frog, a Toad, two Stone Fish and two Inscribed Stone Monuments.

Aside from the two stone monuments, the other fourteen carvings are crafted by different techniques, showing varied styles. It is assumed that they were built for different purposes. "A Hun Intruder Hoofed by a Warhorse" is the most complete showing the most complicated details and the clearest theme. The figure of the

Frog

Horse Trampling on Xiongnu Warrior

Stone Fish

Gold Adornment Showing Wolfs Attacking a Bull, the Warring States Period

Painted Pottery Boshan Censer with Hunting Patterns, the Western Han Dynasty

Hun intruder is richly depicted, probably for demonstrating Huo's feats; a Monster Preying on a Sheep, a Man and a Bear, and a Stone Man present elements of raw life of the Hun; as for lying carvings, such as a Recumbent Horse, a Recumbent Ox, and a Lying Tiger, some believe that they are just ornaments but some scholars argue that they may be prototypes of guardian beasts. Since the Stone Fish and Frog are installed with a flat top, they may be certain parts of a building.

What are the possible functions of these large stone carvings? A widely accepted view is that the tomb was built into the shape of the Qilian Mountain to celebrate Huo's military achievements; wild animals and livestock were added "to the mountain" to enhance its reality and deliver the atmosphere of the mountainous region. Many scholars also support the theory of the "mountain of immortals", which has placed the tomb against the context of a popular belief of the Western Han Dynasty, and is related to the Boshan censer unearthed also in Maoling. They believe that the tomb symbolizes "the mountain of immortals", and like the animal images on the Boshan censer, the stone carvings are strange creatures living in the mountain. The function of the stone carvings is not to commemorate Huo's feats, but to create a virtual world of immortals, expressing the wish of immortality.

Although the purpose of these carvings has not been determined, their historical significance and artistic value should not be questioned. Represented by A Hun Intruder Hoofed by a Warhorse, these carvings show the strength and national spirit of the Han Dynasty. They have laid the ground work of giant funerary stone carvings in China's burial culture, and have exerted a far-reaching influence on subsequent tombs. From the perspective of China's history of art, they are brilliant jewels of ancient stone carving that have inspired the creativity of later generations.

By Wang Yusu

"Five Stars Rise in the East" Brocade Arm Guard

"Five Stars Rising in the East Favor the Middle Kingdom"

"Five Stars Rise in the East" Brocade Arm Guard

Location: Xinjiang Institute of Archaeology

Age: Han Dynasty

Texture: brocade

Size: 18.5 cm in length, 12.5 cm in width

Buddhist Dagoba Ruins

Niya Ruins

Location of the Coffins M3 and M8

The mountains were not always high, the deserts not always dry. For lost beneath the sands of time, another country lies.

The northern meltwaters from the Kunlun Mountains flow towards the searing Taklamakan Desert in the heart of Xinjiang. They supply the oases that once made the stopping points on the Southern Silk Road. In 1995 a team of archaeologists exploring the lost city of Cadota stumbled across a remarkable find. The site known today as the Niya ruins, yielded the coffin of a wealthy couple from the Han Dynasty. The man was found to be wearing an elaborate guard on his right arm which was in near

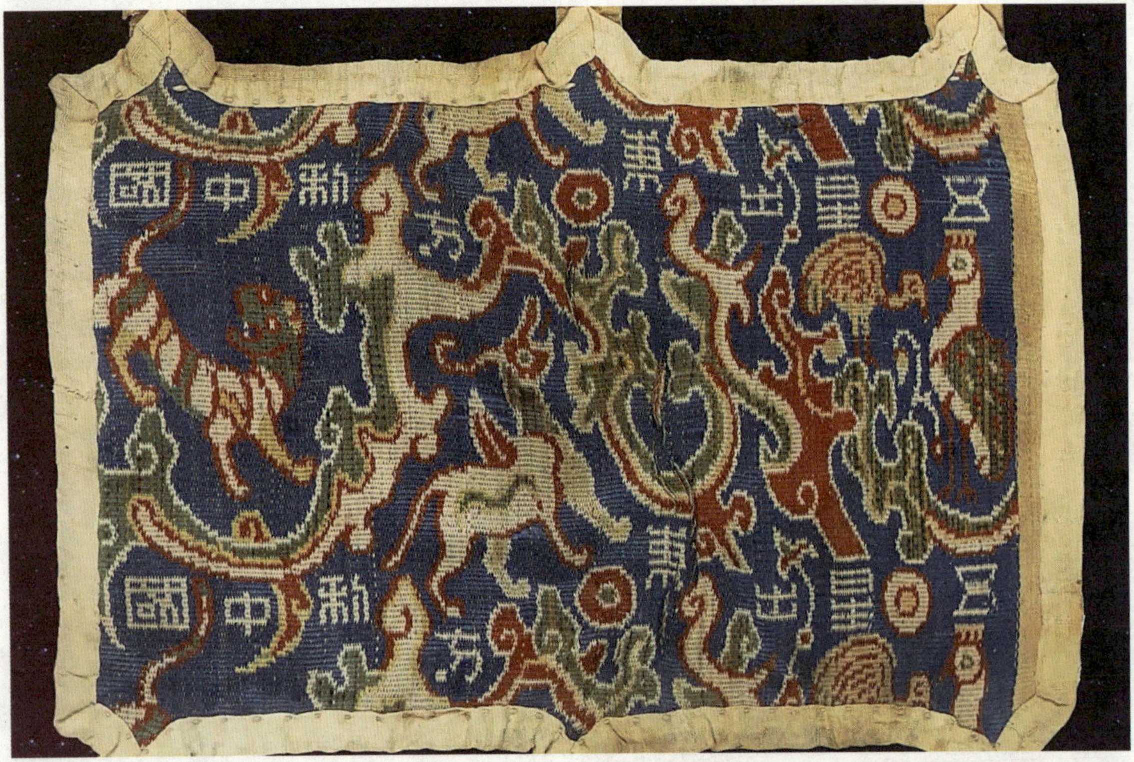

EVERY TREASURE TELLS A STORY

The moment when "Five Stars Rise in the East" Brocade was discovered

perfect condition. The arm guard consists of a five layered brocade with six fastening straps. The brocade was finely decorated with five different colors of thread – blue, green, red, yellow and white – woven into patterns of clouds, mountains, stars, grasses, beasts and birds; a design that symbolizes paradise in Han Dynasty cosmology.

Even more intriguing on the upper and lower quadrants of the guard were eight characters, meaning "Five Stars rising in the east favor the Middle Kingdom" – the middle kingdom refers then, as now, to China. The five stars might refer to the planets Venus, Jupiter, Mercury, Mars and Saturn which, on rare occasion, do all align to rise in the east.

Five interwoven layers make up the piece. The introduction of colored threads builds the images and the characters. There are 220 warps and 48 wefts in each square centimeters of the brocade. The fineness of such a weave indicates the highest standards of craftsmanship in the 2nd - 3rd centuries.

Four jacquard type looms unearthed from Laoguanshan Han Tomb at Chengdu provide a clue as to this past craftsmanship. In 2018 China's National Silk Museum adopted the Han techniques to replicate the five stars brocade. After many months of effort, the images on the ancient brocade were laid anew before the eyes of the public.

Silk travelled far from China, just as woollen fabrics journeyed from the west. They meet halfway, like the east and west winds, in the vast expanses of central Asia. Among the relics of the Silk Road in Xinjiang, the brocade is not the only well-preserved item. There are many strange and exotic scenes foreign to Chinese eyes; a centaur and a soldier on wool tapestry fabric, a fertile goddess on delicate cotton. All tell of the mixing of influences in those ancient desert kingdoms. The culture of our human world is woven from many different strands, east and west, south and north, the strange and the familiar…Lost and lonely in the desert sands are the fragments of history to remind us. All make but one whole fabric under heaven's eye.

Blue-ground Centaur Wool Fabric

Five Elements, Astronomy and Prosperity of the "Middle Kingdom"

This brocade Arm Guard is just over half a *chi* (about 1/3 meter). But with a close look at its form and structure, one can see in it the core wisdom of metaphysics and people's simple understanding of astronomy and meteorology in ancient China.

In terms of colors, this piece of brocade is embroidered with silk threads in the five colors of white, green, blue, red and yellow, which correspond to the Five Elements (*Wu Xing*) which are metal, wood, water, fire and earth. These five elements are the basic substances in which all things exist as perceived by ancient Chinese thinkers. The simple materialism of the Five Elements theory not only incorporated the millennium-old deep-rooted values and world view, but also served as an important basis and means of governing by ruling classes over generations. As an old saying goes, "Movement follows natural laws." Ancient Chinese believed that only by acting in line with "five movements" can one follow natural laws, and finally create prosperity and peace. As a result, a host of metaphors, schools of thoughts and diagrams about Five Elements emerged, influencing every aspect of societal life in ancient China. In addition to silk threads of five colors, this artifact is weaved with auspicious animals including the Phoenix, *Luanniao* (a mythical bird like the phoenix), *Qilin* (a propitious beast) and White Tiger, as well as patterns of the Sun, the Moon, rivers and mountains, which also imply *Yin* and *Yang* as well as the five elements.

Most noteworthy are the eight small characters in seal and clerical scripts running through a variety of patterns: 五星出东方利中国 (Five Stars Rising in the East Favour the Middle Kingdom). Here, "five stars" not only corresponds to the Five Elements, but also represent the development of ancient astronomy and belief in astrology and divination by rulers. According to the *Records of the Grand Historian: Astronomy*, "The five stars divide the world into two halves. When they gather in the east, it is an auspicious sign for the Middle Kingdom; when they gather in the west, it is a good sign for western foreign states. In the latter case, the Middle Kingdom should be on guard against possible war." Here, the Middle Kingdom mainly covers the "Central Plains" primarily inhabited by the Han Chinese in the Han Dynasty, different from today's China. However, the five stars rising simultaneously in the east was an extremely rare phenomenon. The Kangxi Emperor of the Qing Dynasty explicitly pointed out that the five stars ran in the sky at varying degrees and speeds and, therefore, would not be able to gather at one constellation. Though there are relevant records in history books, it is after all unreliable. This reflects that the supreme rulers of the Qing had obtained some scientific understanding of basic astronomy, and kept a rational attitude towards astrology, instead of believing in it blindly. Therefore, it can be said that it embodies the constant progress of the Chinese civilization throughout history.

Auspicious "Brocade" in Ancient Western States

Many other beautiful artifacts were uncovered in the same burial pit as this brocade Arm Guard, including pottery, iron ware, lacquer ware, bows and arrows, textiles, and synthetic beads, among which, textiles best reflect the cultural collision and integration in the exchanges between the west and east.

The textiles buried are mainly the outfits of male and female owners (e.g. robes, head cloth, brocade hats, Arm Guards, gloves, silk ornaments, brocade belts, and boots), pillows, quilts, and blankets. Particularly, the male corpse has its lower jaw closely tied with a plain silk band, its head and neck covered with silk head cloth, body tightly wrapped in a colored blanket and dressed in a right

"Five Stars Rising in the East Favour the Middle Kingdom, Put down South Qiang, Subdue the Minorities, and Bring Chanyu under Control, as Great as Heavens."

"Put down South Qiang" Brocade Relics

lapel robe. Moreover, there is a "Five Stars Rising in the East Favour the Middle Kingdom" brocade Arm Guard on its right arm, a wide colored belt on its waist and the edge of the front decorated with a 13 cm-wide joined patch of brocades embroidered with words "literary greatness", "prolonging life and blessings to off-springs", "suitable for children" and "for peace and happiness". It is worth noting that a piece of brocade buried here is exactly identical with the "Five Stars Rise in the East" brocade Arm Guard in its weaving structure, patterns and material and embroidered with three characters " 讨 南 羌 (put down South Qiang)". It is speculated that this piece of brocade might be from the same piece of fabric as the brocade Arm Guard. So the full text is supposed to be "Five Stars Rising in the East Favour the Middle Kingdom...put down South Qiang..." The words "South Qiang" first appeared in the *Book of Han: Treatise on Geography*, referring in particular to Qiang people living in the south of Qilian Mountains and along the Yellow River and Huangshui River. Thus, "put down South Qiang" expresses the earnest hope of the Middle Kingdom to pacify western areas. As with many words embroidered on brocades unearthed at the Niya ruins, it is a type of message praying for blessings.

"Literary Greatness" Brocade   "Prolonging Life and Blessings to Off-springs" Brocade

Blessings from Ancient Times

Where exactly was the eastern origin of this "silk road"? Seen from the brocades unearthed at the Niya ruins, it is supposedly originated from Shu, today's Sichuan, where the textile industry was most developed then and the best textile workers and state-of-the-art textile-making techniques gathered. One end of silk roads was closely tied to this land of brocade in southwestern China.

What was the political intent of the export of expensive Shu brocade to western regions in history? Delving into historical literature, we can find records of the Han Dynasty adopting a wide range of political strategies towards many western states to placate them at different periods to varying degrees, most common among them were war, peace-making marriage and gift. This piece of "Five Stars Rising in the East Favour the Middle Kingdom (put down South Qiang)" Shu brocade unearthed at the Niya ruins is supposed to be given by the Han imperial court as a high-end gift to the ruling class of the state of Cadota, closely related to suppressing the rebellion by South Qiang.

We can boldly speculate that the owner of this brocade Arm Guard, a man with deep eyes and a high nose, might be a prominent figure who had defended borders in many battles and took up a key position in wars aligning western and eastern states and against the South Qiang. This piece of brocade Arm Guard, a product of the silk roads connecting the east and west and tied to maintaining the peace and stability of the Central Plains and the western regions, was supposed to have accompanied its owner during times of tension and wars, and ended up silently lying beside its owner under the yellow desert for long, solitary thousands of years. Perhaps they have been waiting for the best timing when the five-starred red flag rises above the sky of China, sending out the most brilliant and warmest blessings from ancient western regions to this Oriental land.

By Peng Xiaoyun

Jade Doorknocker with Four Symbols of the Sky

The Dragon, Tiger, Bird, and Tortoise

Jade Doorknocker with Four Symbols of the Sky

Location: Maoling Museum
Age: Western Han Dynasty
Texture: jade
Size: 34.2 cm in height, 35.6 cm in width, 14.7 cm in thickness
Weight: 10.6 kg

Jade Doorknocker with Four Symbols of the Sky

Knockers were common in ancient China. But this piece of jade doorknocker preserved in the Maoling Museum is the only one of its kind. Amidst the clouds emerges the face of a mighty beast. Although the knocking ring is lost, it still maintains an air of grandeur. On its back is a bulging cuboid mortise, for attaching through the door. On the front a pair of bulging eyes radiates intensity vigor. Images of animals can be seen among clouds on upper surfaces. The honorable Dragon of honor, powerful tiger of power, bird of good fortune, and the combined turtle and snake. They as a group have a great name - the symbols of the sky.

The starlit sky fed the rich imagination of the ancients. The 28 ecliptic mansions of the Chinese constellations are evenly divided into four groups in the East, West, South and North, with one deity representing each direction. It is said 'the four symbols guard the world', defending our world from the four directions. The Azure Dragon is the symbol of the East. In the traditional Chinese concept of The Five Phases, it belongs to Wood; the White Tiger guards the West. In the Five Phases theory it belongs to Metal; the Vermilion Bird is the deity controlling the South. It belongs to Fire; the Black Tortoise is the combination of a turtle and a snake. It rules the North and belongs to Water in the Five Phases. Its color is a combination of red and black, a unique color in ancient China.

In the Han Dynasty 2,000 years ago, people believed that the heaven and the earth corresponded to each other. When

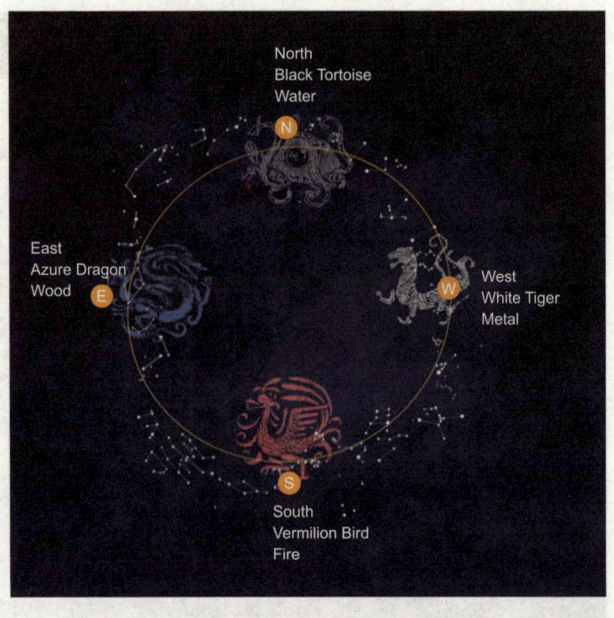

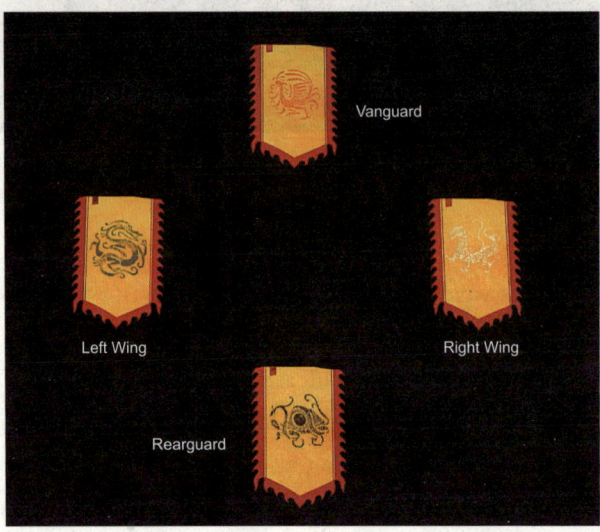

they needed to distinguish directions, they projected the four symbols from heaven to earth. During military expeditions images of the four symbols would be painted on flags. The Vermilion Bird acted as the vanguard, while the Black Tortoise was the rearguard. Left wing would have the Azure Dragon and the right wing, the White Tiger. Thus the army maintained its orientation. The Four symbols appear everywhere. They were carved on the tiles when building city walls and palaces to indicate direction.

They were painted and carved on stone monuments and funeral objects. They also appeared in more intimate settings, guarding over people's lives.

On the jade doorknocker, the positions of the four deities are interchangeable. The northern and southern deities are turning to the right at the two sides of the beast's face, as if they are flying among the clouds, and rendering the fierce visage a sense of tenderness. In the hands of the Han artists, everything becomes romantic.

In China jade is the most precious gift given by the earth. When artists carved the images of the Four Symbols, the jade becomes the connection between the earth and the heaven.

Perhaps the ancients imagined they might be knocking on heaven's door. The Four Symbols imbue a beautiful piece of jade with cosmic meaning. A beautiful piece of jade is the only worthy home for such illustrious deities, guardians of the four directions and guides to the far beyond.

Doorknocker

Animal head applique or doorknocker (*pushou*) is the base of an ancient implement or door leaf to which a ring handle or knocker is attached. They are usually named for their shapes in animal heads. An animal head applique and a knocker held in the animal mouth combined are called "Animal Head Doorknocker". Placed on an implement or utensil, it is a handle; while on a door leaf, it is both a door knob and fastener. Therefore, an animal head doorknocker is both functional and decorative. Its majestic yet ferocious animal face not only adorns, but also wards off evil spirits.

Animal head doorknockers were applied to doors as early as the Spring and Autumn and Warring States periods, and prevailed by the Han Dynasty. Particularly, as lavish funerals prevailed in the Han Dynasty, animal head doorknockers not only appeared on worldly buildings and daily utensils, but were also carried to graves and tombs to guard the dead to rest

Zun with Bull Head and Monster Face, the Shang Dynasty

Inscriptions on Guojizibai Water Vessel, the Western Zhou Dynasty

EVERY TREASURE TELLS A STORY | 154

Gilt Bronze Doorknocker from Tomb of Emperor Yang of Sui

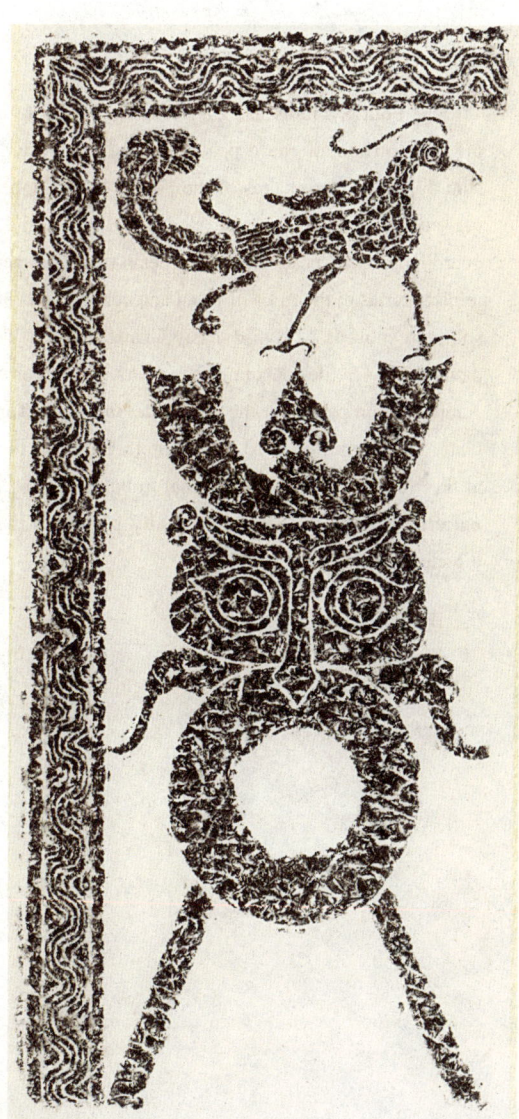

Painting of Vermilion Bird and Animal Head Doorknocker, the Han Dynasty

in peace. They were everywhere from portrait stones to tomb doors and on to funerary objects.

Doorknockers in animal head shapes originate from ancient ancestors' worship of beasts. Ferocious and strong beasts symbolize strength in human eyes. Witchcraft was valued in the Shang Dynasty. Therefore, complex patterns of animal heads appeared on bronze ritual vessels. Such patterns looked frightening and ferocious with mystic, original religious overtones. From the Western Zhou Dynasty to the Spring and Autumn and Warring States periods, the craze for ghost and god worshipping faded. However, animal head appliques passed down for its role in warding off evil spirits and bringing blessings. Its combination with the knocker or ring handle evolved into a stylized "animal head doorknockers". By the Han Dynasty, knocker holders saw enriched images in addition to heads of beasts, such as in combination with the Four Symbols (or Four Mythological Creatures), Fuxi and Nüwa among other patterns. These patterns present romantic ideas of ideal world of afterlife.

Animal head doorknockers are mostly metallic, primarily bronze. There are also golden and silver ones. Jade doorknockers first appeared in the Han Dynasty and were very rare.

Guarding Deities of Four Directions

Four Symbols, or Four Mythological Creatures, are protectors of four directions in ancient Chinese belief. They are four mythological beasts, i.e. Azure Dragon, White Tiger, Vermilion Bird and Black Turtle. They symbolize four directions, seasons and colors. They permeated into all aspects of ancient social life. Four Symbols are masters of the North, East, South and West, and deities guarding human beings.

The Four Symbols find their origin in approximately the Spring and Autumn and Warring States periods, following the theory of Twenty-Eight Mansions. The ancient people grouped these mansions into four groups: East, West, South and North, each of which assigned an animal. By the Han Dynasty, *Yin-yang* and Five Elements theories became popular. The Four Symbols were then matched with four elements, i.e., wood, metal, fire and water, four seasons and four colors, i.e. blue, white, red and black, to form a complete system of ideas. By this point, the images of Azure Dragon, White Tiger, Vermilion Bird and Black Turtle basically had taken shape.

The Four Symbols has auspicious implications as it can ward off evil spirits and guard peace. During the Western and Eastern Han dynasties, the images of the Four Symbols appeared on eaves tiles, bronze mirrors, portrait stones and bricks and tomb murals, guarding people's peace in life and death from all aspects. According to discoveries at the ruins of ritual and ceremonious buildings in the southern suburbs of Han-dynasty Chang'an City, "Four Symbols" patterned eaves tiles decorated the doors of the four walls, with the Azure Dragon pattern at the East Gate, the White Tiger at the West Gate, the Vermillion Bird at the South Gate and the Black Turtle at the North Gate. This shows that in buildings, the Four Symbols patterned eaves tiles were normally placed in their respective directions to dispel the evil.

By Wang Yusu

The Xiping Stone Classics

Broken Yet Awaiting Reunion

Xiping Stone Classics - Fragments of I *Ching*

Location: Xi'an Stele Forest Museum
Age: Eastern Han Dynasty
Texture: stone
Size: 31 cm in length, 66 cm in height

The Xiping Stone Classics

These stone fragments with worn characters have suffered the vicissitudes of time with stoic grace. They are spread in multiple different museum collections across China, but they still speak to one common purpose. Xiping Stone Classics date from the 2nd century AD and the Eastern Han Dynasty. The steles are engraved on both sides and are earliest official editions of China classic texts recorded in this way. There were 46 steles in all, with 7 of the Confucian classics inscribed on them in over 200,000 characters.

The Egyptian pharaohs inscribed their decrees on stele like the Rosetta Stone. The ancient Babylonians inscribed their laws in stone in the *Code of Hammurabi*. Imperial China chose to set in stone the Confucian classics.

Imperial Edict of Pharaoh

The Code of Hammurabi

Since the beginning of the Han Dynasty, ordinary people had been able to climb the social ladder through study. The Confucian classics had been the models for study. There was a substantial state-run education system and a large number of private schools. In the time before the invention of printing, the diffusion of classic works relied on transcription. Over time mistakes were incorporated into texts through human error. In the reign of Emperor Ling of Han, Academician Cai Yong led a group of scholars in petitioning the Emperor in having

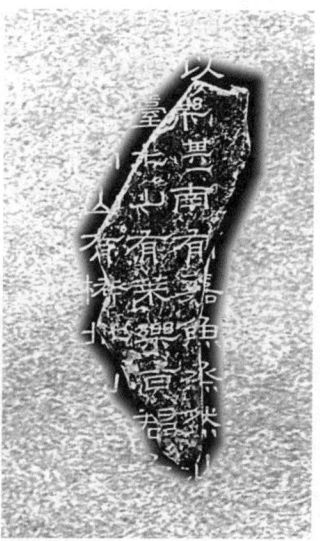

an authoritative version of the classics engraved on stone steles to be erected at the Imperial Academy near the capital. The petition caused a sensation. It meant that students and scholars could make rubbings of the steles as definite copies of the texts to take with them back to their hometowns across the empire. The classics were engraved in the official script of the time, making them masterpieces of both art and calligraphy.

However fortune is fickle, for masterpieces as for men. Two years after the steles were completed (184 A.D.), peasant rebellions began to wrack the empire. Eventually Luoyang was sacked in 191AD and the steles seriously damaged. They were repaired during the Three Kingdoms Period, yet later on they drifted from place to place. During the Southern and Northern dynasties (540

A.D.), they were transferred from Luoyang to the Eastern Wei capital at Yedou. However on route they fell into the Yellow River and when they arrived in Yedou, half were missing. During the Sui Dynasty in the late 6th century they were transferred from Yedou to the Sui capital at Chang'an, but, once there, they were merely used as plinths. In the early Tang Dynasty, when scholar statesman Wei Zheng hoped to restore the stone classics, there were scarcely any left. Since then, in the mid-7th century, there have only been seen as scattered fragments and rubbings, like a disconnected string of pearls.

The contents on this fragment are from the *I Ching, Book of Changes*. Through the centuries the Chinese language has evolved; meaning and pronunciation change but the characters remain the foundation of its civilization. China's "forebears cascade into the future, future generations recognize the past." Xiping Stone Classics pioneered the idea of authorized, government approved, editions of classic texts. Since then every dynasty had had its own official stele inscribed to announce the definitive editions of classic works. "Words set in stone" is more than just a figure of speech in Chinese culture. The steles have proved powerful tools for later generations of scholars and researchers.

The stones are cold, yet the characters still carry profound meanings. Today more than 8,000 characters from the Xiping Stone Classics have been recovered and reassembled. Character by character a culture is reborn, and a window on the past flung wide.

Millenniums of Convergence and Divergence, Inheritance of Civilization

Since its inception, the Xiping Stone Classics have carried on the classical heritage despite becoming displaced and broken over time.

In addition to those collected by Wei Zheng, numerous fragments of these stone classics were unearthed when Luoyang, the eastern capital, was built during the Tang Dynasty. According to the *Anecdotes Told by the Royal Secretary (Shangshu Gushi)*, "When stations for autumn defense purposes were built in the Eastern Capital in recent years, many stone classic inscribed by Cai Yong at the Hongdumen School were excavated. Later, pieces of these stone classics were often found in households in Luoyang."

Afterwards, the Xiping Stone Classics were gradually spread beyond the official circles, and came into the hands of common people as antiques and curios.

However, such stone classics, if shelved and neglected, would become meaningless. As a result, the "original stone classics of the Tang" mostly became lost in the dust of history except for a very few that were passed down.

During the Jiayou reign of the Northern Song Dynasty, many pieces of these stone classics were unearthed again in Luoyang and Chang'an. As noted by Fang Shao in the *Bozhai's Collection (Bozhaibian)*, "The fragments of stone classics ... in those years the gatekeepers in Luoyang reviewed the stone pieces abandoned by the Construction Bureau. They recognized these fragments and collected them. Later they made further searches and gathered tens of paragraphs from the *Book of Documents*, *The Rites* and the *Analects of Confucius*, plus one paragraph from the *Gongyang Tablet*. All those pieces uncovered in Chang'an were much fragmented."

By this time, epigraphy had emerged as a prominent discipline. Many scholar-officials were interested in compiling and writing on bronze and stone inscriptions to pay homage to antiquities of Xia, Shang and

Three-script Stone Classics

Zhou periods and to express their nostalgia for ancient times. The Xiping Stone Classics, though not from the said three dynasties, were appreciated as they were officially recognized and they truthfully and credibly recorded Confucian classics. Therefore, rubbings of original stones scattered all over places during the Sui and Tang dynasties were systematically compiled during this period.

Illustrious masters of epigraphy of the Northern Song and the Southern Song, including Ouyang Xiu, Huang Bosi, Zhao Mingcheng, Hong Shi and Chao Gongwu, all had written on the Xiping Stone Classics. For instance, the *Annotated Inscriptions in Clerical Script (Lishi)* by Hong Shi compiled the remnants of rubbings passed down from the Tang Dynasty to enable future generations to see such stone inscriptions even though they "lived on in spirit though gone in form". Zhao Mingcheng took it further by using the texts on the Xiping Stone Classics to boldly challenge errors fraught in the content of inscriptions popular back then. Zhao wrote in the *Records of Metal and Stone* (Jinshilu) that:

"When collating these ancient texts based on versions of inscriptions passed down by generations, I found that hundreds of words vary, along with varying orders of sections sometimes. If full intact versions existed, we'd work out a full list of variances. Is this not a pity?"

The solemn Chinese calligraphy in clerical script on the Xiping Stone Classics gave Zhao the confidence to challenge classic versions. Unfortunately, his outcry was not followed by a wave of amending classics like the Reformation in western Europe. Zhao's doubt was to be cast over these stone classics, leaving it future generations to answer.

After the Jiayou years of the Northern Song, there were no records on the discovery and writing of stone classics in history books, both official and unofficial. The Xiping Stone Classics disappeared out of sight ever since. "Original stone inscriptions of the Tang and elaborate rubbings of the Song" became invaluable. With a Song rubbing in his hands, one would become instantly famous nationwide.

Fast forward to the 11th year (1922) of the Republic of China period, a large number of inscribed stone tablets were unearthed in Zhugedang village 30 km east of Luoyang City. Scholars recognized that these broken pieces of stone were "Three-script Stone Classics" from the State of Wei period. Soon after, words spread that the remnants of "Xiping Stone Classics" had again come to light. This message shocked the country, pooling together a flood of men of insight.

Early visitors were mostly antique dealers who purchased these stone inscriptions from rural households. Later, as prices of these pieces soared, these dealers began to plan illegal excavations. Due to political turmoil, these stone fragments, after unearthed, were largely scattered and fell into the hands of collectors. Only a small few survived while most went missing.

Fortunately, these stone inscriptions reemerged at just the right time. In late Qing Dynasty and the Republic of China periods, epigraphy regained its prominence. Unlike "recollection and admiration of the antiquities of the early Three Dynasties" by Song-dynasty Confucians, men of insights of the Qianlong and Jiaqing schools of textual research used epigraphy materials to distinguish truth from falsehood and interpreted Confucian classics on an empirical basis. This time produced a galaxy of unprecedented scholars of great learning, including Qian Daxin, Wang Niansun, Wu Dacheng, and Yu Yue. After these stone inscriptions reappeared, they immediately drew great attention from epigraphers. Scholars kept searching for and collecting all fragments that could be seen back then. They repeatedly circulated and rubbed these inscriptions, and compiled them in writing. For example, Luo Zhenyu compiled the *Collection of Fragmented Xiping Stone Inscriptions of the Han Dynasty* for nine times, followed by a succession of additions, supplements and aggregation. Ma Heng devoted his lifetime to sorting, checking, correcting and compiling the rubbings of Han stone inscriptions collected into documented literature for future generations to read. Finally, Ma finished his masterpiece *Collected Inventory of Stone Inscriptions from the Han Dynasty (Han Shijing Jicun)*. In such turbulent times, these great scholars held on to the quintessence of Chinese culture against all odds. Facing these stone classics, Ma Heng once excitedly wrote:

"Various versions of the *Xiping Stone Classics* compiled by Song scholars were up to 1,700 or more characters in length ...

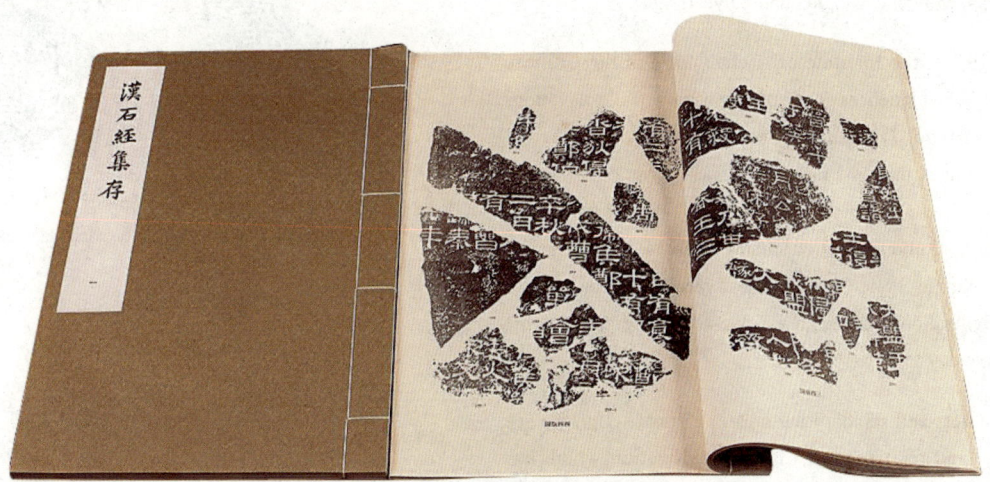

Collected Inventory of Stone Inscriptions from the Han Dynasty

Surprisingly eight centuries later, we were able to see another hundreds of characters. Our generation is indeed luckier than Song scholars to be treated with such a feast for the eyes."

In addition to the great joy that jumps out of the pages, we can also relate to the utter innocence of scholars of old times to wholeheartedly preserve our cultural heritage.

With the introduction of Western sciences, scholars began to adopt a philological approach to studying the Xiping Stone Classics. A comparison between the content of inscriptions and literature passed down revealed contradictions. Perhaps it was due to the fact that pre-Qin classics were mostly written on bamboo and wood scrolls. When the sequence of the slips is incorrect, mismatches may occur. However, Chinese Confucian scholars respected what they were taught and stuck to existing pieces of writing, not daring to make modifications. Thus, mistakes were left uncorrected for centuries. This is the answer to the question posed by Zhao Mingcheng eight hundred years ago.

In the 1970s, the Institute of Archaeology in the Chinese Academy of Social Sciences conducted archaeological excavations in Taixue Village, Dianzhuang Town, Yanshi City, Henan Province, and unearthed 661 pieces of stone inscriptions from the Han Dynasty. These fragments were properly placed in museums and research institutions. Related studies emerged, breathing new life into the Xiping Stone Classics. These pieces of stone classics on which civilization is carried, we believe, will eventually come together some day.

In these neat and standard writings in clerical script, we see the tenacity and resilience of Chinese civilization which has withstood time and gone on continually.

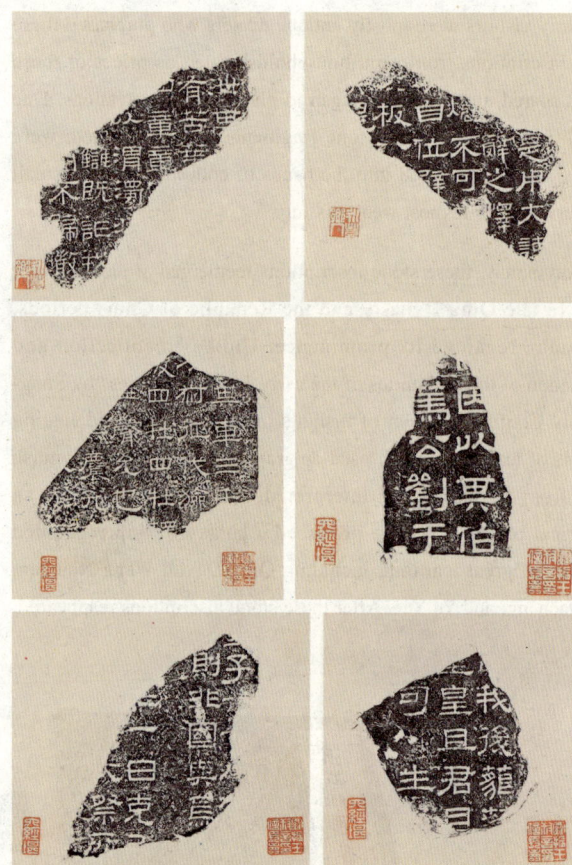

Collection of Fragmented Xiping Stone Inscriptions of the Han Dynasty by Luo Zhenyu

The Chinese civilization will endure just as these stone tablets will not perish.

By Li Kai

Stone Carving of Confucius Meeting Laozi

Tracing Back the Roots

Stone Carving of Confucius Meeting Laozi

Location: Shandong Museum
Age: Eastern Han Dynasty
Texture: stone
Size: 48 cm in height, 111 cm in width, 21 cm in thickness

This Han Dynasty stone relief carving depicts one of the fondest myths of Chinese culture: the meeting between the historical personage of Confucius, and Laozi, the legendary author of the *Tao Te Ching*.

The figure with a wild goose is Confucius. The wild goose is a gift presented to Laozi by Confucius. The figure facing Confucius with his hand resting on a stick is Laozi. "Confucius meeting Laozi" is a common theme in the Han-dynasty carvings. It a type of artwork often used in burial chambers, tombs and coffins during the Han Dynasty. It expresses the way the Han Dynasty sought to integrate differing schools of Chinese philosophy.

When the meeting took place, neither Confucianism nor Daoism, would have existed. It is modeled instead of the visit of a filial junior to a respected senior. In the *Records of the Grand Historian*, Sima Qian makes a detailed description of one of their conversations. Confucius went to Luoyang to ask Laozi about the study of rituals. Laozi said: "As for the ritual you mentioned, the bones of the people who invented it have decayed, and only their remarks remain. A gentleman will make contributions when fortune comes, and if his life is unfortunate, he will drag out an ignoble existence like a grass. Remove your arrogance and excessive desires. Remove the glowing look and expression from your face and untouchable ambitions. These are things that have no benefit for body or mind." After Confucius returned home, he didn't speak for three days. Then he said to his disciples: "The meeting with Laozi was far beyond my imagination. He is like an unpredictable dragon. No one can perceive him completely."

Laozi

Confucius

Stone Relief at the Wu's Tombs Museum

Architecture and Humans, the Eastern Han Dynasty

After Emperor Wu of Han banished the hundred schools of thought in favor of Confucianism, there was still a move to incorporate other schools of philosophy, including those of *Yin-yang* and Five Elements theories. This work mirrors that the exchange and fusion between two thoughts. The Han sought to encapsulate this

Stone Carving of Confucius Meeting Laozi

syncretic inclusivism in stone for time immemorial.

"Gentlemen seek harmony but not uniformity."

"It is such a delight to have friends coming from afar."

"Everything comes from being and being comes from not-being."

"Good fortune follows upon disaster; disaster lurks within good fortune."

From 600 BC to 300 BC, the so-called Axial age, ancient Greece, ancient India, and China all produced great thinkers. The wisdom of Socrates, Plato, Sakyamuni, Confucius, Laozi has influenced human civilization down to this day. Confucius and Laozi are the fonts Confucianism and Daoism. Their philosophies are like two rivers which meet the blood of the Chinese people. It is often observed that they are Confucian in public life and Daoist in their inner hearts. It is a judgment that each can only make for themselves.

Confucius Meeting Laozi—Virtues of Saints Carved on the Stone

Confucius was the founder of Confucianism and Laozi was the originator of the Taoism. The meeting between the two great thinkers was recorded and engraved on the stones, leaving influence on later generations for centuries. The etiquette of showing respect to the senior and the worthy, the atmosphere of learning from each other, and the admiration of the Han people for Confucianism were integrated in this stone carving.

The stone carving is divided into upper and lower parts. The upper part shows the meeting of the two eminent masters, bowing to each other on the right of the stone carving. According to the caption, the person on the left is Confucius and the other is Laozi. The child between them, pulling a cart with one hand and pointing to Confucius with the other hand, is believed to be Xiang Tuo, a prodigy. As for the two people talking to each other behind Confucius, the left one wearing a rooster-like hat is probably Zi Lu, one of Confucius's disciples. There are eight people on the left. A shorter one who wears a sword leads the other seven standing in line, all facing rightward to someone showing a warm welcome. A caption shown above the short character is recognized by some scholars as "Yan Zi". The lower part of the drawing shows a scene of war between two cavalries firing arrows.

Among all Han-dynasty stone carvings, about 30 of them present

this historical meeting, and most of them were found in Shandong, Jiangsu and Shaanxi, although some were discovered in Henan and Sichuan. Shandong boasts a large part of them, probably because it is the origin of Confucianism. Although element arrangement of these stone carvings varies due to different stone textures, carving techniques, aesthetic tastes, and so on, the characters and their portraits are basically the same: with a swan goose in his hand or sleeve, Confucius bows to Laozi, who welcomes him and bows back. Xiang Tuo stands between the two, facing Confucius, pushing a wheelbarrow with one hand and pointing at Confucius with the other. The goose is a gift, which reflects the rites of Zhou. Xiang Tuo is depicted because of a well-known story. It is said that Xiang Tuo was a prodigy of Lu State in the Spring and Autumn period. He asked Confucius three questions and the latter failed to give correct answers, so he respected Xiang Tuo as his teacher. As to the wheelbarrow, researches indicate that it must be a reed-packed cart,

a toy for kids. The artist portrayed it to indicate Xiang Tuo's age; and by pointing at Confucius, he may be asking those challenging questions. Confucius respected Xiang Tuo as his teacher despite his young age (he was only seven years old), so the artist portrayed Xiang Tuo and Laozi on the same side to receive Confucius's greetings, demonstrating Confucius' modesty and humility.

A historical event, the meeting between Confucius and Laozi was recorded in many literatures. Portraying this event in stone, people helped spread the virtue of showing respect to the senior and the worthy, and the spirit of learning from each other encouraged in Confucianism, which is represented by Confucius. The two sages bowing to each other and offering swan goose as a gift well reflects traditional Chinese etiquette, while Confucius seeking advice from Laozi and Xiang Tuo represents the spirit of humility and eagerness to learn advocated by Confucianism. It is worth mentioning that,

in addition to Laozi and Xiang Tuo, Yan Zi portrayed on this stone carving was also a teacher of Confucius. According to *The Spring and Autumn Annals of Master Yan*, Confucius once said to Yan Zi: "I heard that the decent treat the less talented as their friends and those better than them as a teacher. Now I have said some thoughtless words about you, and you criticized me. So you are my teacher." Confucius visiting Laozi, being challenged by Xiang Tuo, and apologizing to Yan Zi were events took place at different times. The artist, however, combined them in the same scene to highlight Confucius's eagerness to learn.

These pictorial stones are a historical testimony of the exchange and complementarity between the Confucianism and Taoism. While advocating different ideas, they do not reject the other. On the contrary, they exchanged and somehow blended to deliver shared values believed by people of the Han Dynasty. At the early stage of the Western Han Dynasty, the rulers followed the Taoist philosophy of "good governance without interferences"; and by the time when Emperor Wu of Han accepted Dong Zhongshu's suggestion and adopted Confucianism alone while suppressing others, the Confucianism actually had evolved to a new form that incorporated many Taoist theories, such as *Yin-yang* and the Five Elements. Some Taoist ideas, such as immortality or eternal life in the afterworld remained influential among common folks and were absorbed as integral parts of social ethics, forming an indigenous Taoist belief. The exchange between Confucianism and Taoism is an important stage in the development of Chinese culture, and such exchange began from the meeting between Confucius and Laozi.

By Wang Yusu

Changxin Palace Lamp

A Light from the Han Dynasty

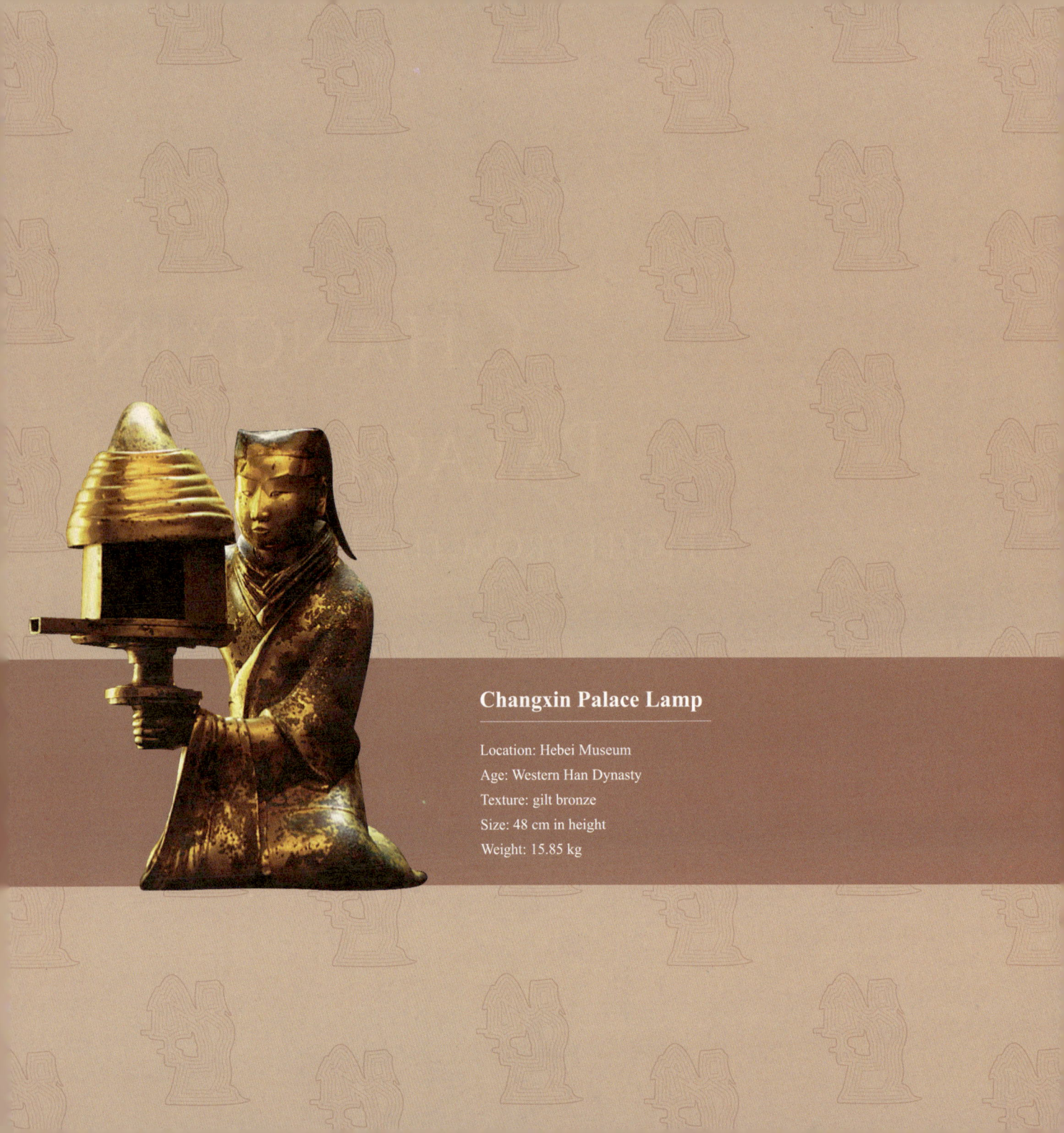

Changxin Palace Lamp

Location: Hebei Museum
Age: Western Han Dynasty
Texture: gilt bronze
Size: 48 cm in height
Weight: 15.85 kg

It's an object of sublime beauty, practicality and a visual pun. This palace maid from the Western Han Dynasty, kneeling barefoot on the ground while holding a lamp, is in fact a lamp holder. For over 2,000 years, she has carried her burden without flinching and today she still illuminates our knowledge of the Western Han Dynasty. While she holds up the lamp with her arms to provide light, like the good maid she is, the rest of her tidies up. The clever design means that smoke and residues from the candle flame are collected inside the body.

Deer Lamp, the Han Dynasty

Gilt Bronze Sheep Lamp, the Han Dynasty

Bronze Bull Lamp Inlaid with Silver, the Han Dynasty

In 1968, on the Lingshan Mountain west to Mancheng County, Hebei Province, two Han tombs were successively found. Dou Wan is the grandniece of the empress of Emperor Wen of Han.

When the bronzes scattered in the tomb were collected and reassembled, the maid's tranquil visage emerged from the dirt. Inscriptions on both the inside and outside of the lamp describe its history. According to the inscription, it was a bathroom lamp in the Changxin

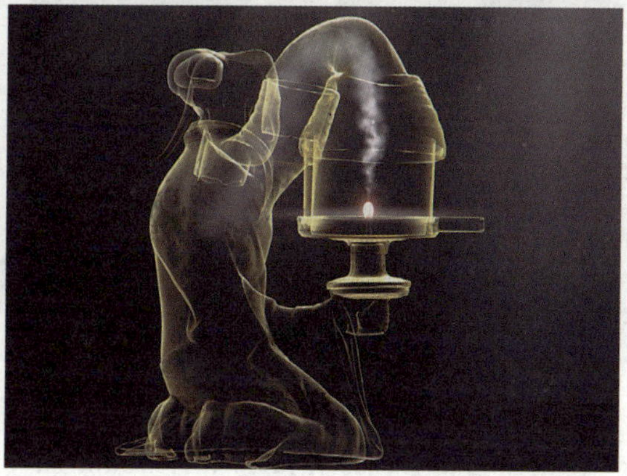

Palace; hence it's name, the 'Changxin Palace Lamp". These bronze lamps lit the chambers of the wealthy and privileged in the second century BC. Among all the various designs, the cylinderlamps are the most intriguing. They usually took the form of animals or other everyday objects. Changxin Palace Lamp is unique in being shaped in human form.

Even without its practical value it would be an object of great beauty. The maid's left hand supports the base of the lamp, while her broad sleeve hangs over the top to make a natural vent to draw away the smoke. There are two sliding panels with a handle on the side of the lamp's tray which allow both the amount and the direction of light emitted to be adjusted.

During Western Han Dynasty, lamp fuel would have been made from rendered animal fats, which often had a pungent odor. The hollow cavity of the maid's body would act as a trap for any noxious emissions from the flame. When the lamp is lit, the heat would draw the air up the sleeve and into the body. The smoky residues would stick to the lamps inner surface. The chamber in which the lamp burned would remain smoke free and fragrant. The components can be dismantled and the base opened up, for ease of cleaning. The practical functions important to the user were wittily incorporated into a delicate and extraordinary creation. It's an insight into the craft and ingenuity of those early empire artisans. A lamp from two millennia past, lights up our imagination. The Changxin Palace Lamp connects us with the genius of the past.

CHANGXIN PALACE LAMP

Unique Han Dynasty Lamps

Modern science and civilization have made it possible for us to enjoy nights ablaze with electric lights. It is thus difficult to imagine the unpredictable, dire circumstances surrounding the nightlife of the ancients who lived in the wilderness. Our smart ancestors finally acquired the expertise of making fire by drilling wood, and used it for cooking, defense, and lighting, offering later generations the possibility of brightness.

It was a long time before the lamp—a lighting tool—was invented. Data now available indicate that the earliest lamps in China appeared in the Spring and Autumn period.

Most ancient lamps were made of pottery or bronze, and a few were made from iron or stone. In the Western Han and Eastern Han dynasties, bronze lamps prevailed and were widely used— especially by the royal family and the nobility. Han-dynasty bronze lamps come in various styles. Some, with the shape of traditional vessels, resemble a plate, a *dou* or a tripod; but those that resemble animals are truly fantastic works of art. The gold-gilded goat lamp (Fig. 1) in the Xi'an Museum is shaped like a robust squatting male goat with spirally-curled horns and a straight neck. Standing on the lamp panel, it is a serene, dignified sculpture ornament. If you lift the back, you can turn on the lamp on the head for lighting purposes. Figure-shaped lamps were rare at the time. The "Changxin Palace Lamp" is perhaps the only discovery. The design of Han-dynasty lamps is evidently more scientific and complicated than that of previous ones. The "oil lamp" embodies the cutting-edge technology of the time. The "Changxin Palace Lamp" is an outstanding "oil lamp" in the Western Han Dynasty. The unique figure-like shape represents the highest bronze-lamp and artistic standards of the time; it is also one precious artifact the civilization of the Western Han and Eastern Han dynasties left to later generations.

The Designer's Innovation

What is an "oil lamp"? It is a lamp with a cylindrical container. It consists of a lamp panel, a lampshade, a smoke pipe and a holder. This design was common in the Han Dynasty. Some of them resemble ancient bronze tripods. For example, the bronze lamp engraved with a dragon of the Western Han Dynasty at the Yangzhou Museum and the tripod-shaped single-cylinder oil lamp unearthed from the Mancheng Han Tomb both have a tripod-shaped holder and a tray with a handle on the tripod. On the tray are two rotating lamp slices. The upper part of the lamp cover is connected with a single cylinder or a pair of cylinder, and the other end of the cylinder is connected to the holder at the bottom. Animal-shaped Han-dynasty oil lamps with the same structure are even more exquisite. The

Gilt Bronze Sheep Lamp, the Han Dynasty

Piped Bronze Lamp with Dragon Pattern, the Western Han Dynasty

Single-piped Tripodal Bronze Lamp with a Shutter, the Western Han Dynasty

Bronze Bull Lamp Inlaid with Silver, the Eastern Han Dynasty

Waterfowl-fish Oil Lamp

"silver-gilded bronze cow oil lamp" at the Nanjing Museum and the "waterfowl-fish oil lamp" unearthed from the Western Han Dynasty Tomb in Pingshuo, Shanxi are typical representatives.

In contrast, a natural style has been adopted in the design of the Changxin Palace Lamp. The oil lamp container resembles the sleeves of palace ladies. What we see is a lamp-carrying feminine figure without any unnecessary ornaments. Therefore, the woman is not only a palace lady who lights the oil lamp, but also an indispensable part of the Palace Lamp being admired when she is seen simply as an artifact. As a behavior, "holding the lamp" has acquired more features and beauty.

Shimmer in the Tomb

Lamps buried in tombs say a lot about the man or woman who was laid to rest. Most of them have accompanied the buried man or woman for a long time, giving light in one corner of the guest room, bedroom, study, or bathroom in each dark night. They were considered favorites by their masters. The "Changxin Palace Lamp" served in Empress Dowager Dou's bathroom in the Changxin Palace. It was unearthed from the tomb of Dou Wan, the wife of Liu Sheng, Prince Jing of Zhongshan, who was the grandson of Empress Dowager Dou. She might have had an intimate relationship with Empress Dowager Dou. Perhaps Empress Dowager Dou bestowed this personal item of hers upon Dou Wan in token of her joy and blessings upon the wedding of the couple. This precious gift became a life-time companion of Dou Wan, and illuminated her path to another world after her death. In addition to the utility and aesthetic value of an ordinary light, the Changxin Palace Lamp, therefore, reflects the close kinship and contacts between the royal family and the aristocrats at the time.

Lamps were buried in the tomb not only because the tomb owner, before his death, had been very fond of them, but also because they could illuminate the tomb chamber. After the tomb chamber was covered over with earth, the entire burial mound was plunged into infinite coldness and darkness, as well as the desolation and horror that came with death. Lamps that could bring light and warmth were believed to illuminate the comfortable life of the dead in another world.

By Peng Xiaoyun

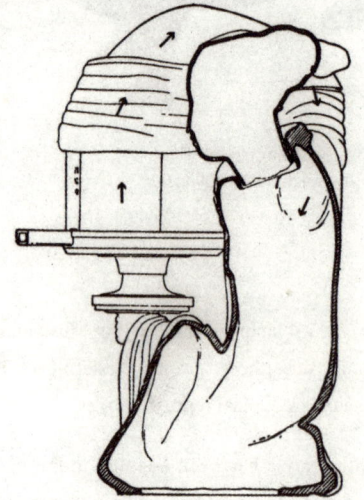

Plain Unlined Gauze Gown

Luxury and Grace

Plain Unlined Gauze Gown

Location: Hunan Museum
Age: Western Han Dynasty
Texture: silk
Size: 128 cm in length, 190 cm in width
Weight: 49 g

Plain Unlined Gauze Gown

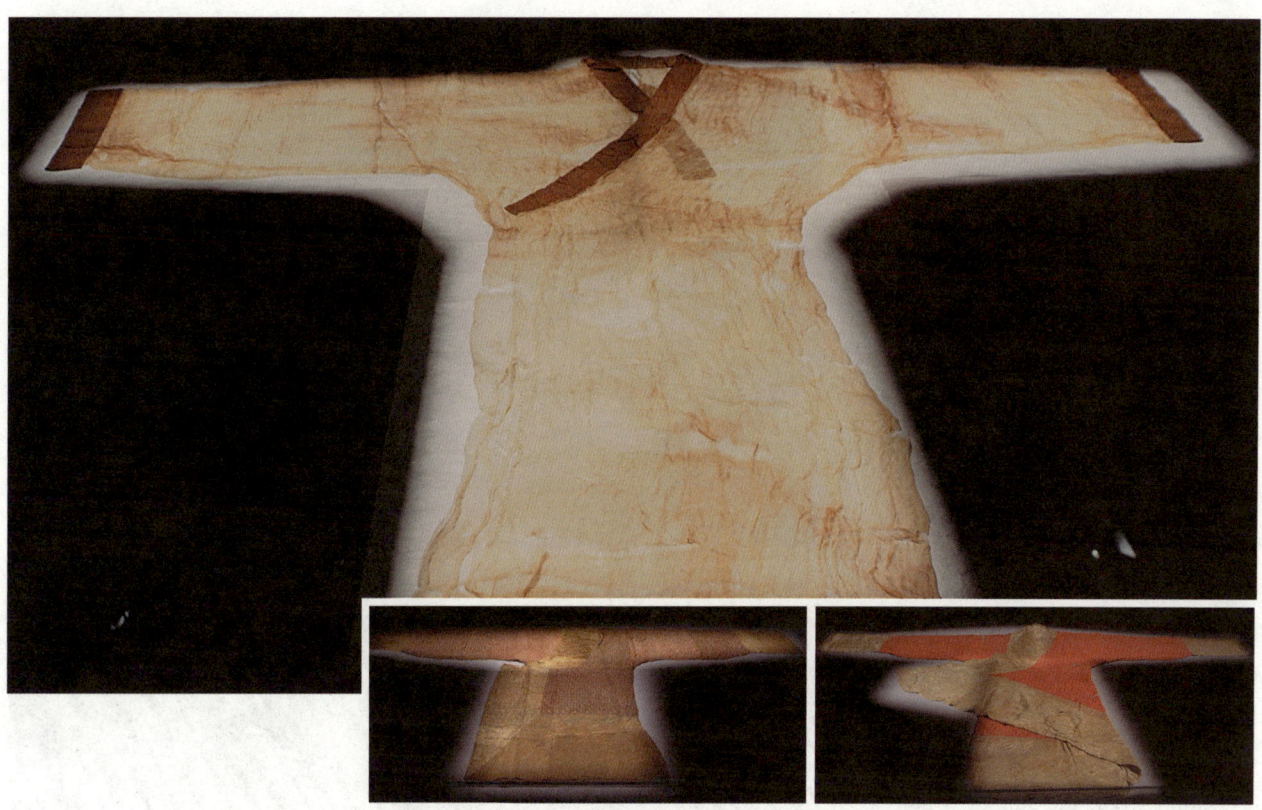

Printed and Painted Silk Padded Gauze Robe

Silk Padded Gown with Lozenge Pattern

In 186 BC, Xin Zhui, widow of the Marquis of Dai, breathed her last. Her husband was the chancellor of the imperial fiefdom of Changsha under the Western Han Dynasty. As such Xin enjoyed a life of extreme luxury. Many of her treasures, she took with her into the afterlife. Among her clothes, this piece was her favorite. It is unlined, soft and light. Worn over other garments it would add an air of elegance and mystery as the colors and patterns below were partially revealed. This is plain unlined gauze gown.

The plain unlined gauze gown from two thousand years could seem to be a forerunner of many contemporary fashion styles.

"Overlapping collar, square shoulders, wide sleeves, and a straight body. It is not tight fitting; there is a gap between the clothes and the human body, which allows the air to circulate" said Li Wei, a professor of Tsinghua University.

Xin Zhui's tomb was packed with over one thousand artifacts to help her in the afterlife. In clothing terms it is like a Han-dynasty fashion show. Hundreds of pieces of silk were recovered between 1972 and 1974, the star of which is the plain unlined gauze gown. After 2,000 years the delicate silk has become very fragile. Today we can only study its original appearance by making replicas.

This garment is 1.28 meters long. The distance from cuff to cuff

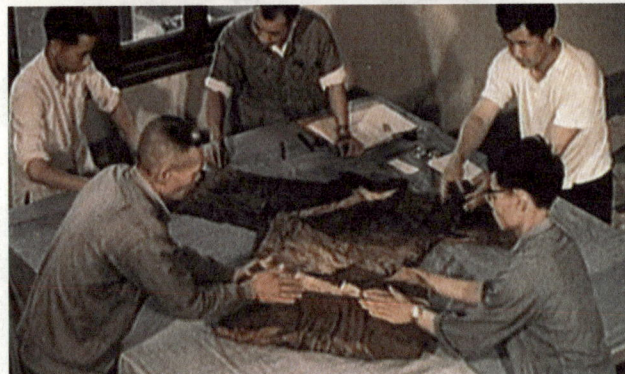

is 1.9 meters. Despite the beautifully designed collar, cuffs and lappet, the whole piece only weighs 49 grams. The Nanjing Yunjin Brocade Research Institute is attempting a second replica. The first was heavier than the original. 9,000 meters of this type of silk thread weighs one gram. This means that the original garment weighs just 11.2 grams. Today even the finest silk can only achieve a denier of 14. This

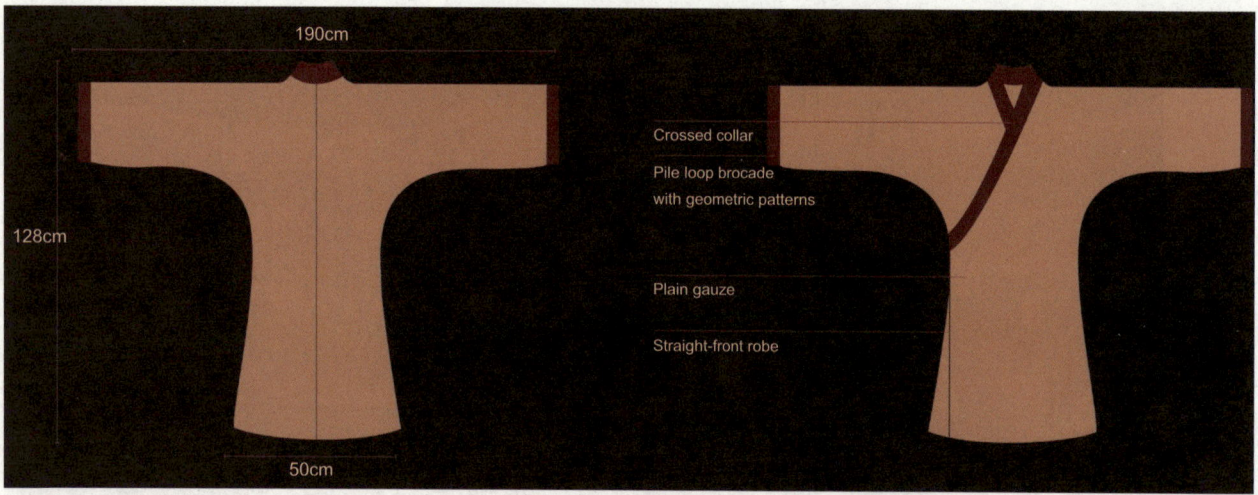

is because today's silkworms have been bred to be stronger, producing thicker threads. Sadly, no matter how much they work out, today's silkworms can never revert to the trim of their ancestors. To the Ancient Greeks and Romans "Serica" was the land at the eastern most extent of the known world. The name means the land where silk comes from. Silk was not just a commodity for trade; it helped define the character of a nation.

Everyone may find yourself through clothes. With the overlapping lapels and the wide, straight body, the gown looks graceful yet casual. It would allow free movement for activities like dancing.

"The gauze gown gives freedom to the human body. People feel at ease. They feel calm and confident.

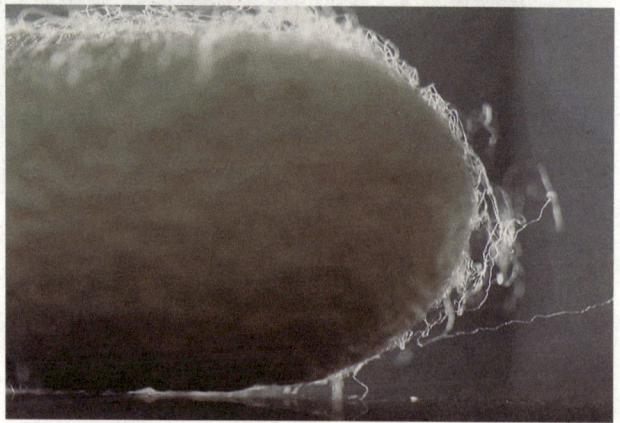

I believe this is freedom." said Li Wei, professor of Tsinghua University

China is a state of ancient refinement and culture. The Plain Unlined Gauze Gown belongs to that ancient time; yet it still influences people today. It is an archetype of Chinese design style. In its sense of freedom and romance, it expresses the way Chinese people dream of living.

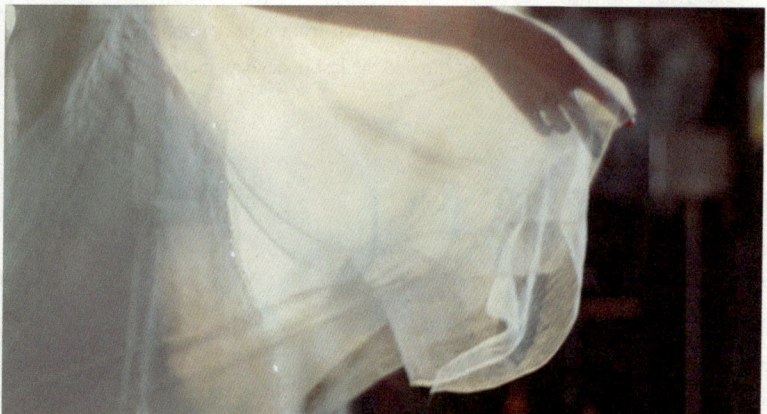

Lady Dai's Fancy Garment and Cosmetic Set

One day in 169 BC, Lady Dai (Xin Zhui), the 50-year-old wife of Li Cang, the first marquis of Dai and Chancellor of the Kingdom of Changsha during the early Han Dynasty, was enjoying the fresh honeydew melon on the table. At that time, she was suffering severe coronary heart disease and gallstone due to her very good living conditions and sedentary lifestyle. She suffered from acute biliary colic after having unconsciously swallowed the last honeydew melon seed, which caused her sudden death from acute myocardial ischemia.

Lady Dai was buried in a ceremonious way after her death. Her body was completely and elegantly preserved in the central coffin in the tomb, which was covered by successive layers of sealed soil, rammed soil and white paste. Her skin was still kept soft and elastic even when her corpse was excavated after more than 2,000 years.

Line Drawing of Lady Dai in the T-shaped Silk Painting from Mawangdui Han Tomb No. 1

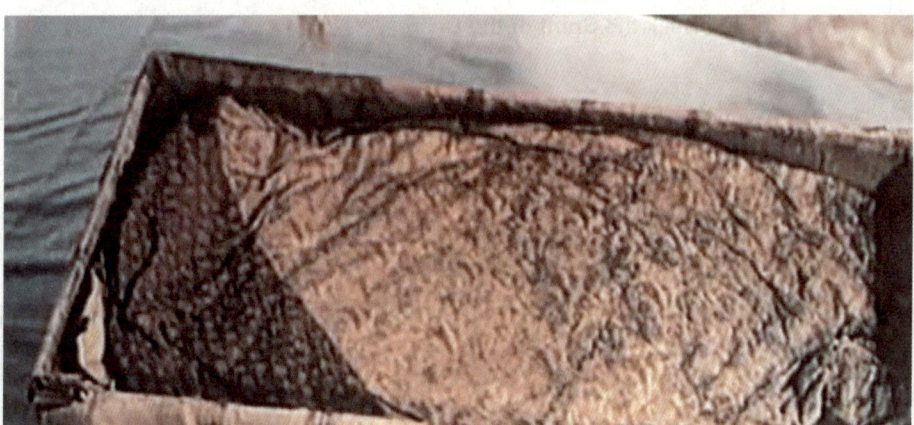

Around the wooden coffin were buried many different articles, such as lacquer ware, bamboo slips, potteries, wooden tomb figures and clothes. Amongst these funerary objects, the silk fabrics are known for their fine craftsmanship, which are made of different materials, including gauze, tough silk, brocade, faille, embroidery, damask, and linen.

According to uses, these silk fabrics consist of: apparel and accessories (e.g., unlined clothes, gown, overskirt, socks, silk shoe, glove, perfumed medicine bag and silk hat); bedding (e.g., pillow and pillow towel); and some special accessories (e.g., the black silk wigs twined with the real hairs on Lady Dai's head). From the standing image of Lady Dai in the tomb's silk painting and the restored portrait, we can imagine that Lady Dai, with her prominent social status, must have been a middle-aged woman with a soft and round face and petite figure. She cared about her clothing and appearance, and could always wear enviable fancy clothes as a result of her husband's pampering and wealth. In case of any important occasion, she would wear long robe with elaborate patterns, thin unlined clothes, and double-pointed square shoes made of blue silk. In her waist, special pearls and a perfumed medicine bag were hanged. Her thick and beautiful hair was twisted with black silk wigs into a bun and inserted with a few hairpins giving her an elegant and dignified appearance. While this embroidered brocade represents the highest standard of weaving industry in the south of Yangtze River during the Western Han Dynasty, the plain unlined gauze gown is recognized as a rare treasure that is hardly possible to be reproduced.

Plain Gown to Call Back the Spirit of the Dead

The two plain unlined gazed gowns unearthed from Mawangdui Han Tomb are called "rare treasures", as they are so thin and light that they cannot even be readily reproduced with modern silk reeling process. It cannot be overstated that the gown is "as thin as cicada's wings and as light as clouds". It was not until 1990 that Hunan Museum worked with Nanjing Yunjin Brocade Research Institute to spend 13 years in reproducing a plain unlined gauze gown, which weighs 49.5g, although it is still 0.5g heavier than the original one. The original plain unlined gauze gown has, therefore, become the genuine "thinnest and lightest clothes in the world".

So how was the tight and narrow *quju* (a skirt in a different shape) worn? It was commonly believed that *quju* was worn outside the bright-colored, brocaded robe, making the clothing look hazy and be full of layers. However, some have argued that the plain unlined gauze gown was too small to feel comfortable if it was worn outside the loose robe. In addition to being used as the clothing of daily use, it might also be used as the ghost suit for funeral to call back the spirit of the dead in the ceremony of offering sacrifices to the ghosts.

During the Qin and Han dynasties, the soul was believed to be the spirit of a person. When a person died, his soul would be separated from his physical body and linger about in the vicinity. A ceremony of calling back the spirit of the dead was held at that time, hoping to bring back to life the person who had just died. This was called the "Ceremony

Light Yellow Silk Surface Cotton Gown with Bird and Flower Embroidery from Mashan Tomb No. 1

Plain Unlined Gauze Gown | 195

Light Yellow Silk Surface Cotton Gown with Bird and Flower Embroidery, Restored Image

of Rebirth". According to the *Book of Rites*, when a woman died, a ceremony of rebirth would be held for her. However, special "Clothes for Rebirth", most of which were the clothes which she had worn before her death, would be used, rather than the formal dress she had worn in her marriage. Prior to the ceremony, all those present were required to wail and mourn the body of the dead woman. At the ceremony, the person presiding over the funeral ceremony would hold the clothes to the living place of the dead woman or the place she often visited in her lifetime to call back her spirit. During the whole process, however, the person could only call the courtesy name of the dead woman rather her given name. It remains unknown whether the two plain unlined gauze gowns discovered in Lady Dai's tomb were used as the clothes she had worn before her death, or were specially made for her funeral ceremony. One thing, however is certain: the family of Lady Dai buried the exquisitely-made gowns in her tomb to express their deep love and respect to her.

By Peng Xiaoyun

The Twenty-Eight Mansions Cosmic Plates and Sundial

Cycles of Time

The Twenty-Eight Mansions Cosmic Plates and Sundial

Location: Fuyang City Museum
Age: Western Han Dynasty
Texture: wooden lacquerware

The Twenty-Eight Mansions Cosmic Plates and Sundial

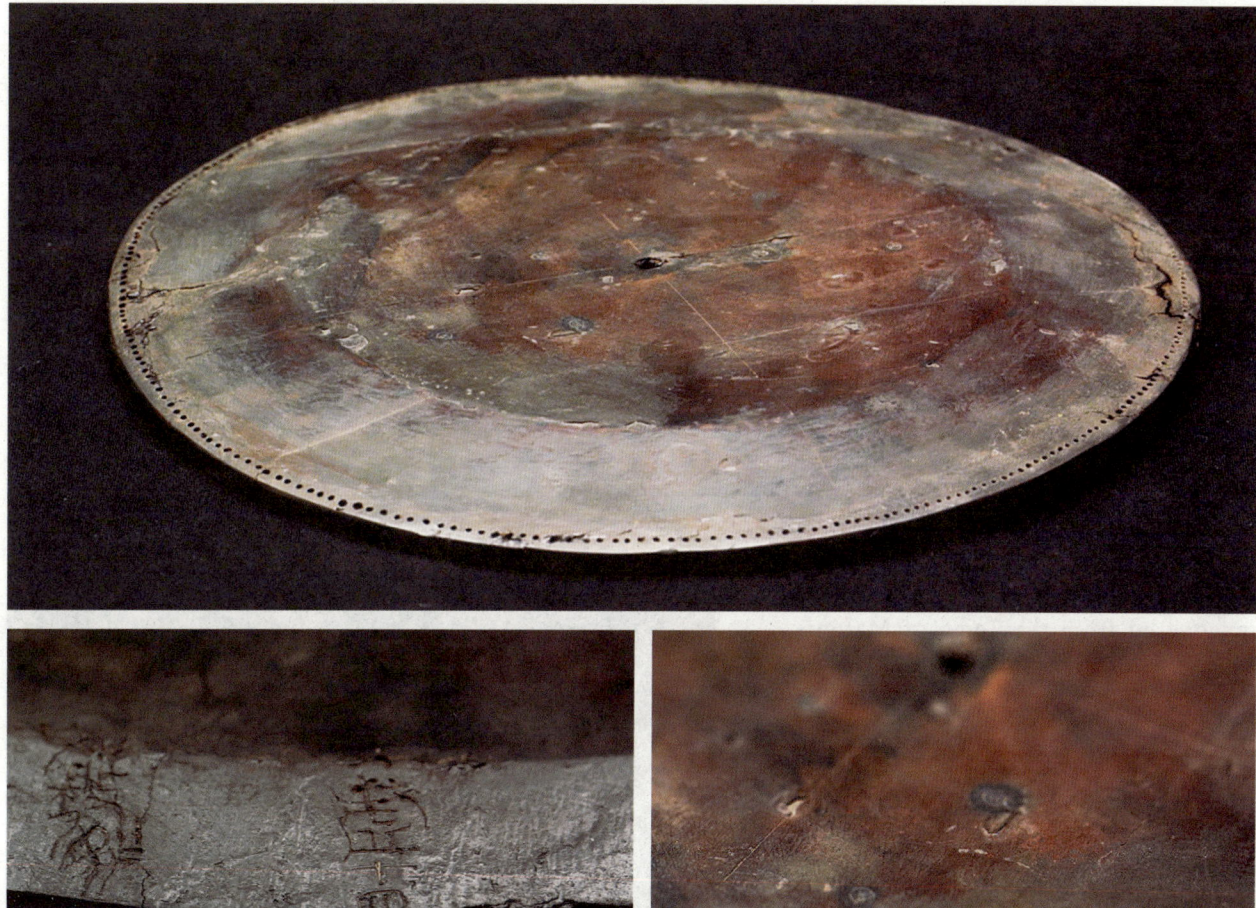

By the beginning of the first millennium BCE Chinese astronomers had divided the heavens in to twenty-eight mansions. Along the edge of this lacquer plate are carved the names of the mansions and measurements of distance.

Another plate has the Big Dipper marked on it. There are 365 small holes around the rim. There are concentric holes in the center of each plate.

"We made a copy of the lacquer plate set discovered from the Tomb of Marquis Ruyin. They are used overlapping. There should be a needle in the middle. How do you use it to observe the stars? The key is another object discovered from the same tomb. It looks like a box. And it forms a structure like this. The plate is set in this position. If it's not steady we can tie it with string." Prof. Shi Yunli of University of Science and Technology of China showed us how to use the lacquer plate set.

The angle of the plate is preset for use in Fuyang. The plate is parallel to the

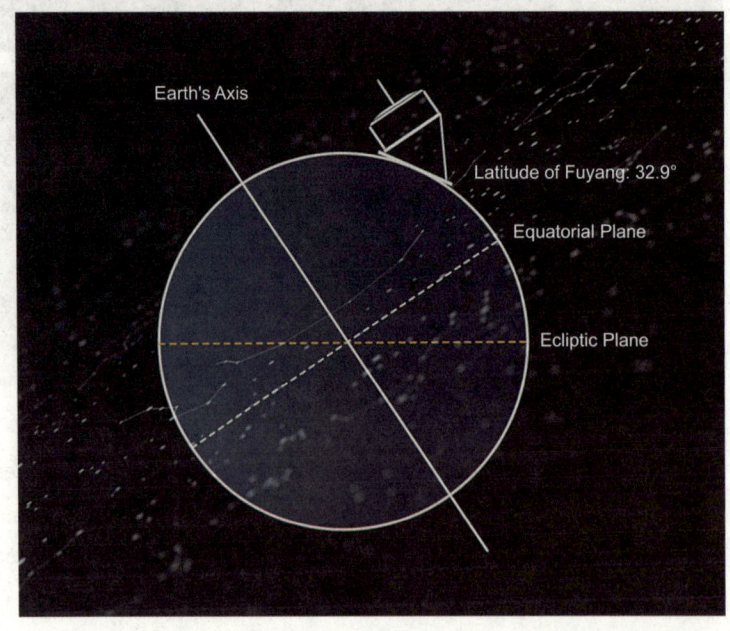

equatorial plane. The needle is pointed to the north star and the angle between it and the ground plane is set to the local latitude. The twenty-eight mansions are coordinates in the sky, divided unevenly around a circle marked into 365 degrees. It measures the position of celestial bodies in relation to the earth's equator along with the positions of the sun, moon and the five planets.

"We made a working model of the device using modern methods. We put a needle in the hole corresponding to the position of pointer from Star A. We put another needle on the extended point of Star B. Counting the holes between the two needles, we can measure the distance between the stars. Observation like this was very important for the calculation of the ancient Chinese calendar." said a narrator of Anhui Museum.

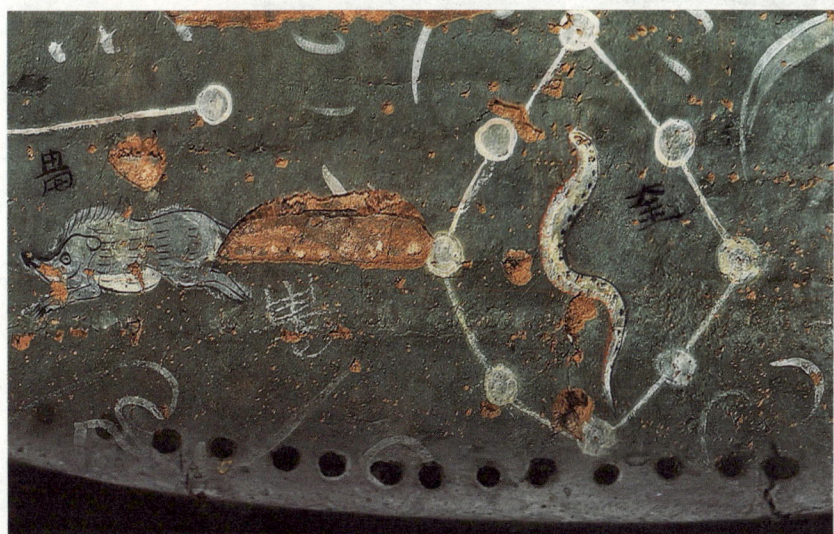

Astronomical Chart from Qushuhao Han Tomb, the Eastern Han Dynasty

Day after day, year after year, Chinese astronomers took careful note of the changing heavens. This was important for calculating the calendar but also for divination – what messages heaven had for those on earth.

"This is another lacquer item discovered in the Tomb of the Marquis of Ruyin. We open the box and erect the inner leaves. Then by placing this small rod between them, we can measure the four most important solar

Sundial 2018

Sundial 1977

Astronomical Chart from Qushuhao Han Tomb, the Eastern Han Dynasty

terms." said the narrator of Anhui Museum.

On Summer Solstice, the Solar Elevation Angle is highest in the northern hemisphere. The shadow is shortest and the hours of daylight at their longest. On the Spring Center and the Autumn Center, there are equal hours of day and night: the equinoxes. On the Winter Solstice, the shadow is longest and the day time is at its shortest. When the Summer Solstice comes round again, the sun has been through a full solar year. The lunar cycle is twenty nine and a half days, with 7 extra leap months in every 19 years.

Based on astronomy and the observation of weather and nature, the Han Dynasty divided the year into 24 solar terms and 72 climates. In spring, we plant; in summer,

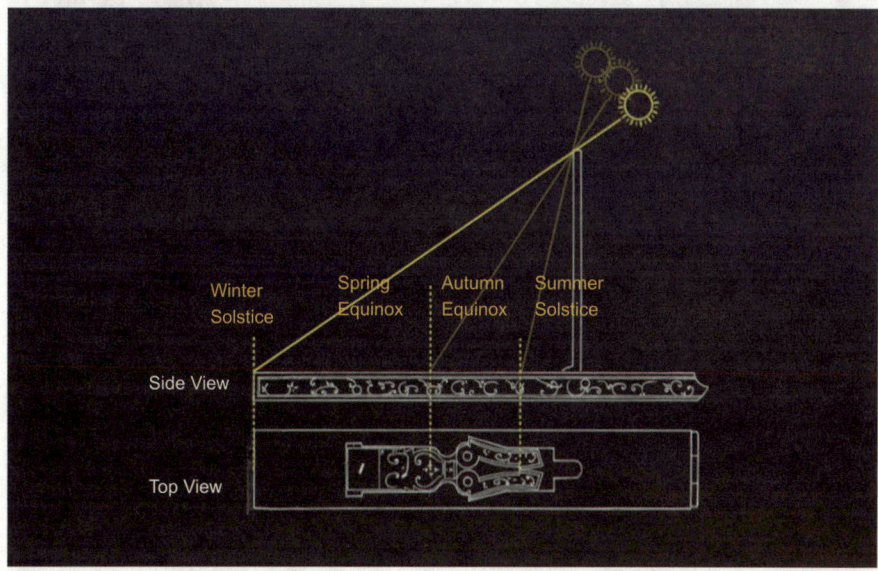

plants grow; in autumn, we harvest; and in winter, we store. Following this weather pattern regulated people's lives and established the foundation of agricultural civilization. This combined solar-lunar calendar is still used today.

The wood has rotted but the lacquer survives. Time and space extend into a boundless universe. Our sun is just one star among the 10,000 visible dotted in the sky. Heaven follows its own laws, the cycles of time ebb and flow. To keep our pace with them is nature's grace.

Loyal and Faithful as Time

"After the Clear and Bright Festival, it is time to sow melon and fruit seeds" is an agricultural proverb that is well known in northern China. This is because the ground temperature during the Clear and Bright or Tomb-sweeping Festival is suitable for seed germination. According to their growth period, the high temperature and rainy season is optimal for their growth. Therefore, this is the best time to plant melon and fruit seeds. There are many similar proverbs, such as "It is suitable to plant wheat during the Tomb-sweeping Festival and plant field crops during the Grain Rain", "It is suitable to plant cotton before the Grain Rain to promote its smooth growth." These proverbs reflect the features of China's agricultural civilization.

The Twenty-four solar terms were a summary of our ancestors in the creation of Chinese traditional calendars and practical experience. For ancient China, with a focus on agriculture, the timing of agricultural production activities was particularly important and might be decisive in whether a harvest is good or not, and determine the basic standards of living of a family. In China's history, a host of

Ancient Astronomical Observatory, Dengfeng, Henan

dynasties were overturned in famine and uprisings by refugees, so it is no exaggeration to say that agricultural timing could determine the fate of a dynasty to some extent. Agricultural production should follow the sun's motion, so the twenty-four solar terms that could separately reflect the solar cycle were added in the ancient calendar. In ancient China, an ancient astronomical instrument called the sundial was used to determine the solar terms. The sundial consists of two parts: the straight pole or stone column perpendicular to the ground is called the "sundial", and a scale plate placed due north/south parallel to the ground and used to measure the shadow length is called the "ruler". A small sundial, only a few tens of centimeters long, is portable. The Star Observation Platform in Dengfeng, Henan is a large-scale sundial of brick and stone structure. The platform is 12.6 m high and the ground stone is 31.2 m long. These sundials, regardless of size, determined the solar terms by measuring the length of the midday shadow. Every year, the longest shadow of the day is "long solstice" (also known as the Winter Solstice), and the shortest shadow of the day is "short solstice" (also known as Summer Solstice). These time nodes are determined by the included angle between the solar rays and the Earth, which determines the relationship between different solar terms and temperatures, thus providing a reliable basis for production activities.

Both the solar calendar and the lunar calendar are faced with the need for a correctional leap month because the total number of days in a year is not an integer, and a correction is required when the deviations accumulate. The measurement method based solely on the sun is relatively fixed, so it is not too early or too late to rely on solar terms for agricultural production. As it is a method drawn from practical experience, the ancient people were also convinced of the solar calendar. As the Book of Rites: Music states: "Heaven convinces people without any words." The Way of Loyalty and Good Faith in the Guodian Chu Slips also states: "Be loyal and faithful as time that will definitely come without an end". Although people had no agreement with time, but it often came as scheduled and circularly guided people in farming without an end. These proverbs are the ancestors' praise to the loyalty and faith of the solar terms.

In addition to agricultural production, the ancestors also applied this Chinese-style solar calendar to the characteristic Chinese zodiac rotation. Many think that the conversion of the Chinese zodiac is from the Lunar New Year, that is, the Spring Festival. Although the Spring Festival is the Lunar New Year, it is not a replacement node of the zodiac. As mentioned earlier, a leap month problem lies in both the solar calendar and the lunar calendar. As a result, the Chinese zodiac may be inconsistent in probability, and the number of people with the birthday in the leap month may increase. In fact, the zodiac replacement starts from the Beginning of Spring, so the length of each year is about 365.25 days, and the number of people of each zodiac is basically consistent. As the Beginning of Spring

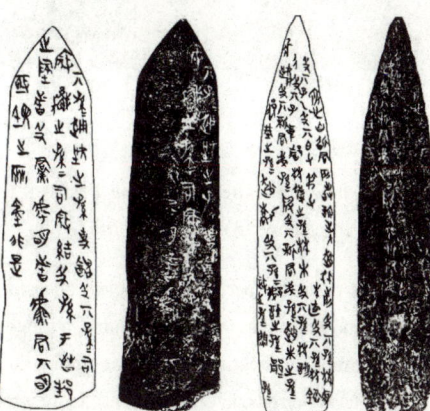

Rubbing of The Houma Allied Oath

Houma Allied Oath

sometimes comes before or after the Spring Festival, the zodiac cannot completely correspond to the year of birth.

Moreover, it is precisely because the ancient ancestors had the concept of "loyal and faithful as time", the sundial, a time-measuring tool, became a symbol of integrity. During the Spring and Autumn and the Warring States periods, in order to consolidate internal unity and fight against hostile forces, the governors and ministers often made an oath of alliance, where the convention signed by the oath of alliance was called the Allied Oath. An allied oath was usually made in duplicate, one kept in the feudal government, one buried in the ground or sunk in the river to win the trust of the ghosts and gods. The Houma Allied Oath, unearthed from the Jin site of Houma City, Shanxi Province in the 1960s, is an allied oath of the late Spring and Autumn period, which was signed between Zhao Yang, an aristocrat official of Jin, and Jian Ju, a minister of Jin in the 15th to 23rd year of Duke Ding of Jin (497 BC-489 BC). The Houma Allied Oath was written on jade pieces with a brush, with the writing mainly in vermilion and the minority in black. These jade pieces were mostly in the shape of a ruler, and the largest one was 32 cm long and nearly 4 cm wide, and the smallest one 18 cm long and less than 2 cm wide. For the oath of alliance, what is more important than the oath is whether both parties that signed the oath could keep their promises in a persistent way. Therefore, the text of the oath was written on the jade rulers which were used as a time-measuring tool with the concept of "loyal and faithful as time", in order to enhance the reliability of the oath.

On November 30, 2016, China's "Twenty-Four Solar Terms" were officially included in the UNESCO Representative List of the Intangible Cultural Heritage of Humanity. This is the recognition of the wisdom of the ancient Chinese ancestors by people all over the world. At present, the Chinese character "圭" in the commonly used idiom "奉为圭臬" (to regard something as the standard by which to compare) refers to Sundial for measuring time. The Chinese civilization has a history of thousands of years, shaping and influencing our lives. It is also embodied in our daily manners and customs, and is handed down from generation to generation.

By Wei Zhen

Lacquer Dish with the Leopard Cat Pattern

The Kittens on the Lacquer Dish

Lacquer Dish with the Leopard Cat Pattern

Location: Hunan Museum
Age: Western Han Dynasty
Texture: wooden lacquerware
Size: 6.2 cm in height, 27.8 cm in caliber

Lacquer Dish with the Leopard Cat Pattern

A Cat on the Lacquer Dish with Leopard Cat Pattern

After the Han Dynasty came to power in 202 BC, China enjoyed a long period of peace and increasing prosperity. In the south, the household of chancellor for the imperial fiefdom of Changsha enjoyed many luxurious items; like this lacquer dish with leopard cat pattern. Round eyed and round bodied, with pointy ears and scratchy claws, these leopard cats seem rather like the domestic moggies we keep as pets today. Yet their appearance as a pattern is not so simple. Their forepaws are grounded firmly, in perfect calm. Both ears are cocked, and on alert. Their tails are pointed high, as reflects their proud nature. Their fierce eyes are marked in vermilion, giving us a glimpse of their ruthless feral hearts.

Such vivid and amusing feline imagery is a novelty of its times. In the Western Zhou Dynasty the belly of the Boju Bronze Cooking Vessel was decorated with bull's heads, to express the power and majesty of the monarchs. But as the empire prospered under the Han a new lightness and playful frivolity became part of the spirit of the age.

Symmetrical Structure, Creepy Eyes

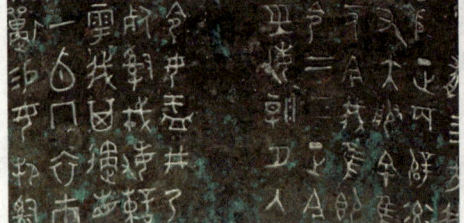
Numerous characters

Boju Bronze Cooking Vessel, the Western Zhou Dynasty

The lacquer dish bears three characters, "Jun Xing Shi". If translated into modern Chinese, it means "eat well, drink well". The cute kitties and simple message sit well together, both in practicality and aesthetic value. The cats which would have been seen as unbecoming to grace the tables of the aristocracy in previous ages are the sign of their times; the development of moderately hedonistic society.

The woman at the centre of the silk painting is the owner of the dish, Xin Zhui, the widow of the Marquise of Dai. Her corpse was so well preserved that it was able to be autopsied. She died of a heart attack, aged around fifty. She suffered from coronary heart disease and gallstones. Her husband had died some twenty three years previously. From the autopsy it emerged that Xin Zhui's lavish lifestyle and rich diet was the main cause of her undoing, though for her times she could be considered quite long-lived. However, among her legacy are items of striking and stylish beauty, which offer a unique insight into the lives of the Han-dynasty aristocracy and the aesthetics of southern Chinese culture. The simple blessing and playful cats would have brought a touch of warmth for Xin Zhui at her table.

"Eat well, drink well" is a phrase as richly Chinese as it is universal. "Eat well, drink well" is a blessing we all hope to enjoy and share.

Portrait of Lady Dai in the T-shaped Silk Painting from Mawangdui Han Tomb No. 1

Restored Image of Lady Dai

Winged Cup with Cloud Design

Eat Well and Drink Well

Archaeological Traces of the Feline Species

As one of the most loved pets in modern society, cats are connected with humans much closer than many other animals. They are beautiful and strong at the same time, and their walking posture is mimicked by human models on the cat walk. Though a lovely friend, this cute creature has not stayed with us for long, occupying a short period of time in the million-year history of human society.

As a species, however, cats have a long history but for a long period of time did not develop a symbiotic relationship with humans. Among other varieties, domesticated cats are actually accepted in our everyday life. The earliest cats which coexisted with humans were discovered in 2004, when archaeologists were excavating a 9,500-year-old tomb burying a human body and a cat buddy in Cyprus, an island country in the Eastern Mediterranean. In the same confined pit, remains of an 8-month-old cat were found only 40 cm away from an adult skeleton, both heading to the west. After careful measurement and comparison of physique, teeth and other bones, scientists believed that it was biologically closer to African wild cats than modern domestic cats. This is the earliest evidence of the coexistence of humans and cats.

In addition to archaeological findings, some scientists have applied biotechnology in attempts to study the origin of domestic cats. Drisko et al. collected and studied DNA samples of 979 wild and domestic cats, and five geographically distinct clades were identified, namely European wild cats, Chinese wild cats, Central Asian wild cats, South African wild cats, and African wild cats living in the Near East. Among them, African wild cats share the same clade with domestic cats. The result indicates that the African wild cat living in the Near East is the ancestor of domestic cat. The result is also similar to archaeological findings.

The domestication of cats features an extremely complex and lengthy process, particularly in the early stages when biometrics were difficult to distinguish. However, more evidence was found to prove their existence as the human society evolved. It is now generally accepted that ancient Egyptians started cat domestication earlier, as proved by paintings of the New Kingdom of Egypt (began about 3,600 years ago), the oldest and most credible evidences of fully domesticated cats. Cats in those paintings usually sit under a chair, some wearing a collar or a sling, and some eating from the bowl. A number of cat-themed paintings at the time have been discovered, meaning that cats were already members of Egyptian families.

It is noteworthy that among the gods of ancient Egyptian mythology, Bastet is a special cat-headed goddess. She is the goddess of the Bubastis, the god of music and family, the daughter of the Sun God. She has a complex character, exhibiting the gentleness of Bastet, and the fierceness of Sekhmet when she gets angry. This quality well agrees with the character of a cat. Among other gods in the ancient Egyptian tombs, Bastet is responsible for guarding the peace of the tomb occupant.

It was generally believed that Chinese domestic cats were introduced from Europe some 2,000 years ago. However, archaeologists recently discovered remains of cats at the 5,300-year relics of Quanhu Village, Huaxian County, Shaanxi Province. Scientific identification and measurement indicated that their size was smaller than that of European wild cats and similar to European domestic cats, meaning the cats found in Quanhu must have been domesticated. Results of stable carbon and nitrogen isotope analysis

A Cat in the Wall Painting of Ancient Egypt

A Mummified Cat at Egyptian Museum of Florence

of humans, cats and rats at the relics clearly showed that they all ingested a certain amount of C4-containing food, which means those animals might have either been foraging in domestic wastes or fed by ancient people for a long time.

Nevertheless, archaeological discoveries were limited about cats before the Qin and Han dynasties. The *Book of Rites: Single Victim at the Border Sacrifices* recorded that "In the past, a decent man would reward whoever had helped him. Cats and tigers are honored with sacrifices because they hunt field mice and boars, respectively." These animals were respected and rewarded as deities in the end-of-year rite by the king for their behaviors were good for crops. However, we could not prove that the cats mentioned in such an old book are actually the domesticated cats of modern times. It's possible that they are wild leopard cats and are therefore put beside tigers. Dongfang Shuo, a great scholar in the Han dynasty once said: "Qiji, Lyuer, Feihong, and Hualiu are all top-notch horses in the world. However, a crippled cat would beat them at catching mice in the palace." Apparently, cats in a palace must be domesticated ones. In addition to the lacquer dish discovered at Mawangdui, images of cat are also found at other sites, such as a wooden sculpture of cat unearthed from Mozuizi Tomb in Gansu Province, and cat bones from relics of Han Chang'an City in Xi'an and Dabaotai Han Tomb in Beijing.

Cats gradually came to occupy an elevated position in ancient society of China. Many have wondered why the rat is among the list of Chinese zodiac signs but not the cat. It may simply because the cat was not so important in people's lives when the list was developed. In other words, the list had been formed so early and the cat only became a part of human life at a much later historical stage. Even in the Tang Dynasty, when China traded frequently with

A Cat Wooden Sculpture from Tomb of Mozuizi, Wuwei, Gansu

foreign countries, descriptions about cat were extremely limited in the Tang poetry. The situation started to change from the Song Dynasty because cats are more described in the Song poetry. Many types of cats we know today are exotic, such as the Persian cat, the name indicates its origin from West Asia. It should be noted that, unlike pigs, horses, cattle and other livestock domesticated by humans, cats maintained their ability to survive independently during the process of domestication. Known as the world's most successful hunter, the cat is born to be a good predator. Even today, cats can live well without human feeding them. This may be the reason why they are always proud in front of human beings.

By Wei Zhen

Counting Rods

A System of Numbers

Counting Rods

Location: Yunnan Provincial Museum
Age: Western Han Dynasty
Texture: ivory
Size: 13.5 cm in length, 0.4 cm in diameter

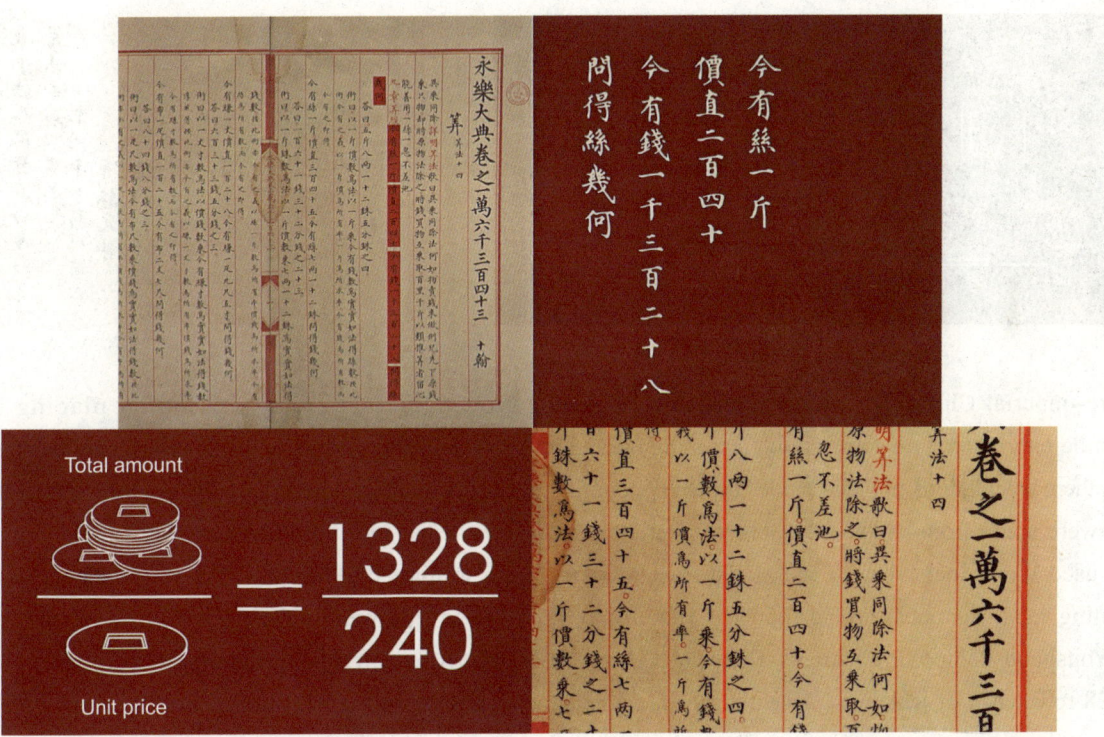

If 0.5kg of silk is worth 240 yuan, how much silk can we buy for 1,328 yuan? This question appears in *The Nine Chapters on the Mathematical Art*, a Chinese mathematics book composed between the tenth and second centuries BC. It worked on the decimal system we still use today, so they could easily deal with these complicated calculations.

The decimal numeral system uses ten decimal digits, from zero to nine, and a "place value system" to denote values of ten or above. Every natural number can be constructed in tens. From right to left, the first digit is its value multiplied by ten to the zeroth power, the second digit is its value multiplied by ten to the first power and so on, each place to the left represents a ten times multiple of the numeral to its right. So, 8 times ten to the power of zero, plus 1 which is multiplied by ten to the 1st power plus 0 which is multiplied by ten to the 2nd power and plus 2 which is multiplied by ten to the 3rd power gives the figure two thousand and eighteen.

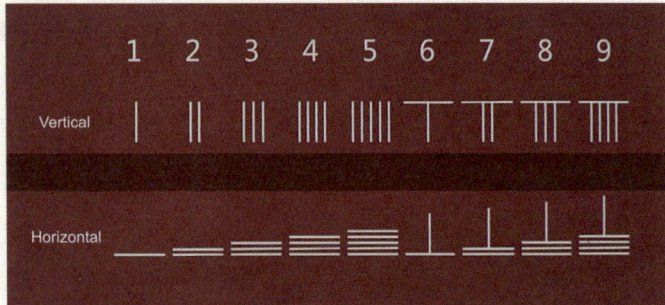 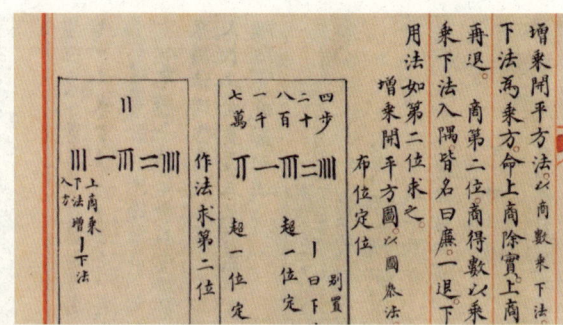

In pre-imperial China such seemingly abstract figures could be expressed with some simple counting rods and from them calculations of value made. Typically counting rods were made from bamboo, but other materials were also used like bone, ivory or metal. This set of ivory counting rods was unearthed in the No.1 Han Tomb of the Yousheng Palace in Shaanxi's Xunyang County. It has 28 rods, each of which is 0.4 centimeter in diameter, 13.5 centimeters in length. They are all equal in size and length.

Rod numerals are expressed by placing the rods either in the perpendicular or horizontal planes. In the perpendicular, when representing numbers from one to five, each rod represents one digit. For numbers from six to nine, one rod placed horizontally represents five, and the perpendicular rods placed below, represent one. Alternatively the numerals can be expressed by horizontal placement taking priority. Only five rods are ever used. When denoting multi-digit numbers, each digit is displayed from left to right in descending value,

  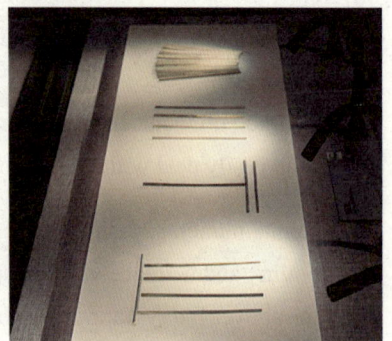

with perpendicular and horizontal placings alternated to differentiate each numeral. "Zero" is expressed by a gap. Once mastered, this method can represent any number, no matter how large. For example, 2018. Calculation with counting rods follows the same principles as the decimal system – "add 1 into the higher digit when the sum of lower digits is over 10; and 1 borrowed from the higher digit is regarded as 10". When 1,643 and 375 are added together, the 4 and 7 on the ten position digit make 11. After we add 1 onto the hundred position, it rolls up to 10, so the thousand position also needs a 1 to be added, so we get 2018. When the rods can be handled fluently they can be used to calculate the answer to many practical problems in building, agriculture, logistics and warfare.

In the sixteenth century the era of the counting rods came to an end to be completely replaced by the abacus. Though the rods were replaced by beads, the decimal system rules remained unchanged. The new technologies and improved tools have simplified calculation to the touch of a button. But an understanding of the basis of the system remains essential. In inscriptions on bones or tortoise shells more than 3,000 years ago, merchants could use the thirteen characters for the numbers from one to ten, the hundred, the thousand and the ten thousand, to notate any natural number up to 100,000. Although recording methods have changed, the decimal system has triumphed throughout.

It is everywhere in our lives. Decimal measurements can be used to express all the patterns and principles of science and society. From everyday activities like shopping, to high finance and artificial intelligence, it's all just numbers. Numbers that we usually take as for granted as a simple bundle of sticks.

Figures in Various Civilizations

In ancient China, the counting rods used for counting and calculation were not only found in the form of physical objects in archaeological discoveries, but also recorded in the numerous volumes of ancient Chinese literature. As Laozi's *Tao Te Ching* states: "A good reckoner makes use of no counters," which means that "counters" is a method of calculation, and the people "adept at counting" do not rely on tools; the extended meaning is to persuade people not to care too much about gains and losses. The Shushu Jiyi by Xu Yue from the Eastern Han Dynasty states: "...only a counting rod is needed with the length of five cun...", which was the earliest documentary record that described the shape of the counting rod. The book also records an algorithm using fingers and counting rods, with the measurable unit up to the level of "100 million". Unfortunately, among the 14 algorithms recorded in the book, only Zhusuan has survived to the present.

The above description points out that the counting rod is a tool for counting the number. How did human beings come to know the numerals? Where did the concept of the logarithm come from? It is commonly believed that human beings had an abstract understanding of the objective world from the long-term life practice. At the beginning, they counted with fingers, recorded the prey numbers by the number of stones, and "governed successfully by the use of knotted cords" as recorded in the *Book of Changes*, and then abstracted to the colored drawing or carved marks on potteries, or the numeric symbols with which we are familiar.

There are many records of the numerals on oracle bones, especially the sacrifice-related content. The collection of "Wangwei Banbu" tortoise shell in the National Museum of China is a complete oracle tortoise shell. It recorded that in the middle and late period of the Shang Dynasty, Wu Ding, the aristocratic minister "Ban" often went on expeditions following the order of the king, and the king of Shang Dynasty practiced divination for him to predict whether there was a disaster to him. The reverse side of the tortoise plastron was drilled; the frontal face was engraved with 17 words and a circle of numerals ranging 1 to 7 in two groups.

The Front Side of "Wangweiban Divination" Plastron   The Back Side of "Wangweiban Divination" Plastron

The " 一 ", " 二 ", " 三 ", etc. on oracle bones may be the abstract symbols that were established by usage before the formation of characters. In the numerals recorded in the oracle inscriptions, the multiples of ten, one hundred, one thousand, and ten thousand were often written as "combined texts". For example, ten was symbolized as " l ", twenty as " ∪ ", ten thousand as " Ƴ ", and thirty thousand as " Ⱡ ".

Besides Chinese oracle bones, what is the situation in other global civilizations in terms of numerals?

COUNTING RODS | 223

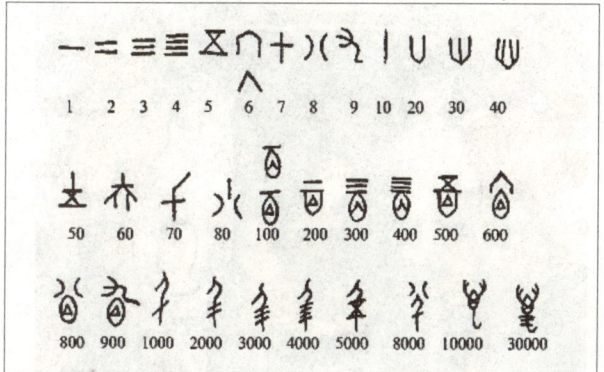

A comparison of ancient and modern form of numbers. All may not be correct due to irregular inscription.

In the "Great World Civilization" exhibition of the China Millennium Monument, there was a trade record clay tablet of the Mesopotamian Civilization, which was also called "Onion File" by Assyrian linguists because it mainly recorded the shipment of onions. This clay tablet belonged to the Dynasty of Akkad (2334 BC-2154 BC) and recorded the total amount of onions shipped. The combination of the circle and the crescent moon diagram was numerals, different from those in the traditional cuneiform.

The Roman numerals later than Oracle bones have seven numeric symbols, which are corresponding to Arabic numerals as follows:

Roman alphabet	I	V	X	L	C	D	M
Arabic numerals	1	5	10	50	100	500	1000

There are roughly three ways to count Roman numerals:

1. Reuse the same numeric symbol (generally at most three times) to indicate the multiple. For example, the number 30 is symbolized as three repeated 10 "X", that is, "XXX";

2. Right plus and left minus: If 6 is symbolized as the number 5 "V" plus 1 "I" on the right, that is, "VI", and 9 as 10 "X" minus 1 "I" on the left, that is, "IX";

3. A numeric symbol is added with a horizontal sign to indicate 1000 times.

For example,

23: XXIII; 233: CCXXXIII; 2,333: MMCCCXXXIII; 23,333: XXIIICCCXXXIII;

233,333: CCXXXIIICCCXXXIII ;

233,333,333: CCXXXIIICCCXXXIIICCCXXXIII

In the custom-made altarpieces of the Italian nobility, Mary embraced the little Jesus sitting on the throne of the center of the picture, and the words on the base of the throne marked the date of completion of the work: "A.D M.CCCCC VIIII". Where, A.D represents to the Christian era, the vacancy between CCCCC and

VIIII represents zero, and "M.CCCCC VIIII" represents 1509, and the date is followed by the author's signature.

Regardless of the complex or simple numeric representation methods, Chinese and Western civilizations achieve unity in mathematical theorems. The Pythagorean Theorem, which was introduced in the Zhoubi Suanjing, became the theorem of the later generations after being proved by the mathematician Zhao Shuang from the Three Kingdoms period. This Theorem is widely used in land and building measurement, and even astronomical calculation. According to the theorem which is similar to the Pythagorean Theorem, "the square of the hypotenuse of a right triangle is equal to the sum of the squares of the two orthogonal sides", which was discovered, proposed and universally proven by the Pythagorean School in Greek mathematics.

Numerals are not only the cornerstone of mathematics, but also contain profound philosophical principles. Mathematicians and philosophers have a series of views on the exact scope and definition of mathematics. The Shuowen Jiezi states: "It is that the start of the Great Begin of the Way is based upon Unity. It divides Heaven and Earth and forms the ten thousand creations". The same understanding is also manifested in the Taoist thoughts. For example, Laozi's *Tao Te Ching* says: "Dao begets One (nothingness; or reason of being), One begets Two (yin and yang), Two begets Three (Heaven, Earth and Man; or yin, yang and breath qi), Three begets all things." The Pythagorean School in ancient Greece upheld the motto of "All is Number", and they reckoned that "One is original, two is movement, and three is the universe". In their view, mathematics is equivalent to the universe.

Mathematics also plays an irreplaceable role in the development of human history and social life. Mathematics has been closely

The Virgin and Child with St. Peter, St. Catherine of Alexandria, St. Agatha and St. Paul

related to our life for as long as we could remember from numeracy, counting, simple calculation to binary, decimal, and geometric calculus. Maybe you questioned the purpose of learning mathematics when you are plagued by some difficult mathematical problems in your schooldays, but it may not affect your joy in successfully solving a complex mathematical problem. You may enjoy learning mathematics, in a bid to establish a more solid foundation of computational science or mathematical research, or use it as a pure knowledge.

By Chen Kun

Gold-inlaid Bronze Hill Censer

The Calculation of Clouds

Gold-inlaid Bronze Hill Censer

Location: Hebei Museum
Age: Western Han Dynasty
Texture: gold-inlaid bronze ware
Size: 26 cm in height, 15.5 cm in abdominal diameter

Gold-Inlaid Bronze Hill Censer

Tigers, leopards and boars roam the mountains. A hunter stealthily approaches. Monkeys watch the drama from above. This hunting scene from two thousand years ago is captured on a gold-inlaid bronze censer. It was a treasured possession of King Jing of the State of Zhongshan. The design of the censer's lid in the form of a sacred mountain has gifted it a unique place in art history.

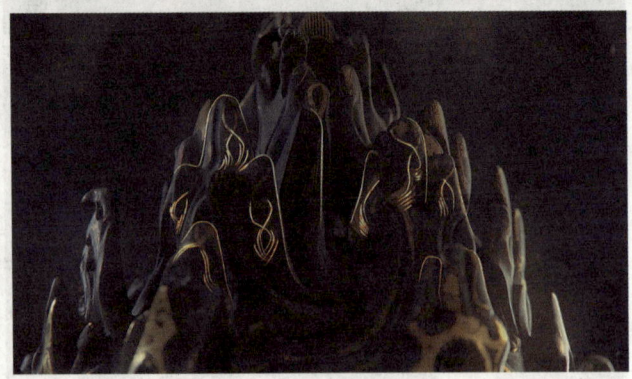

Gold-inlaid Bronze Hill Censer

The censer is 26cm tall. On the base three dragons rear their heads to support the gourd-like bowl. The peaks on the lid resemble frozen tongues of flame. The craftsman inlaid clouds to mark the summits. The inlay technique makes the clouds look flowing and mysterious, an eye-catching rendering of a sense of the divine. If you look closely, the clouds and rock integrate to form a whole. The tips of the clouds are as frozen as stone, while the mountains rise up into the sky like plumes of smoke. It is hard to tell whether patterns at the foot of the hill represent clouds or waves. But perhaps the designer blurred the distinction of the two on purpose, to leave people's imaginations to create beauty from nebulousness. Like the blank spaces in traditional Chinese painting, this type of artistic expression can encompass the whole cosmos in its emptiness.

Similar designs became common in the art of the Han Dynasty. There are no written records of why the Han were so fixated on mountains and their images. Most likely is that it reflected the belief that mountains were the home of gods and immortals, and a place from where the elixir of eternal life might be obtained. From the Sixth Dynasties onwards they were referred to in poetry as "Boshan censers": literally "universal mountain censers".

The incense smoke rises from the holes. Eventually, the hill censer becomes a dreamland in miniature. The animals seem to move, becoming more vivid amidst the white mist. The golden clouds stretch further as the smoke rises. Although there are no celestial beings on it, the censer has an auspicious air. In the moment, the hill censer is not merely an incense burner, but with its combination of imagery and odor, it becomes a celestial mountain rising from the sea.

Gold and Silver Inlaid Bronze Crossbow, the Han Dynasty

Gold-inlaid Bronze Hill Censer

Long before the mountains and rivers became the popular subject for scroll paintings, Han artists had already expressed the mystery of mountains in a solid three dimensional form. The viewer, two thousand years on, travels through time on the flowing smoke. Time marks the trajectory between life and death. Evanescent mist and cloud mark the sound, color and shape of everything on earth, as well as the distance between the secular world and the heavens.

EVERY TREASURE TELLS A STORY | 232

A Brief History of Censers

Incense has a long history in China. It has been widely used as early as the Spring and Autumn and Warring States periods. Incense could be used to expel insects, treat clothes and season food, but more importantly, it was a symbol of social status and lifestyle. In his poem *On Encountering Sorrow* (Lisao), Qu Yuan frequently dotted his flowery and gorgeous verses with herbs, mostly native scented plants. The pleasant aroma is either emitted by the herbs in their own right or through heating or burning. In this case, censers were often required to have unobstructed holes as smoke outlets.

By the time of Emperor Wu of Han, as Zhang Qian blazed the trail to western regions, silk roads spanning the Eurasian continent were established. A variety of exotic aromatic herbs and drugs found their way into China along with camel caravans, including

Line Drawing of Gold-inlaid Bronze Hill Censer

sandalwood, silver-mouth turban, frankincense, eaglewood, borneol, styrax, and ambergris to name just a few. It was in exchange for such rare exotic items that bolts of silk were transported to the West.

Compared with native sweet herbs, these resin spices from the West and south seas have richer, more lingering aroma, thus much sought after by the nobles. Accordingly, silk roads thrived due to these luxurious goods.

However, better-quality exotic incense required particular burning methods, driving changes in the shapes and forms of censers. Incense was ground to powders and evenly scattered into a hill censer beneath which charcoal fire could be lit. The fire could only smolder due to lack of fresh air. As a result, the incense burned slowly, emitting faintly lingering aroma that permeates the whole room.

Such ingenuity was not a native invention. The shapes and forms of hill censers were closely associated with cross-cultural exchanges. According to foreign Sinologists, covered censers, the predecessor of hill censers, were first used by Assyrians, and brought into Chinese-speaking regions via silk roads by Scythians and other ethnic groups from Siberia or Central Asia. As incense swept across the Eurasian continent, similar censers were found in Greece, Rome, Iran, Egypt, and India, among other places. While, hill censers, rooted in China, were also spread to Korea and the wider Eastern Asia. As recorded in the *Xuanhe Fengshi Gaoli Tujing* (Illustrated Record of an Embassy to Korea in the Xuanhe Reign Period by Song scholar Xu Jing, "Boshan censers originated from Han...The Korean

Three Incense Things in the Painting of the Qing Dynasty

versions, though similar at the top, have three legs, which differs greatly from Yuan shapes but is desirable in terms of workmanship." A hill censer gives us a glimpse into the great integration and interaction between civilizations on the Eurasian continent.

Liu Sheng, King Jing of Zhongshan, is supposed to be an incense expert at that time. After he died, an exquisite censer was ordered to be placed in his stone tomb in a deep mountain cave. In his final resting place, the gold-inlaid bronze hill censer emitted lingering fragrance, as if evoking a hint of attachment to this worldly life.

Hill censers, with its singular shapes, have historically been praised by the literati as a legend. By the Jin Dynasty, Boshan censer became an exclusive name for such censers. Bronze hill censers enjoyed enduring popularity among the royalty and nobles. At the same time, a large number of celadon hill censers with similar shapes were discovered among tombs of the Six Dynasties. These porcelain censers, more cost-effective, were widely favored by scholar-officials and commoners. Porcelain censers were originally well-disciplined imitation of bronze ones. Later, as its shapes grew richer, a distinct artistic style developed. Particularly, after Buddhism was introduced to China, the "hill" component of Boshan censers became increasingly blurred and abstract, incorporating new ornamental elements like lotus.

By the Tang and Song dynasties, incense burning changed again, bringing about innovations in the forms of censers. Tang people blended incense powders into pills or cakes according to various formulas. During the Northern Song Dynasty, incense stick was made by combining incense with fuel. Ever since, hill censers had gradually gone out of sight and been replaced by "three incense things" commonly seen in recent times, i.e. incense burner, incense case, and a stand and shovel bottle. Incense was no longer a mystic medium for otherworldly experience, but a worldly necessity for men of letters to pursue meditation and for pious believers to worship the divine.

The gold-inlaid bronze hill censer, a calculator of fleeting smoke and clouds, is like the origin of coordinates, with the horizontal axis representing spatial cross-cultural exchanges while the vertical axis representing temporal incense history. Although it is no longer used to burn incense to create fairyland, we may still lose ourselves in appreciating it.

By Li Kai

Green-glazed Lotus Petal and Curled-up Dragon Hill Censer, the Sui Dynasty

"Forever Forget Me Not" Silver Belt Hook

A Secret Oath Worn Close to the Heart

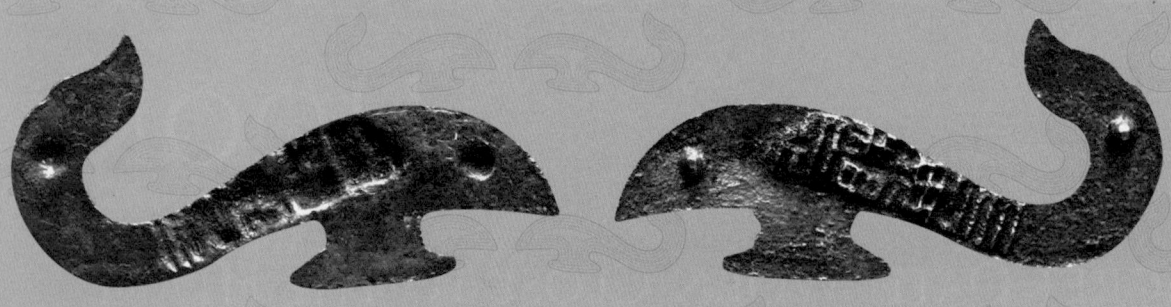

"Forever Forget Me Not" Silver Belt Hook

Location: Nanjing Museum
Age: Western Han Dynasty
Texture: silver
Size: 3.7 cm in length, 1.8 cm in height

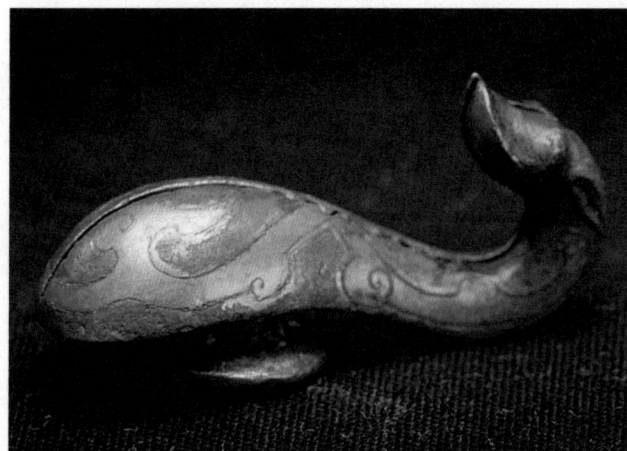 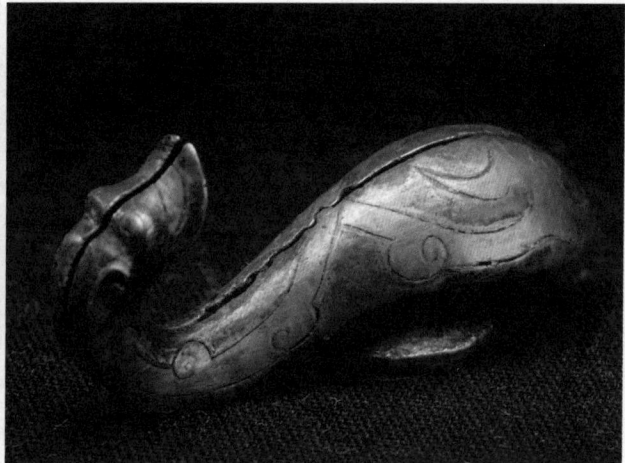

When mountains fall, rivers run dry, thunder shakes the winter air with summer snows, while heaven and earth conjoin, only then dare I part from my lord.

—— *Yuefu Songs*, Han Dynasty

This silver belt hook held more than its owners robes fast to her body. It belonged to Chunyu Ying'er, one of the Western Han aristocrat's most favored concubines, and was buried with her two thousand years ago. She took her secret oath of love and loyalty with her to the grave. The secret pledge was not revealed until 2009, two thousand years on from her passing.

The belthook is composed of two matching halves. On the inside of each are engraved four characters; "Chang Wu Xiang Wang" meaning "Everlasting Love" or "Forever Forget Me Not". The pledge, secretly inscribed on the inside of the hook, seems to indicate that this was a special private commitment between the pair, that they didn't wish to make public.

Such discretion was unusual in the Han Dynasty. Characters were frequently carved or embossed onto everyday objects, but they were open to view, embodying the owners' desire for good fortune, wealth, health, beauty or love, or even to proclaim moral and ethical virtues. A bronze mirror inscribed with words of longing for a loved one reads: "In the light of day, under heaven's bright sun, even serving the great master, in all of time, we'll never forget each other." A seal carved with the words "Sincerity and Honesty" serves as an admonishment to and from its owner. They not only expressed their owner's aspirations for "Wealth and Rank", but tackled consolations for sadness and the transience of life.

Inscription of "Forever Forget Me Not"

"Integrity" Bronze Seal, the Han Dynasty

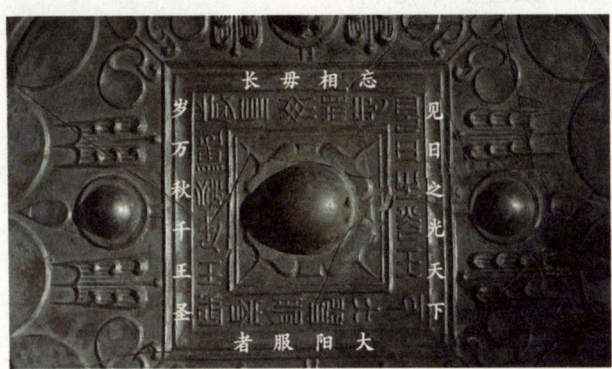

Inscription on the Bronze Mirror with Leaf Patterns, the Han Dynasty

Inscription on Bronze Mirror with Flower Patterns, the Han Dynasty

A Variety of Han Belt Hooks

The belt hook first appeared on clothing around six hundred years earlier. It quickly became a fashionable item allowing people to express their personal style. They came in all different materials and shapes. Animal designs were among the most popular – and if the hook wasn't worn with the belt, it could be used to hang other objects. Looking at this cheerful ensemble of terracotta dancers and musicians, we can imagine a fashionable crowd among who belt hooks were there to be displayed, showing off the wearer's character and taste.

In contrast, Chunyu Ying'er's was small and quite plain in appearance. Its head is a simplified dragonhead with protruding eyes and up standing ears. The body of the hook is decorated with a gilded cloud pattern, specific to the Han Dynasty. Unlike the candid expressions of the commoners, a secret oath made in a royal palace was not for display. Undue favoritism to a lowly concubine could cause ructions in the aristocratic household. Instead the pair carried their secret together close to the heart.

Directness and secretiveness both abound in Chinese culture. The public imprecations for love and good fortune are matched by private expressions not to be shared with others. Chunyu Ying'er's belt hook kept her secret for two millennia, hidden in an object of beauty that never left her body in life and in death.

And so we remember her, for her "Everlasting Love".

Love Stories Discovered in Archaeological Excavations

Love is an eternal topic. Archeology captures the material and spiritual dimensions of the ancient world. Archaeologists are often inadvertently moved by ancient love stories in their numerous dialogs with the ancient world. According to the British newspaper *The Sun*, archaeologists recently discovered in a tomb in the village of Petrykiv, Ukraine a couple holding each other in a tight embrace Studies show that they were Vysotskayan prehistoric humans in the Bronze Age. Archaeologist Mykola Bandrivsky pointed out that the male lay flat and the woman lay on her side. She embraced the man with her right arm and placed her right hand on the man's right shoulder. The two put their heads together. The woman's legs, slightly bent, lay on top of the man's legs, which are also slightly bent. Bandrivsky indicated that it would have been impossible for the woman to maintain such an intimate posture if she had been buried after death. Bandrivsky and other archaeologists speculated that the woman might have chosen to be buried alive so that she could remain with the man she loved. Love in that era seemed pure and passionate, despite the fact that it was not a time of affluence and easy life.

The ancients lived and died together in a manifestation of their love for each other. Beside this direct way, they also had their unique, indirect way of showing love, such as the "forget me not" inscription in the belt hook, which is often hard to notice. The "Forget Me Not" is a silver belt hook kept as a keepsake. Soon after the founding of the People's Republic of China, archaeologists found hundreds of Han-dynasty tombs in Shaogou Village, Luoyang City. On March 8, 1953, however, two Neolithic tombs numbered 38a and 38b caught the attention of archaeologists. The two juxtaposed burial chambers share the same tomb passage. In archaeological

An Ancient Vysotskayan Couple

terms, it is a "tomb with two chambers"—mostly for the burial of couples. The coffin chamber is not a particularly large one, and few burial objects were found in it. They include pottery tripods, pottery kettles, pottery pots and other utensils for daily use. The remains of three people have been found in this tomb. Chamber A contains two coffins and Chamber B contains only one coffin. Shattered bronze mirrors are sometimes unearthed from Han-dynasty tombs. A half bronze mirror was found near the head of the skeleton in the left coffin in Chamber A and in the coffin of Chamber B. Amazingly, the archaeologists saw something magical when they put the two halves together. These two bronze mirror halves seamlessly fit into each other—they combined to form a complete Han-dynasty four-beast talisman mirror. The restored bronze mirror has a diameter of 15 cm and a thickness of 0.5 cm. Construction of this bronze mirror did not involve any special technology. However, the fact that a complete mirror was split into two and buried separately embodies the hope of this 2,000-year-old couple that they would be together again in their afterlife. This was the first archaeological event in the history of China in which "a broken mirror was joined together".

Archeology has continued to tell us stories of "a broken mirror being joined together". In 1985, archaeologists discovered a half bronze mirror in two Tang-dynasty tombs which were three meters apart in Huaining County, Anhui Province. When they put the two halves together, this Tang-dynasty mirror inscribed with a prostrating turtle and a flying crane once again showed itself in its entirety. In 1990, farmers fetching earth in Wangjiawan, Ansai County, Shaanxi Province, discovered a husband-wife tomb dating back to the Xin Dynasty. Archaeologists unearthed the two halves of a *zhaoming* mirror: one half was found near the head of the man buried in the tomb and the other half was found near the head of the woman. The mirror halves found to be held separately by husband and wife in archaeological excavations do reflect ancient people's commitment to love and their aspiration to reunite in afterlife.

Love has never been an easy thing. Some ancients were also disappointed in love. This Tang-dynasty celadon-glazed brown kettle with poetic inscriptions reminds us of the bitterness that ancients experienced in love. This porcelain kettle among the collection of

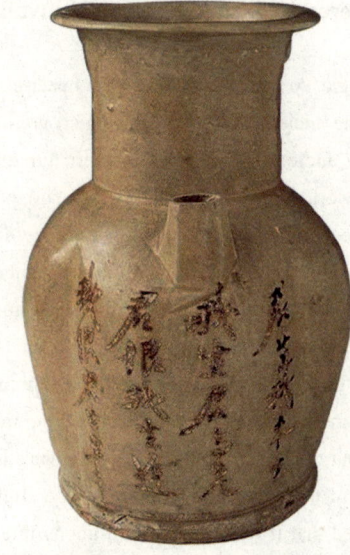

Green and Brown Glazed Pot with Poem Inscription, Changsha Kiln of Tang Dynasty

Changsha Museum is inscribed with a poem:

I was born after you,

When I was born, you were already too old.

You regret that I was born late,

But I regret that you were born too early.

The melancholy that comes with the inaccessibility of love or the regret that love has come too late is most thoroughly depicted in this poem. It resonates with us even today. The bitterness of love overwhelms us from a distant location; it is set to accompany us in the future. People in love expect to live happily together and enjoy the tenderness of love until death, whatever the circumstances.

By Wei Zhen

Gold and Silver Inlay Cloud-patterned Rhinoceros Vessel

The Spirited Beast

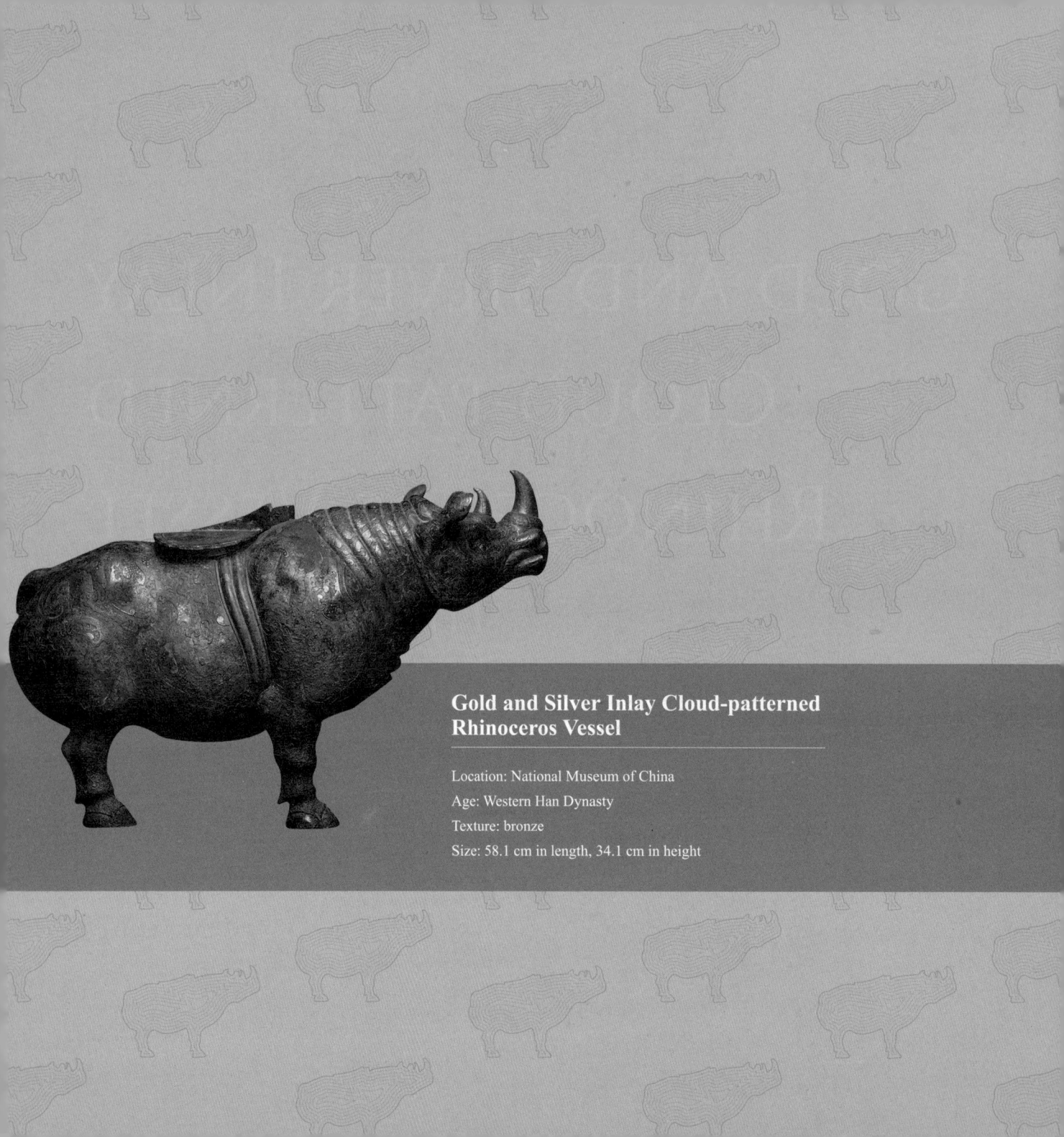

Gold and Silver Inlay Cloud-patterned Rhinoceros Vessel

Location: National Museum of China
Age: Western Han Dynasty
Texture: bronze
Size: 58.1 cm in length, 34.1 cm in height

Gold and Silver Inlay Cloud-Patterned Rhinoceros Vessel

A rhinoceros found in Shaanxi Province, the dust wiped from its body and it looks defiantly ahead. Once it spent its days full of liquor, but lives in more sober times now. Its given purpose in life was as a wine vessel. Its haunches and tail are curled like a hook. One can hold the tail and use the hoofs as support when the wine is poured. The vessel's lid on its back looks like a saddle. There are layers of wrinkles around its neck and a pair of horns adorns its snout. Its eyeballs are of the deepest black. Its bones and muscles are well structured. Its four hooves stand securely grounded, each with three clear toes. It shows the craftsman knew his beast.

Sparkling gold and silver lines swirling like rainforest mist, turn into clouds or bunches of hair, in true Sumatran fashion. The gold and silver inlay technique means carving grooves on the surface of a bronze in which to inlay the gold or silver filament. It creates magnificent decorative patterns. On this crossbow mechanism, over 20 animals including birds, snakes, deer, tigers and pigs are all clearly defined. A tiger striped in gold, with upturned head and long tail. Complex craft and durable materials demonstrate a harmony between man and nature. Different animals in many forms brought together to create vivid images of life.

Across the ages, countless lives came and went before humans appeared on earth. Images from life are as old as human civilization itself. People made images of what

Gold and Silver Inlay Cloud-Patterned Rhinoceros Vessel | 249

Gilt Copper Rhinoceros and Rhinoceros Trainer Figurine, the Western Han Dynasty

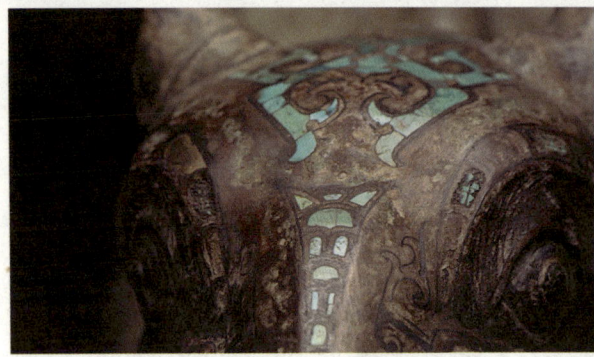

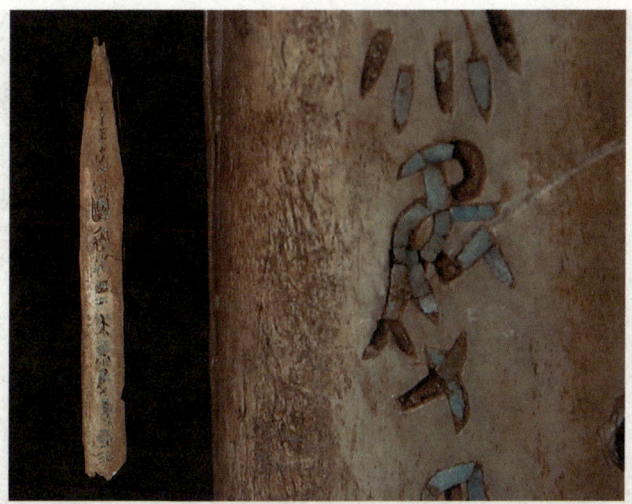

Zaifeng Bone Dagger, the Shang Dynasty

they saw around them with whatever came to hand. Over 3,000 years ago the footprints of the rhinoceros was stamped across the land of China. It was a time when the climate was warm and humid, full of grass and trees. The Kings of the Shang Dynasty are recorded as hunting rhinoceroses on the oracle bones inscriptions, the pregnant females and juveniles were off limits. 2,000 years ago people in the Han Dynasty would have come across Rhinoceroses in Sichuan and the southwest of China. They were likely similar to today's Sumatran Rhinoceros. As the smallest species in the rhinoceros family, it is a shy and solitary creature. After the Western Han Dynasty, with a cooling climate and increased human population, the rhinoceroses were forced further south. Today their range is restricted to a few isolated patches of tropical rainforest.

Despite their banishment from China, this spirited beast still leaves its mark in memory, history and culture. All things may pass but the spirit is immortal.

Rhinoceros Horn

A bronze liquor vessel with inlaid gold and silver cloud patterns was unearthed in Wuxiang Town, Xingping County, Shaanxi Province in 1963. The most fascinating aspect of this liquor vessel is not its bronze craftsmanship nor its volume, but its life-like shape of a rhinoceros.

This rhinoceros vessel, 58.1cm long, 34.1cm high and weighing 13.5kg, is now in the collections of the National Museum of China. A closer look at this vessel will find the physical appearance of the rhinoceros strong, its forelegs and rump muscular with smooth lines, and its facial expression focused with eyes staring ahead, as if facing the world with its animal pride.

Although bronze animal-shaped liquor vessels are not uncommon, the shape of this vessel is quite exquisite and realistic. Scholars, therefore, treasure it very much. The shape of this vessel is accurate in every aspect. The rhinoceros' cheekbones, spine, and joints are vividly sculpted, and muscles at every part finely textured. It can be speculated that the craftsman who made it could not have done it so well merely by imagination.

Tapirus-shaped *zun* Pig-shaped *zun* Rabbit-shaped *zun*

During the Warring States period or earlier, rhinoceroses inhabited ancient China like other animals. Archaeologists discovered rhinoceros skeletons at a Neolithic site in Hemudu Town, Yuyao City, Zhejiang Province. This proved that there were rhinoceroses living within the Chinese territory as early as the Neolithic Age. According to research by scholars, the rhinoceros shape of this vessel is based on a Sumatran rhinoceros species which inhabits many islands of Indonesia and once inhabited various places across ancient China. In addition to Zhejiang, many rhinoceros bones had been discovered in places north of the Yangtze River. For example, there are some rhinoceros bones among animal bones unearthed at the Tomb of Fuhao in Anyang City, Henan Province.

In ancient times, animal-shaped liquor vessels were very common. A large number of animal-shaped bronze vessels were unearthed in Baoji. These animal shapes are varied, including elephants, rabbits, dragons, fish, pigs, birds, and tigers. However, the rhinoceros form is quite rare among animal-shaped liquor vessels. Scholars have pondered why ancient people used such animal-shaped vessels to hold liquor. Some believe that during the Western Zhou period, people not only hunted wild animals, but also domesticated them. As a result, they understood the physical structures of these animals quite well, and started to feature domesticated animals in their artistic creation.

However, this theory could only explain when people modeled liquor vessels after domesticated animals, such as poultry and birds. The rhinoceros lives in the wild, and its meat is not tender enough for people to eat, so why exactly did ancient people hunt the rhinoceros?

One theory is that people hunted large animals for their hides which could be used to make armor. As Qu Yuan wrote in the *Nine Song: For Those Fallen For Their Country*, "We take our southern spears and don our coats of mail. When chariot axles clash, with daggers we assail." The "coats of mail" in this verse were made of the hides of rhinoceroses which people had hunted. Scholars speculate that animal-shaped liquor vessels were for sacrificial purposes after people successfully hunted animals. Animal-shaped bronze liquor vessels, finely crafted in themselves, reflect ancient people's awe of and faith in deities.

There is another theory about the production of sacrificial utensils in the shape of the rhinoceros. Ancient people viewed the rhinoceros as a mythical creature which could ward off floods. According to the *Annals of the King of Shu* by Yang Xiong of the Han Dynasty, "To control river floods, Li Bing, governor of Shu, had five stone rhinoceroses (*xiniu* in Chinese) made, and ordered the placement of two in the government office, one under the city bridge, and two in the river to deter evil water spirits. So this place was named Xiniuli." Also, *the Chronicles of Ancient Southwest China* (*Huayang Guozhi*): *Annals of Shu* records that, "Li Bing had five stone rhinoceroses made to ward off evil water spirits." This might have had something to do with ancient people's practice of making liquor vessels in the shape of the rhinoceros.

Rhinoceros horn is also viewed as sacred. The *Book of the Master Who Embraces Simplicity* (*Baopuzi*) by Ge Hong of the Eastern Jin Dynasty records, "If a person acquires three *cun* or more of real rhinoceros horn which has access to Heaven, and carves it into the shape of fish and jumps into a river with it, the river would make way for him instead of drowning him." It is obvious that both the rhinoceros and its horn were closely related to water. This corroborates the theory that ancient people believed that rhinoceros had flood deterrence functions. Cut open a rhinoceros horn, we can see there is a vein like a white thread running through to connect both ends of the horn. As Li Shangyin, a famous poet of the Tang Dynasty, wrote in a poem, "We wingless could not fly like shiny phoenix's side by side; the magic line of rhinoceros horn but linked us heart to heart." This is a metaphor that two people perfectly understand each other without saying a single word, and their hearts beat in harmony as if connected by the magic white thread in a rhinoceros horn.

To this day, rhinoceros horn, still seen as sacred and magic, is a precious material in traditional Chinese medicine. The Miao people in Guizhou, Hunan and Guangxi, among other places, still worship the rhinoceros. They take the rhinoceros as their tribal totem which can been seen in various sacrificial rites. Unfortunately, wild rhinoceroses can no longer been seen in China today. According to the *Convention on International Trade in Endangered Species of Wild Fauna and Flora (CITES)*, any trade in rhinoceros products is banned. We should then leave the rhinoceros story here for good appreciation within museums.

By Lian Yongxin

Tomb Figurine of a Storyteller

The Show Must Go On Forever

Tomb Figurine of a Storyteller

Location: National Museum of China
Age: Eastern Han Dynasty
Texture: pottery
Size: 56 cm in height

My eyes are like the waxing moon. My smile like a rippling pool. My pudgy cheeks are like ripened apples. Such is my cheery face. People call me a Storyteller Figurine. Though an unknown, I am still a star at the National Museum of China.

I am a storyteller from Sichuan during the Eastern Han Dynasty, frozen at the moment my performance reaches its climax. Holding a drum in my left hand and a stick in the right, I lean forward with my back curved like a bow. I lift up my leg high to wave my wide flat foot at my audience. That always gets a laugh. People like me are common in Sichuan. People called us "Pai You", which means comedian, as you would call us today. Laughter is our game.

But it not all laughs for us. Look at my colleague. Three bands of wrinkles on his forehead, sticking out his tongue, trying his best to get a laugh. But he was not blessed by his curved spine and a malnutrition that has left his arms short and thin, only fit to clown around. We were born with deformities, which make our bodies different from others. Self-inflicted mockery is the best way to secure our lives and livelihood. We turn our defects into a talent to amuse. But I'm lucky. I am immortal.

Two thousand years ago, my colleagues and I were confined to eternal darkness.

Pottery Comedian Figurine

Pottery Comedian Figurine

Then one day I saw sunlight again. The beautiful colors of my favorite hat have faded, though my pants are still tight at my waist. Even with nothing to eat or drink for 2,000 years, I still maintain my figure. Losing weight was never so hard. Chengdu is still as warm and delightful as it always was. We are blessed with a rich and prosperous culture; fine food, fine art, witty repartee and an easy going attitude to life – who would not envy us?

Pottery Comedian Figurine

Long, even before my time, some distinguished man wrote: "a full record of history requires both the written works and the oral telling". So there you have it, I'm a scholar to boot. In our stories live the founding emperor's sword, the flying general's bow, and the heart of an innocent girl. Passed on from generation to generation, these stories become the collective memory of the nation. My back is bowed by the weight of histories I must carry. This is why I am so carefully looked after here. And I am have been given a name, Y328A. I am the official representative of Han-dynasty folk art. My spirit has never died. It becomes a type of art, a way of thinking, and a subject of philosophy. I am common, but noble. I am an individual, but represent all. I laugh, but my purpose is serious.

Terracotta Dancers and Musicians

Pottery Figurine Culture

Pottery figurines are funerary objects made of pottery clay and fired into shape. Over its long history, it has played a key role in the funeral rites of ancient China.

Chinese ancestors had the notion of afterlife very early on. They believed that death was the beginning of life in another world, and hoped that they could live the same life after death. Funerary objects including gold and silver ware, porcelains and pottery figurines, as ancient people believed, could be brought to and used in the other world. This notion shaped the custom of lavish funeral. Among the funerary objects were many pottery figurines, with the images of servants, maids and warriors, for serving the dead. Therefore, these pottery figurines extant to date down generations constitute a main pathway through which we can learn about past societies.

The birth of pottery figurine had something to do with the ancient practice of burying living people with the dead. By the Spring and Autumn period, people started to replace living people

Pottery Female Dancer Figurine, the Eastern Han Dynasty

Pottery Painted Male Actor Figurine, the Period of Five Dynasties

Tricolor-glazed Pottery Hun Figurine of the Tang Dynasty

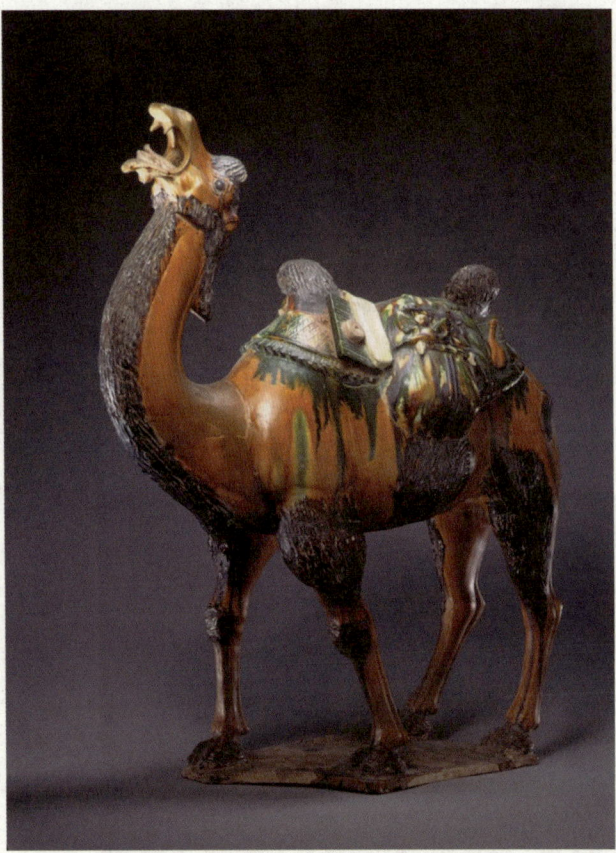
Tricolor-glazed Pottery Camel Figurine of the Tang Dynasty

with wooden figurines, then soon pottery ones. The creation of pottery figurines changed the primary burial notion of human sacrifice, driving ancient civilization a huge step forward. Compared with wooden figurines, pottery ones were less fragile and more flexible, so they were quickly applied in more and more tombs of the nobles. As pottery figurine making techniques evolved and ancient people mastered them with proficiency, by the Qin Dynasty, there came the spectacle of terracotta warriors buried in the Mausoleum of Qin Shi Huang.

Into the Han Dynasty, as society stabilized and economy grew, prevalent social needs drove increasingly sophisticated pottery figurine making techniques. Production grew over time and new images such as artists, chefs, and mystical animals appeared, then spread widely to all social classes. By the end of the seventh century, there were the tricolor-glazed pottery figurines of the Tang Dynasty. In addition to various human images, there were famous horses adored by the nobles, camels traveling the silk roads, and a wide range of other images. These figurines fully reflected the lifestyle and interests of Tang nobility. By the Song Dynasty, pottery figurines underwent a shift towards realism with greater details which revealed the lifestyle of different periods including costume. This trend continued to the Qing Dynasty. By late Qing, people started to use wooden or cloth figurines, or cut paper into human figures. From then on, pottery figurine culture gradually disappeared.

Han Figurine Making

The most impressive part of Chinese pottery figurine culture is Han figurines. In the Han Dynasty, it was common that pottery figurines were buried in mausoleums of emperors and high ministers or the tombs of ordinary people. This reflects the general practice of using pottery figurines as funerary objects, a cultural phenomenon peculiar to the Han society. Such wide application of pottery figurines suggests that figurines could be mass produced by then to meet the needs of all social classes.

Seen from the extant Han pottery figurines, molding techniques at that time had been used, which was a major driver for the sheer volume of Han figurines. There are several steps in figurine making: firstly, soak the clay in water, mix it and let it precipitate, then select fine mud; secondly, shape the mold of pottery figurine, and remold the upper part of the mold; third, paste pottery clay on the exterior, press it into shape and trim and style it with laminating, portrayal and other techniques.

Pottery Figurines from Yangling Mausoleum of the Han Dynasty

Pottery figurines must be fired into shape at a temperature from 800 to 1,000 degrees Celsius. The firing temperature decides the quality of figurines. Figurine molds unloaded from the kiln then are painted, a process that gives figurines verisimilitude. Figurines fired in the same mold, upon coloring, would differ in their looks.

Who made these pottery figurines? A review of historical records would reveal that the Han Dynasty had *dong yuan jiang* (literally, East Garden Master), an official position in charge of making coffin, pottery figurines, earthenware and other funerary objects. Emperors often gave officials objects made by the East Garden, as a gesture of favor or respect. Seen from the many pottery figurines and other funerary objects unearthed, it may be assumed that a funeral industry developed in private too, along with craftsmen who made pottery figurines, earthenware, lacquered wooden ware, and weaved bamboo ware. It is these craftsmen who facilitated the evolution of pottery figurine production techniques and influenced Tang tricolor glazed pottery.

Han Performance Art

As economy and culture developed and evolved in the Han dynasty, people's minds were emancipated and no longer rigidly adhered to rites and music systems of the Shang and Zhou dynasties. Driven by this realization, performance art of the Han saw unprecedented progress in both form and content. On pottery figurines, portrait stones and other cultural relics, many pictures record the prevailing forms of performance art at that time, including music and dance scenes, acrobatics, sports, and masquerades, giving us important access to peeping into Han social life.

Han dances were mostly small song and dance events. Common among these were Dance on Tray and Drum, Jian Drum Dance, Long-Sleeve Dance, and Handkerchief Dance. These dance scenes were generally depicted at halls, courtyards, shops, squares and working sites. Long-Sleeve Dance was most popular in the Han Dynasty. The dancing girls would wave their long sleeves as they danced in a soft and lovely way, expressing complicated thoughts and feelings. Handkerchief dancers would hold long handkerchiefs with short sticks wrapped inside to create various dance patterns. In Jian Drum Dance, Jian means "erect", i.e. erecting a drum with wooden pillars with the drum surface facing the audience, while the dancer would beat the drum and dance at the same time, rendering a powerful performance.

Pictures on cultural relics show that Han music bands varied in size and standard, including solos, accompaniment, ensemble and other forms of performance. Music was performed at various rituals and ceremonies including emperor outings, victory celebrations, and suburban and temple sacrifices. Moreover, the performance scenes outnumbered all others are about emperors treating officials with feast and music, and officials and gentry entertaining guests with banquets. Songs and dances were prevalent in the Han Dynasty. From the ruling class to the nobles, officials, and rich people, all were given to song and dance luxuries. This trend gave rise to chamber music and songs and dances accompanied by music.

Han also saw the rise of acrobatics, illusion, comedian and

Long-sleeve Dance

Handkerchief Dance

Jian Drum Dance

Juggling

Ropewalking

Handstand on Overlapped Tables

dwarf shows, wrestling, beast training and other shows. Comedians, or pai you, were common in Han performances. They were professional artists of music, dance and jest. They would dance while beating drums. They probably had songs or lyrics in their performances. Moreover, in many music, dance and variety show pictures on Han brick portraits, there are scenes of short and stout funny-looking dwarfs with their upper body naked performing alongside female dancers. These dwarfs often danced in impromptu comic gestures and performed acrobatics. These performers' movements are funny or amusing, suggesting that they were generally also good at singing, dancing and acrobatics performances.

It is obvious that Han performance art gradually matured in both its content and forms. Particularly, singing, dancing and music were highly developed, and they were complemented by acrobatics, illusion, comic shows, and beast training. These forms of performance co-evolved and shaped future dance, opera, acrobatics and other performance arts. This laid a solid foundation for future branches of art and played a key role in the establishment, development and improvement of traditional Chinese performance arts system.

Dance on Tray and Drum and Juggling, Stone Relief of the Eastern Han Dynasty

Galloping Bronze Horse

The Celestial Steed

Galloping Bronze Horse

Location: Gansu Provincial Museum
Age: Eastern Han Dynasty
Texture: bronze
Size: 45 cm in length, 34.5 cm in height

This is a wild and willful steed. It transcends its earthly brethren, leaping into the clouds, to join the birds in the sky.

The unique bronze comes from Leitai, a rammed earth platform situated in Wuwei, Gansu Province. In 1969 an Eastern Han tomb was discovered under the platform. The owner of the tomb was a general named Zhang. The brick-chambered tomb was lined with spectacular ceremonial chariots and horses. In the Han Dynasty, the possession of such a team of horses and chariots was a mark of honor and distinction. The whole team of bronzes includes 17 warriors, 28 servants, 14 chariots, 1 bull and 39 horses.

Tomb of the Eastern Han Dynasty, Wuwei City, Gansu Province

Among the horses, one horse in particular stands out. Viewed from any angle, its body shape is appealing, suggesting energy and strength while its head tilts to the side. It is both bursting with vigor, and yet strangely relaxed. This is a heavenly horse which transcends the mortal world, rids itself of saddle and bridle, and bolts skyward for freedom. Emperor Wu of Han, no less, wrote in eulogy of the heavenly horse, which gallops through the clouds, battling with dragons, evincing such power it can only sweat blood. During the Han Dynasty, Gansu's Hexi

Servant Figurine

Bronze Standing Horse

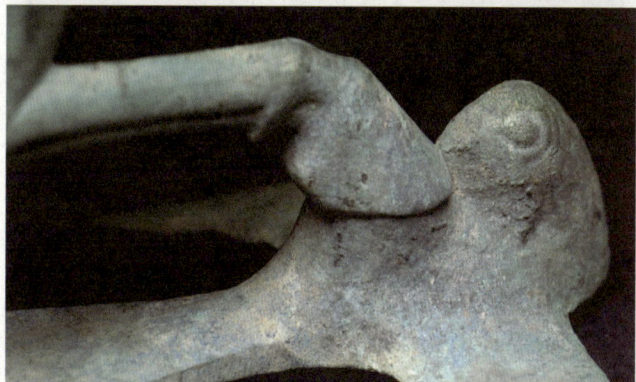

Corridor was both a battleground and a hunting ground. Outposts like Wuwei and Zhangye were surrounded by grass and water, providing rich pastures for grazing. At the end of the 2nd century BC the Han sent out multiple orders to seek out heavenly horses from the far northwest. Han emperors compared the mortal steeds from the Altai and beyond to heavenly horses. They were a vital asset in the Han's struggle with the Xiongnu. These heavenly horses allowed Han cavalry armies to campaign successfully beyond the great wall and into the barbarian heartlands. Their success is celebrated in this spectacular bronze.

The mouth, eyes, and nose of the horse are wide open and had been painted with vermilion. The rising mane and tail seem to carry the echoes of its neighing and whinnying on the wind of time. The sole hoof which supports the body is stood gently on the back of a flying bird, which turns around in startled amazement. It is an incomparably dramatic masterpiece of bronze craftsmanship. The posture of the horse, stretching up and dashing forward, at the same time expresses its hauteur and passion.

Horses are beautiful creatures on the earth. This heavenly horse represents them as well as being a divine messenger from the heavens. Our heavenly horse holds its head high, and even without wings, it is able to soar among the clouds.

Leitai Han Tomb and Its Disappointing Facts

Leitai Han Tomb in Wuwei City, Gansu Province is a major archaeological discovery following the founding of the People's Republic of China. It was discovered by local peasants who were digging earth in October 1969. A rammed earth platform 8.5m tall, 106m long north-south and 60m wide west-east, Leitai rises up 15-20cm layer by layer. As this platform was built on heap earth over the mound, it was to protect this tomb from robbing. In spite of this, two holes dug by robbers were found in excavation, one at the upper part on the east wall of the mid-chamber and the other in the passage.

Judging from the accretion in the chamber, the two robberies happened not long after the burial, followed by obvious traces of mends to these holes. Though it did not go through any disastrous plunder later, the said two robberies stole a large number of valuable cultural relics that disappeared forever. And we will never know what was lost. Tomb robbery has been a huge challenge facing archaeologists. One important reason lies in the fact that such robberies would rob tombs of many cultural relics of great historic, cultural and informational value on the one hand, and damage the primitive environments of tombs on the other. China has historically valued filial piety, so ritual processes varied in funerals by historical period, generating different remains. These remains, once unearthed, would give us a glimpse into ancient societies and cultures. However, this environment, if damaged, would confuse, and worse, mislead our judgments. A case in point is the discovery of Leitai Han Tomb. Before the archaeological team arrived, some of the public had search and taken articles out of their unique chamber environment, significantly reducing the information carried by them. This has ever since been a great disappointment of this archaeological discovery.

For example, the procession of bronze chariots and horses unearthed in this discovery was taken out of its original place, which means that though without any loss in quantity and mass, the order of this procession is totally messed up. Now audience can see the procession restored in order at the Gansu Provincial Museum, but it is merely based on the recalls by the people who first saw them. We have no way to make sure if this is the way it should be. Also, we cannot be sure if this bronze galloping horse should be in front of the procession or not. Though the restoration based on such recalls is basically reliable, the truth is still thinly veiled. If these objects had been extracted by archaeologists, they would have been recorded in detail before withdrawal, both in photos and words, so that their true face could have been restored to the greatest extent.

It is the failure to extract cultural relics according to scientific processes that gives rise to another disappointment of the Leitai Han Tomb -- the identity of the owner has yet to be pinpointed to date. Four silver seals with turtle-shaped knobs were unearthed that reflect the identity of the owner, but the texts on the seals were damaged. Although, in combination with the inscriptions on some bronze chariots and horses, we can speculate that the owner is a general Zhang, the public offices as inscribed on the four seals are inconsistent. It is possible that a Han official had more than one seal. Plus, the practice of burying multiple people of different generations in one tomb was popular in the Han Dynasty, we are not sure that this tomb buried only a couple. Furthermore, the information that there are only traces of two coffins was provided by the crowd upon impression, which greatly reduces its reliability. If this archaeological excavation was detailed enough, we could have identified the exact locations of the four seals and the traces of

Restoration of Bronze Chariots and Horses in Gansu Provincial Museum

coffins in the tomb, which would have helped us confirm how many people were buried here. The past cannot be redone. What a pity.

For this reason, archaeologists approach each and every excavation with awe and respect to history, acting meticulously so as not to miss a single historic detail. More importantly, they would never do this work for novelty or treasure hunting purposes, because every excavation is essentially a damage. Therefore, the most majority of archaeological excavations are intended to coordinate with general economic development and salvage the cultural legacies that have been robbed. Archaeologists are fully aware that tangible cultural legacies are unique while every excavation gets only one shot and can never be redone. In this sense, we can understand why the well-known cultural heritages such as the Mausoleum of Qin Shi Huang and the Qianling Mausoleum have not been actively excavated. All of us know that there are many rare treasures in such mausoleums, but we should also realize that these heritages do not exclusively belong to our generation, but also belong to future generations of Chinese.

Some say cinematography is an art form with regrets, while archaeology is a science with regrets. As a branch of science, archaeology has its initiative. Even if some intuitive information is still missing, we are able to meticulously delve deep and deduce to restore historic truths to the greatest extent. However, no matter how hard we try, all we can see is merely part of the truth. Such obsession to truth is exactly where the appeal of archaeology lies. As noted by Mr. Zhang Zhongpei, a renowned archaeologist, "Generations of people have sought for truths in history. However, all they could do is to get closer to truths. They can never touch the true face of history, let alone a full understanding of it. Nevertheless, the pursuit of truths is as tricky as it is fascinating! And it makes history, and archaeology in particular, a branch of science forever young!"

By Wei Zhen

Appendix:
Chronological Table of the Chinese Dynasities

The Paleolithic Period	Approx. 1,700,000–10,000 years ago
The Neolithic Age	Approx. 10,000–4,000 years ago
Xia Dynasty	2070–1600 BC
Shang Dynasty	1600–1046 BC
Western Zhou Dynasty	1046–771 BC
Spring and Autumn Period	770–476 BC
Warring States Period	475–221 BC
Qin Dynasty	221–206 BC
Western Han Dynasty	206 BC–AD 25
Eastern Han Dynasty	25–220
Three Kingdoms	220–280
Western Jin Dynasty	265–317
Eastern Jin Dynasty	317–420
Northern and Southern Dynasties	420–589
Sui Dynasty	581–618
Tang Dynasty	618–907
Five Dynasties	907–960
Northern Song Dynasty	960–1127
Southern Song Dynasty	1127–1279
Yuan Dynasty	1206–1368
Ming Dynasty	1368–1644
Qing Dynasty	1936–1912
Republic of China	1912–1949
People's Republic of China	Founded in 1949

A Dialogue across Time and Space

Every Treasure Tells A Story is a well-liked documentary about Chinese cultural relics and the China Intercontinental Press is about to publish its book under the same title. Personally, I think this is of great significance for us and we should adapt important cultural traditions into today's culture, and blend them into modern society. I would be more than happy to make a few humble remarks.

Culture is the soul of a nation. Blessed with extraordinary cultural creativity, the Chinese nation has written a splendid history and created a great civilization that has lasted for thousands of years, all of which is embodied in national treasures born centuries ago. They are our invaluable heritage, full of vitality despite the erosion of time. With the help of our national treasures, we can develop a clear perception of our past, our present and our future. We can base our efforts on Chinese culture, pass down our cultural characteristics, demonstrate Chinese aesthetics, and nurture common emotion and value, as well as our shared ideals and spirit.

President Xi Jinping said that we should "bring life to the cultural relics collected in the forbidden palace, the heritage standing on the vast land, and the characters written in the ancient books"; "vitalize the cultural spirits that break down the barriers of space and time, spread across borders, and have eternal enchantment and contemporary values; and hand out the fruits of our cultural innovations that combine traditional merits and modern values, and feature universal qualities deriving from our homeland". This book, *Every Treasure Tells A Story*, has delved into how to achieve such goals.

A hundred of treasures have been carefully selected for the book *Every Treasure Tells A Story*, each telling a legendary tale. The book introduces each of the treasures and talks about from their relationships to the civilizations embodied in those artifacts. It also celebrates the unique creativity, developmental path, and values of Chinese culture through the telling of breathtaking stories of the treasures, presenting extensive pictures and providing an appealing, knowledgeable narrative, which is both meaningful and interesting.

Today, there is growing interest in the heritage of China. Many want to learn more about our country. Some are interested in perceptions, opinions, emotions and the aesthetic tastes of our people, and some want to get acquainted with Chinese traditions, customs, and our national ethos. I believe that our treasures, as well as this richly illustrated and narrated book, will open the very window for our foreign friends to have a glance at Chinese culture. Hopefully, they may feel the distinctive enchantment of Chinese culture from the moment they focus on any one of the treasures in a museum, and come away with a deeper understanding of our culture, which would be wonderful.

Thank you.

Shan Jixiang

the former director of the Palace Museum

图书在版编目（CIP）数据

如果国宝会说话. 第二季：英文/《如果国宝会说话》节目组著；
李奕锋,(美)斯杜尔特·J.摩根译. --
北京：五洲传播出版社, 2019.8
ISBN 978-7-5085-4275-1

Ⅰ.①如… Ⅱ.①如…②李…③斯… Ⅲ.①历史文物 - 中国 - 通俗读物 - 英文 Ⅳ.①K87-49

中国版本图书馆CIP数据核字(2019)第154872号

如果国宝会说话 第二季

著　　者：《如果国宝会说话》节目组
出 版 人：荆孝敏
知识链接：智朴 等
知识链接翻译：李奕锋　[美]斯杜尔特·J.摩根
责任编辑：樊程旭
设计总监：闫志杰
装帧设计：王春晓　玄元武
设计制作：北京正视文化艺术有限责任公司
出版发行：五洲传播出版社
地　　址：北京市海淀区北三环中路31号生产力大楼B座6层
邮　　编：100088
发行电话：010-82005927，010-82007837
网　　址：http://www.cicc.org.cn，http://www.thatsbooks.com
印　　刷：北京市海天舜日印刷有限公司
版　　次：2019年12月第1版第1次印刷
开　　本：889x1194　1/20
印　　张：14
字　　数：200千
定　　价：118.00元